Reconceptualising Feedback in Higher Education

WILLIAM HARVEY LIBRARY
WITHDRAWN
GETEC
GEORGE ELIOT HOSPITAL NHS TRUST
COLLEGE STREET, NUNEATON CV10 7DJ

WILLIAM HARVEY LIBRARY

Feedback is a crucial element of teac[...] however, substantial evidence that st[...] there is growing impetus for change.

Student surveys have indicated that feedback is one of the most problematic aspects of the student experience, and so particularly in need of further scrutiny. Current practices waste both student learning potential and staff resources. Up until now the way of addressing these problems has been through relatively minor interventions based on the established model of feedback providing information, but the change that is required is more fundamental and far reaching.

Reconceptualising Feedback in Higher Education, coming from a think-tank composed of specialist expertise in assessment feedback, is a direct and more fundamental response to the impetus for change. Its purpose is to challenge established beliefs and practices through critical evaluation of evidence and discussion of the renewal of current feedback practices. In promoting a new conceptualisation and a repositioning of assessment feedback within an enhanced and more coherent paradigm of student learning, this book:

* analyses the current issues in feedback practice and their implications for student learning;
* identifies the key characteristics of effective feedback practices;
* explores the changes to feedback practice that are needed and how they can be brought about;
* illustrates through examples how processes to promote and sustain effective feedback practices can be embedded in modern mass higher education.

Provoking academics to think afresh about the way they conceptualise and utilise feedback, this book will help those with responsibility for strategic development of assessment at an institutional level, educational developers, course management teams, researchers, tutors and student representatives.

Stephen Merry is Senior Lecturer in Cell Biology in the Faculty of Computing, Engineering and Sciences at Staffordshire University.

GEORGE ELIOT CENTRE LIBRARY
T12827

Margaret Price is Professor in Learning and Assessment at Oxford Brookes University.

David Carless is Professor of Educational Assessment at the University of Hong Kong.

Maddalena Taras is Senior Lecturer in the Faculty of Education and Society at the University of Sunderland.

Reconceptualising Feedback in Higher Education

Developing dialogue with students

Edited by Stephen Merry, Margaret Price, David Carless and Maddalena Taras

Routledge
Taylor & Francis Group

LONDON AND NEW YORK

First published 2013
by Routledge
2 Park Square, Milton Park, Abingdon, Oxon OX14 4RN

Simultaneously published in the USA and Canada
by Routledge
711 Third Avenue, New York, NY 10017

Routledge is an imprint of the Taylor & Francis Group, an informa business

© 2013 Stephen Merry, Margaret Price, David Carless and Maddalena Taras

The right of the editors to be identified as the authors of the editorial
material, and of the authors for their individual chapters, has been asserted
in accordance with sections 77 and 78 of the Copyright, Designs and Patents
Act 1988.

All rights reserved. No part of this book may be reprinted or reproduced
or utilised in any form or by any electronic, mechanical, or other means,
now known or hereafter invented, including photocopying and recording,
or in any information storage or retrieval system, without permission in
writing from the publishers.

Trademark notice: Product or corporate names may be trademarks or
registered trademarks, and are used only for identification and explanation
without intent to infringe.

British Library Cataloguing in Publication Data
A catalogue record for this book is available from the British Library

Library of Congress Cataloging in Publication Data
Reconceptualising feedback in higher education : developing dialogue
with students / edited by Stephen Merry, Margaret Price, David Carless,
Maddalena Taras.
    p. cm.
Includes bibliographical references and index.
1. Communication in education. 2. Feedback (Psychology) 3. Education,
Higher. I. Merry, Stephen. II. Yorke, Mantz. Surveys of 'the student
experience' and the politics of feedback. III. Title: Reconceptualizing
feedback in higher education.
LB1033.5.R425 2013
371.102'2—dc23   2012043180

ISBN: 978-0-415-69234-2 (hbk)
ISBN: 978-0-415-69235-9 (pbk)
ISBN: 978-0-203-52281-3 (ebk)

Typeset in Bembo
by Keystroke, Station Road, Codsall, Wolverhampton

Contents

List of figures	ix
List of tables	xi
Notes on contributors	xiii
Foreword	xv
MARCIA MENTKOWSKI	
Preface	xix
STEPHEN MERRY	

PART I
Current thinking   **1**

Overview	3
MADDALENA TARAS	

Section A: The student voice   **6**

1 Surveys of 'the student experience' and the politics of feedback	6
MANTZ YORKE	
2 Feedback – what students want	19
ALEX BOLS AND KATE WICKLOW	

Section B: The wider picture - challenges to preconceptions   **30**

3 Feedback on feedback: uncrossing wires across sectors	30
MADDALENA TARAS	
4 Assessment feedback: an Agenda for Change	41
MARGARET PRICE, KAREN HANDLEY, BERRY O'DONOVAN,	
CHRIS RUST AND JILL MILLAR	

Section C: Principles and practices   54

5   Opening up feedback: teaching learners to see   54
D. ROYCE SADLER

6   Building 'standards' frameworks: the role of guidance and feedback in supporting the achievement of learners   64
SUE BLOXHAM

PART II
Enhancing the student role in the feedback process   75

Overview   77
DAVID CARLESS

Section A: Students   80

7   Involving students in the scholarship of assessment: student voices on the feedback agenda for change   80
KAY SAMBELL

8   Feedback unbound: from master to usher   92
JAN MCARTHUR AND MARK HUXHAM

9   Feedback and feedforward: student responses and their implications   103
MIRABELLE WALKER

Section B: Tutors   113

10   Sustainable feedback and the development of student self-evaluative capacities   113
DAVID CARLESS

11   Students' social learning practice as a way of learning from tutor feedback   123
PAUL ORSMOND, STEPHEN MERRY AND KAREN HANDLEY

12   Integrating feedback with classroom teaching: using exemplars to scaffold learning   133
GRAHAM HENDRY

PART III
Fostering institutional change   **143**

Overview   145
MARGARET PRICE

13 An assessment compact: changing the way an institution thinks about assessment and feedback   147
CHRIS RUST, MARGARET PRICE, KAREN HANDLEY,
BERRY O'DONOVAN AND JILL MILLAR

14 Fostering institutional change in feedback practice through partnership   160
GRAHAM HOLDEN AND CHRIS GLOVER

15 Making learning-oriented assessment the experience of all our students: supporting institutional change   172
MARK RUSSELL, DOMINIC BYGATE AND HELEN BAREFOOT

16 Achieving transformational or sustainable educational change   190
STEVE DRAPER AND DAVID NICOL

Conclusion and reflections   204
STEPHEN MERRY, MARGARET PRICE, DAVID CARLESS AND
MADDALENA TARAS

Index   211

Figures

1.1 First-year Australian students' responses to the statement 'Teaching staff usually give me helpful feedback on my progress'   12

1.2 Global scores for the 2009 NSS 'core' items   13

1.3 First-year students' responses to feedback items   14

1.4 Percentage agreement with the NSS item 'Feedback on my work has been prompt', for subject areas in a particular institution in 2010   15

13.1 The Oxford Brookes University Assessment Compact   150–51

14.1 'How do you use yours?' campaign poster   167

14.2 Prize draw cards   167

14.3 Bookmarks handed out to students   167

15.1 ESCAPE project work packages   174

15.2 ESCAPE project process   177

15.3 Linking the ESCAPE themes to existing assessment and feedback principles   179

15.4 Part case study overlaid with the ESCAPE themes   181

15.5 Examples of assessment patterns – making more of feedback   183

15.6 Examples of assessment patterns – a programme view of assessment   184

15.7 An example of a student-facing postcard   186

15.8 Student-focused ESCAPE feedback hierarchy   187

15.9 Teacher-focused ESCAPE feedback hierarchy   188

Tables

 9.1 The most frequently occurring response themes   105
 9.2 The most frequently occurring response themes, with the two
      types of 'useful/helpful' response separated out   105
14.1 Outline design of the Feedback for Learning Campaign   166
16.1 An example of the relationship of design decisions to resources
      for persuasion in the course-level REAP project   201

Notes on contributors

Helen Barefoot, Deputy Head of the Learning and Teaching Institute, University of Hertfordshire, UK.

Sue Bloxham, Professor of Academic Practice and Head of Educational Research, University of Cumbria, UK.

Alex Bols, formerly Assistant Director (Research) and Head of Higher Education, National Union of Students, UK.

Dominic Bygate, ESCAPE Project Manager, University of Hertfordshire, UK.

David Carless, Professor of Educational Assessment, Faculty of Education, University of Hong Kong, Hong Kong.

Steve Draper, Senior University Teacher, School of Psychology, University of Glasgow, UK.

Chris Glover, formerly Co-ordinator (The Assessment for Learning Initiative), Learning and Teaching Institute, Sheffield Hallam University, UK.

Karen Handley, Reader in Organisational Studies, Business School, Oxford Brookes University, UK.

Graham Hendry, Senior Lecturer, Institute for Teaching and Learning, University of Sydney, Australia.

Graham Holden, Head of Quality Enhancement, Student and Learning Services, Sheffield Hallam University, UK.

Mark Huxham, Professor of Teaching and Research in Environmental Biology, Faculty of Health, Life and Social Sciences, Edinburgh Napier University, UK.

Jan McArthur, Lecturer, the Moray House School of Education, University of Edinburgh, UK.

Marcia Mentkowski, Senior Scholar for Educational Research and Professor of Psychology, Educational Research and Evaluation Department, Alverno College, USA.

Stephen Merry, Senior Lecturer in Cell Biology, Faculty of Computing, Engineering and Sciences, Staffordshire University, UK.

Jill Millar, Associate Lecturer and Researcher, Pedagogy Research Centre, Oxford Brookes University, UK.

David Nicol, Emeritus Professor of Higher Education, Centre for Academic Practice and Learning Enhancement, University of Strathclyde, UK.

Berry O'Donovan, Principal Lecturer and Deputy Director, Pedagogy Research Centre, Oxford Brookes University, UK.

Paul Orsmond, Senior Lecturer, Faculty of Computing, Engineering and Sciences, Staffordshire University, UK.

Margaret Price, Professor of Learning and Assessment, Director of Pedagogy Research Centre, Oxford Brookes University, UK.

Mark Russell, Professor of Learning and Assessment in Higher Education, Director of Technology Enhanced Learning, King's College London, UK.

Chris Rust, Professor of Higher Education and Associate Dean (Academic Policy), Oxford Brookes University, UK.

D. Royce Sadler, Senior Assessment Scholar, Teaching and Educational Development Institute, University of Queensland, Australia.

Kay Sambell, Professor of Learning and Teaching, Faculty of Health and Life Sciences, Northumbria University, UK.

Maddalena Taras, Senior Lecturer, Faculty of Education and Society, University of Sunderland, UK.

Mirabelle Walker, Lecturer, Faculty of Mathematics, Computing and Technology, Open University, UK.

Kate Wicklow, Head of Quality and Student Engagement, National Union of Students, UK.

Mantz Yorke, Visiting Professor, Department of Educational Research, Lancaster University, UK.

Foreword

Feedback is an essential element in a student's learning process. The authors of this excellent volume take up this assumption and put it through a rigorous analysis that is tested in relation to experience. The book will benefit academics as scholars and practitioners alike. Readers will begin to appreciate why the editors and authors arrive at this perspective: feedback-for-learning is an essential part of an instructional and assessment process. As more staff learn to provide feedback effectively, and more students learn to engage with feedback productively, both tutors and learners may use it for reaching their goals. Feedback is not only a source of critique for goals that academics and learners have set, but also a source for discussion about subject matter and skills. Thus, feedback stimulates conversations about core academic work and moves toward another benefit – more sophisticated goals and a search for continuous improvement towards further learning and mastery.

Conversations about student work involving students and staff, and students and their peers, sometimes only happen occasionally. These authors, however, are committed to fulfilling a long-expressed dream of educators and learners alike; that educators provide effective and engaging feedback and model the feedback process for students to carry out with their peers. The authors are also deeply mindful of the broader issues that arise in how to design, adapt and institutionalise the structures and innovative assessments that make feedback more feasible, more effective and more engaging for academics and students.

Thus, several authors delve into wide-ranging theories that capture and integrate recent research studies about feedback. They integrate frameworks, evidence and their own experience. The result is a strong case for interactive dialogical feedback for supporting individual learners as they interact with their teachers. Social learning theories emerge with many dimensions. For me, this is convincing. For example, students may discuss their reasoning underlying an argument, ideas that seemed untenable at first, or what happened in a setting where students tried on a professional role. In each situation, over time and interactively with instructors, learners gradually develop ways to take up more sophisticated feedback, especially when it is tied to their level of current abilities. Students may also develop further their ability to create observed performances for assessments that re-energise their learning and assist them to seek ways to use, adapt or improve what they have learned.

The authors provide many themes and examples of effective and engaging feedback as common practices in teaching, learning and assessment. I have selected a few of the authors' themes in this foreword that struck me as particularly useful, merging their practices with my own research and experience. Perhaps these might illuminate what we have in common for the reader.

Feedback as opportunity to learn. When students experience feedback only as marks on assignments or assessments, they are less likely to see it as another opportunity to learn. Many academics in recent years have struggled to distance feedback from marks and grade levels. Creating this distance is challenging when a system of assessment continues to treat all samples of student performance as a chance for marking. Rather, feedback is an opportunity to learn without fear of what some students may see as reprisal.

Feedback as continual and coherent. Effective feedback is frequent and integrative. It can take place during assignments, after assessments, when students are evaluating their own work, or are planning their further learning. Yet instructors know that students do not necessarily come to learning contexts with a clear understanding of what it means to connect feedback over time. Students can gradually learn to find coherence – as well as surprises and insights – by reflecting on feedback from various instructors across their coursework. Effective feedback processes may also help students to develop and sharpen their goal-setting strategies.

Feedback as interactive and dialogical. Beginning students may experience feedback only as evaluation, as a general affirmation or rejection of the self. Emotions elicited by feedback, even when feedback is given calmly and carefully, may derail insight into a sample of her or his performance, or alternatively, heighten attention to feedback. A student may comment, 'But I worked so hard on that.' This signals an instructor to engage the learner interactively with a question, perhaps 'What are you thinking about what I said?' A student might then reply 'Well you said I have to do it all again and I don't have time. I have all these other classes.' Interactive feedback assists a learner to see value in separating an initial emotional response by engaging with an instructor's thoughts. Stepping back or attempting some distance from a perceived slight or a high mark may allow for rethinking what an instructor had written: 'In this essay you showed real progress in your thinking about your ideas. In this other one, you might benefit from further developing just these two ideas. Would you be willing to try that?'

Students who are learning to accept criticism and suggestions on assignments are probably likely to view feedback as a way to get specific information on their progress. That insight could be unlearned unless they seek out formative feedback, rather than waiting for a summative assessment. Thus, students who act on feedback and expect feedback that helps them take charge of their own learning may show disappointment when beginning academics treat a search for feedback as holding them up. Students often intuit that their feedback stands in the way of an instructor getting to the next class or writing a journal article. They become frustrated. Thus, dialogical feedback throughout a class where instructors model question-asking can often seek out those students who expect feedback to help them see patterns and relationships with thoughts and actions gleaned from other classes as well. These students are also modelling responses to effective and engaging feedback for others when they show how it commits them to improvement across coursework.

Feedback as anonymous marking. This suggestion (which has its pros and cons) came from students who created the National Union of Students *Charter on Feedback and Assessment.* I especially understand their concern about diverse students being marked fairly. Each of us is different in some way, and may be confused by expectations from a dominant culture, wherever one is, in whatever country across the world. In my experience, not only diverse students but also others may be rightly concerned if there is a lack of explicit criteria – or criteria they do not yet understand – for performing on an assessment. So a guideline for anonymity seeks fairness in the marking and grading process.

Feedback as developmental. Perhaps the need for explicit, public criteria has a developmental quality for both academics and students to strive for. Beginning students seem to need specific, public criteria for assessment, especially if they are beginning to learn in a new environment. When an instructor compares student examples to more specific criteria, a student may comment, 'Now I get the material and how to use it.' Beginning academics may be trapped by concern for covering subjects and use criteria that are too specific, so that learners lag behind their peers in making inferences from feedback.

Intermediate student users of feedback seem energised by and perform better in structured situations with broader yet explicit, public criteria. Even if criteria are less specific, students learning at an intermediate level are able to envision what to do in an assessment – especially where students are learning how to perform. Students who seem to know already what to do to improve and take initiative in using class resources to improve their learning, for example, are probably more advanced in seeing patterns and relationships and seeking feedback when they need another perspective on their work from an academic or peer.

Feedback as self-assessment and integrative learning. Several authors in this volume point out that students who expect feedback following assignments and final assessments are the active seekers of feedback that experienced academics prefer. Some seekers may be interested in integrating subject matter, skills and academic values from a current module with other modules. Other students may be hoping to engage in some form of self-reflection or peer review. These students will also be appreciative of learning from their teachers how to conduct a self-assessment process explicitly, at least at first. Community professionals who attend training sessions to provide students with opportunities to deepen their learning through feedback, and who also comment on students' ability to critique their own work in relation to standards, are appreciated by learners who anticipate taking on professional roles in the future.

Feedback as critique. Each academic is aware of when a student disagrees, sometimes argumentatively, with a critique of their work. The student may be surprised when a final assessment does not meet a faculty's or a profession's set of standards, especially if the learner has not been able to use feedback for improvement along the way. I myself often recall the disappointment when I have received a rejection of an article and then I am grateful for anonymous feedback. Sometimes students will ask for feedback in anonymous formats (different from anonymous marking), or seek a second opinion from someone else in an academic department. We as learners-in-common need distance from a feedback event to deal fully with a critique using our own reflective thinking. The nature of academic work involves sound critique, and it needs to be acknowledged that critical analysis of feedback is an essential part of using it to improve.

Feedback as ethical. Feedback is a moral act and that is why it is an essential part of humane teaching and assessment. My colleague, Georgine Loacker, has reminded me often that the act of assessment is derived from the Latin word *assidere*, meaning 'to sit down beside'. Thus, assessing means, literally and figuratively, to sit with learners and provide our best efforts at feedback. The authors model discussing, rethinking, and seriously studying what it means to each student to provide effective and engaging feedback. A further goal for students is learning how to provide feedback for others as another perspective on others' self-assessments. Feedback is a step forward, a more civil life of the mind and heart, as we ourselves as learners engage privately and publicly with other learners for whom we take responsibility.

Marcia Mentkowski
Alverno College

Preface

It is recognised that effective feedback is an integral component of successful teaching, learning and assessment processes. However, there is substantial evidence of dissatisfaction with feedback processes in higher education (HE) from both student surveys and educational literature. National Student Surveys have indicated that feedback is one of the most problematic aspects of the student experience and hence a particular target for further scrutiny. Problems in current feedback practice for students include interpretation, utility and clear opportunities to apply their feedback. The common assumption that feedback is uni-directional in nature severely limits its scope and, together with confusion over its multiple purposes, leads to ineffective feedback practices. Staff are often engaged in the time-consuming task of crafting good feedback, but the methods used to measure its effectiveness are often fairly limited and simplistic. This situation generates justified dissatisfaction, which is feeding a growing impetus for change.

To consider these issues and their resolution a group of 23 researchers and writers with specialist expertise in assessment feedback were brought together for two days in June 2009 by a UK Centre for Excellence in Teaching and Learning, ASKe. To be known as the Osney Grange Group, they produced an Agenda for Change to be used to inform national and institutional assessment policy and feedback practices in the Higher Education sector. The Agenda for Change is discussed in detail in Chapter 4 and has many of the contributors of this book as signatories.

This book seeks to outline the case for reconceptualisation of feedback. It does so in three parts:

1   *Current thinking* outlines the current issues and context of feedback practice. It considers the need for change and provides some theoretical underpinning for that change. Its role is to provide an informed analysis of the current situation concerning feedback practices in higher education and to explain why changes are imperative.
2   *Enhancing the student role in the feedback process* considers how students might be encouraged to be participants in, rather than simply recipients of,

feedback processes. It explores from the student perspective how feedback can be made more meaningful and considers ways by which tutors might support the process. Its role is to use examples of practice to emphasise how learning can be enhanced through feedback.

3   *Fostering institutional change* explores the feasibility of the widespread adoption of such changes in feedback practice within the current HE system. Through analysis of several feedback change initiatives it highlights key aspects of the adoption process that are critical to success.

These three parts, together with their supporting overviews, provide an exploration of the nature of feedback and how it can be improved through initiatives at both course and institutional levels.

The book, overall, emphasises the need for HE stakeholders to fundamentally re-think the role and purpose of feedback. Many current practices waste both student learning potential and staff resources. Furthermore, the situation has been exacerbated by the expansion of higher education with the concomitant changes to its purpose and its ways of working. Up until now the problems identified with feedback have been tackled through relatively minor interventions based on established models, but this book argues that the change that is required is more fundamental and far reaching. This book recognises that high level and complex learning is best developed when feedback is seen as a relational process that takes place over time, is dialogic, and is integral to learning and teaching. Within a resource-constrained educational environment this may be considered difficult to achieve, but valuable and effective feedback can come from varied sources and, in particular, students themselves. If students do not learn to evaluate their own work they will remain dependent upon others. The abilities to self- and peer-review are therefore essential graduate attributes.

This book therefore outlines current thinking by active researchers in the field. It presents evidence-based arguments grounded in theory and shows that the problems with feedback are unlikely to be solved by working within current feedback paradigms. The objectives of the book are as follows:

- to outline the current issues in feedback practice and analyse the implications for student learning;
- to identify the key characteristics of effective feedback practice;
- to explore the changes needed to feedback practice;
- to present an argument for a reconceptualisation of feedback;
- to illustrate through examples how processes to promote and sustain effective feedback practices can be embedded in modern mass higher education.

The book represents more than a collection of research papers or case studies. It has brought together into a single synthesis the views of a wider variety of contributors than previous publications. The chapter authors have a range of experience and disciplinary backgrounds. They are well-recognised lecturers, student representatives, researchers and educational developers based in England, Scotland, Australia and Hong Kong and they have drawn on international literature and practice such that there is explicit evidence that issues discussed are equally relevant to many European, Australasian and North American Universities. The book highlights some of the current myths and misconceptions concerning feedback practices and seeks to challenge the status quo. The analysis of feedback that it presents shows that a range of writers are reaching similar conclusions and calling for an agreed change of direction towards a workable solution to the long-running dissatisfaction with feedback. The authors have come together to promote the ideas in the Agenda for Change that provided the impetus for this book.

Stephen Merry
September 2012

Part I

Current thinking

Overview

Maddalena Taras

Part I provides an overview of the wider aspects of the student voice, current engagement, thinking and conceptualisations of feedback. Feedback is a much used and abused term, particularly in its adoption at the services of learning: exploring our collective conceptualisations and understandings of feedback is necessary at every level of education for future developments. This book serves such a function.

Government offices have developed questionnaires to measure and monitor the efficacy of institutional support of feedback to students in an attempt to link feedback processes with learning and 'customer' satisfaction.

In Section A ('The student voice'), Yorke, and Bols and Wicklow evaluate inter/national surveys on aspects of assessment feedback. Yorke, at an international level, examines student surveys and the limited use of feedback data that impact on major national and institutional decisions. Bols and Wicklow delve deeper at national level into student wishes on feedback.

More specifically, Yorke examines government-led surveys to enable accountability and comparability in higher education institutions. He highlights the politicisation of feedback in the national undergraduate student surveys in Australia and the UK and comes to two main conclusions: First, two or three questions on feedback in a survey cannot hope to provide meaningful data on such a complex process. Second, despite the paucity of these data, results are often used as stop-gap, short-term remedial measures by institutions, often by-passing and neglecting long-term planning to support and sustain developmental strategies that are embedded and part of learning. This perceived official student voice, despite the limited data that is used to represent it, has substantial impact, particularly at institutional level.

Bols and Wicklow evaluate what students want in relation to feedback as reported in the NUS/HSBC UK Student Experience Research. In the context of a wider assessment and learning context, they seek feedback integrated into a developmental and communicative framework to support both formative and summative assessments. There are five essential things that students want: feedback situated within support of learning, effective feedback, innovative assessment approaches, anonymous marking, learning focused assessment and accessible, legible submission methods.

In Section B ('The wider picture'), Taras examines theories of formative assessment across educational sectors, with the ensuing implications for feedback in a world where divisions are meaningless with the internationalisation of research communications and communities. Price *et al.* provide a detailed rationale for a new understanding of feedback that has provided the Osney Grange Group agenda and instigated this book.

Taras explores differences in theories of formative assessment across sectors through an evaluation of the definitions of feedback. Feedback appears to be described in its own terms, that is, unrelated to standards, outcomes and criteria (which are often implicit and covert understandings) or feedback against a standard, outcomes and criteria (explicit). Across sectors, the roles of feedback and formative assessment are linked variously to learning and require differing roles from tutors and learners. This is problematic as we have common terms and literature. Furthermore, five self-assessment models are identified and used to demonstrate degrees of learner-centredness and participation in dialogue. How feedback is arrived at impacts on the quality, ethical aspect and the communicability of the consequences.

Price *et al.* outline changing epistemologies of feedback as product to feedback as a dialogic process for negotiation of meaning within assessment, learning and teaching. Mandatory peer- and self-assessment are part of the contextual factors that support our new epistemological understandings of learning and negotiation of meaning. Learners cannot be excluded from assessment (of which feedback is just one aspect), otherwise they are excluded from learning. All artefacts that are used to mediate and reflect quality need to be 'peer' assessed to clarify these elusive 'qualities'.

In Section C ('Principles and practices'), Sadler and Bloxham examine the details of new processes, practices and conceptualisations. Sadler focuses on peer feedback in order to develop expertise on criteria, which is necessary for learners to become cognisant of evaluative processes, initiated into the higher education assessment community and develop an understanding of standards. Similarly, Bloxham examines how students can be enabled to develop a comparable understanding of standards as tutors in order to be helped with assignment production.

Section C provides two examples of supporting students' initiation to assessment cultures and understanding of standards. Sadler uses peer feedback in a discussion process to develop shared understandings of criteria, standards and quality. Students prepare, share and compare their work, as does the tutor. Through assessment practice and discussion, they make implicit understandings of their own standards into explicit comparisons. Without initial explicit criteria or guidance as to what to do, students learn to use their past knowledge and experience and so become clearer on their own perceptions and understandings as a basis for new shared and explicit learning. Bloxham uses research to clarify and support best practices in enabling students to understand requirements of assessment, task compliance and knowledge of standards. The natural processes of learning and acquiring this knowledge and skills through practice and experience are the usual means by which lecturers are initiated into the assessment community. This process is also recommended as being the most efficient and expedient for inducting students to assessment processes, understandings and protocols, so that these align with those of their tutors.

Chapter 1

Surveys of 'the student experience' and the politics of feedback

Mantz Yorke

The politics of feedback

Governments around the world acknowledge the importance of higher education for national economic performance. With varying levels of intensity, they also appear to view students as acting as rational 'consumers' or 'customers' of higher education, asserting that an individual investment in higher education pays off in terms of better career prospects and other life-benefits. The idea of student choice has, as a consequence, become a significant element in political rhetoric. The consumerist perspective, however, underplays two major considerations – that higher education contributes significantly to the social good, and that students have to contribute their own energies to their development.

In Australia and the United Kingdom, the focal countries of this chapter, governments invest considerably in higher education, even though students are required to contribute substantially to the costs of their studies. National surveys of students' perceptions of their experience have been undertaken since 1993 in Australia (focusing on graduates a short time after they have completed their programmes, and based on the Course Experience Questionnaire [CEQ]) and from 2005 in the UK, though in this case focusing on students towards the end of their final year's studies. These surveys were introduced for various reasons relating to accountability, such as justifying the investment of public money and assuring the quality of provision to a range of stakeholders, as well as making a contribution to informing potential students regarding their choice of institution.

As part of the 'consumer choice' agenda, the data are made available to the public, although in differing amounts of detail: CEQ data are published annually by Graduate Careers Australia (e.g. GCA 2010), and annual data from the UK National Student Survey (NSS) (previously made available through the national 'Unistats' website) is integrated into 'Key Information Sets' pertaining to all courses.

These surveys are politically and economically important to institutions as they seek to position themselves in the market for students. It is unclear how much use students make of the survey data, but 'league tables' or rankings of institutions (which incorporate survey data with varying degrees of detail) may for many be treated as proxies for the quality of 'the student experience'. Feedback on students' work is a significant component of the perceptions of the value obtained from the money invested in higher education programmes by students or their sponsors. Satisfaction with feedback is one of the 'measures' incorporated into the league table of universities published by the *Guardian*, and that newspaper's disaggregated tables focusing specifically on subject disciplines. In contrast, the league tables published by *The Times* and the *Independent*, along with their subject-specific disaggregations, use merely a global 'measure' of student satisfaction, to which perceptions relating to feedback contribute. In Australia *The Good Universities Guide* (Hobsons 2010) gives an indication of whether a field of study at a university has teaching quality, 'generic skills' achievement of its students and overall satisfaction that are average, or better or worse than average, based on CEQ ratings.[1]

Institutional performance in general, as measured by national surveys, is palpably of national and international political and economic significance. There is also an intra-institutional micropolitical dimension to institutional performance in that differences between ratings given to academic organisational units can affect institutional strategy, with some units being privileged and others penalised.

This chapter focuses on surveys of first degree students in Australia and the UK, though surveys are also administered to postgraduate students in both countries.

Brief political histories

Australia

The National Inquiry into Education, Training and Employment raised the twin issues of the quality and efficiency of the Australian educational system, on which public expenditure had increased greatly (Williams 1979, Volume 1, para. 18.1). In the Williams Report there are hints of the interest in performance indicators that was to develop over the succeeding decade and a half: for example, Question (h) of a suggested checklist relating to tertiary education asked:

> What arrangements are there to review methods of teaching and examining, and curricula, in the light of examination results, and comments from students, professional or para-professional associations, and employers?
>
> Williams (1979, Volume 1, para R18.23)

In the succeeding years, political interest in evaluating the higher education system increased. Amongst the relevant policy documents were:

• reports from the Commonwealth Tertiary Education Commission (CTEC) for the 1979–81 and 1982–84 triennia, which stressed the need for improved evaluative practices within higher education;

- two studies supported by the CTEC – Linke *et al.* (1984) and Bourke (1986), the latter of which noted 'the absence of systematic and routine scrutiny of performance at the departmental level' (p.23);
- the *Review of Efficiency and Effectiveness in Higher Education* (Commonwealth Tertiary Education Commission 1986), which was charged, inter alia, with examining 'measures to monitor performance and productivity in higher education institutions, to assist institutions to improve their efficiency and accountability' (p. xv);
- the government White Paper, *Higher Education: a policy statement* (Dawkins 1988), which supported the development of a set of indicators that would include, inter alia, the quality of teaching (see pp.85–6);
- a response from the two bodies representative of the leaders of Australian universities and colleges (AVCC/ACDP 1988) in which a number of possible indicators were set out. Of relevance to this chapter is the suggestion that the quality of teaching should be evaluated through the use of a short student survey, though feedback was not explicitly mentioned in this broadly couched document (see pp.10–11).

This steadily intensifying policy interest in performance indicators led to the commissioning, by the Commonwealth's Department of Employment, Education and Training, of a feasibility study into a number of possible indicators. The outcome was the two-volume report *Performance Indicators in Higher Education* (Linke 1991).

One of the indicators whose utility was researched was the Course Experience Questionnaire, a 30-item instrument focusing upon students' perceptions of teaching quality in higher education. The Linke Report recommended that an indicator (initially along the lines of the trialled version of the CEQ) be included in any national system of performance indicators: this instrument could be incorporated in, or administered in conjunction with, the annual survey of graduates that was conducted by the (then) Graduate Careers Council of Australia (Linke 1991, Volume 1, pp.63, 65). The policy substrate to the CEQ was made apparent when its designer, Paul Ramsden, acknowledged that performance indicators entailed

> the collection of data at different levels of aggregation to aid managerial judgements – judgements which may be made either within institutions, or at the level of the higher education system as a whole.
>
> (Ramsden 1991, p.129)

In a paper circulated in 1989 to clarify various issues relating to the CEQ during its trial period, the importance was acknowledged of the CEQ producing findings that would allow appropriate comparisons to be made across the higher education sector:

[The CEQ's] guiding design principle has been a requirement to produce, as economically as possible, quantitative data which permit ordinal ranking of units in different institutions, within comparable subject areas, in terms of perceived teaching quality.

(Linke 1991, Volume 2, p.81)

United Kingdom

The political desire for performance indicators relating to higher education in the UK can be tracked back at least as far as the Jarratt Report (CVCP 1985), which recommended that the then University Grants Committee (UGC) and the Committee of Vice Chancellors and Principals (CVCP, the representative body of the universities of that time) should develop performance indicators. A joint working group of the two organisations produced two statements on performance indicators (CVCP and UGC 1986; 1987) and during the ensuing decade the statements were followed up with compilations of university management statistics and performance indicators that evolved over time (see, for example, the last in the series: CVCP 1995). The Polytechnics and Colleges Funding Council (PCFC), which was established in 1988 together with the Universities Funding Council (UFC) (which had replaced the UGC), produced a report on performance indicators (PCFC 1990) whose intention was, inter alia, to support public accountability.

When the two sectors of higher education were merged in 1992, funding councils in England, Scotland and Wales[2] took over from the UFC and PCFC. The Higher Education Funding Council for England (HEFCE) led further development on sectoral performance indicators, initially producing a report (HEFCE 1999) and subsequently publishing annual statistics on the widening of participation, retention and completion, and research performance. These statistics, which have become more detailed since they were first published in 1999, have been made available since 2004 by the Higher Education Statistics Agency.

Running alongside the development of institutional performance indicators, there was a political concern to provide stakeholders in higher education with information about quality and standards in the sector. Over the years, various approaches to quality audit and assessment were adopted that gave rise to reports that have been placed in the public domain by the Quality Assurance Agency for Higher Education. However, the generality in the content of such reports prompted investigations of the information that intending students (and others) might find useful. The consultancy firm Segal Quince Wicksteed (SQW) found that the quality of teaching was influential in the choices made by roughly two-thirds of their sample of intending and actual students, although it was rarely accorded the status of the single most important factor in decisions: that turned out to be the course and/or its component modules (SQW 1999, para. 2.12ff). A web-based survey showed that, of the six areas of reporting on quality then in use in England, 'Teaching, Learning and Assessment' was the most frequently cited as influential. In due course, a Task Group reported on ways in which information on quality and standards could be provided (HEFCE 2002). The idea of a national survey of student opinion was first publicly mooted in this report, and subsequently the idea was taken up (for a fuller chronology of relevant events, see Brown *et al.* 2007).

The NSS, considerably influenced by Australian experience with the CEQ, underwent a substantial trial with recent graduates (Richardson 2004). A large number of changes were made to the instrument for its first full-scale administration in 2005, in which the focus of the instrument was switched from recent graduates to final-year students: the outcomes led to further refinement in 2006.

The NSS consists of 21 items covering six aspects of the student experience:

- teaching and learning (4 items);
- assessment and feedback (5);
- academic support (3);
- organisation and management (3);
- learning resources (3);
- personal development (3),

together with an item focusing on overall satisfaction. Latterly, these 22 'core' items have been supplemented by a set of items specific to students funded by the National Health Service and a bank of optional items from which institutions can select those of greatest interest to them. Beyond the 'core' items, data from only the supplementary items relating to the NHS-funded students are publicly available.

In addition to its original purpose of providing information to the public, the NSS quickly accrued a second purpose – the enhancement of learning and teaching in institutions (see HEFCE 2006). Institutions that fare badly on publicly reported surveys of student opinion find themselves challenged to improve their performance, and have striven to improve their position – in some cases in a manner tantamount to seeking a 'quick fix'. After all, no institution likes to appear at the bottom of a 'league table', even if such tables are of questionable methodological merit.

What surveys say about feedback

Surveys during the first year of the student 'life-cycle' and also towards, or just after, its end show that feedback has on the whole been rated relatively less highly than other aspects of 'the student experience'.

The Course Experience Questionnaire (Australia)

The development and testing of the original version of the CEQ is described in some detail in Linke (1991,Volume 2, pp.1–85), a shorter account being given in Ramsden (1991).

Analysis of responses to the CEQ confirmed the appropriateness of the five scales identified from previous work, namely:

- good teaching (8 items);
- clear goals and standards (5);
- appropriate workload (5);
- appropriate assessment (6);
- emphasis on independence (6).

The trialled version of the CEQ had three items relating to feedback:

7 Staff here put a lot of time into commenting on students' work.
17 Teaching staff here normally give helpful feedback on how you are going.
23 Feedback on student work is usually provided *only* in the form of marks or grades.

The first two of these fell into the 'good teaching' sub-scale whereas the third fell into the 'appropriate assessment' sub-scale. This separation would seem to reflect something of the difference between formative and summative assessment.

The version of the CEQ currently in use with recent graduates is an extended version of the original, with 48 items spread across ten scales plus the single 'overall satisfaction' item (see GCA 2010). Feedback now appears only in the two items in the 'good teaching' scale (GTS), with textual modifications as follows:

GTS01 The staff put a lot of time into commenting on my work.
GTS03 The teaching staff normally gave me helpful feedback on how I was going.

Since the administration of the CEQ to graduates in 1993 both items have shown a marked upward trend, GTS01 particularly so. Agreement with each of the items is currently in the region of 50 per cent (see GCA 2010, Table F14). GTS01 is technically unsatisfactory since it invites responses at a remove from the graduates' actual experience. The time-commitment of staff can only be inferred from the feedback received: an item asking about the actual amount of commenting would have greater validity, though this would not cover the quality of the feedback. Graduates are in a better position to respond to GTS03.

Surveys of the first-year experience (Australia)

In the series of studies of the first-year experience in Australia that have been run quinquennially since 1994, students were asked to respond to a single statement specifically related to feedback: 'Teaching staff usually give me helpful feedback on my progress'. Agreement with the statement has hovered around 30 per cent (Figure 1.1).

The Australasian Survey of Student Engagement, AUSSE (Australia and New Zealand)

The AUSSE, developed from the National Survey of Student Engagement [NSSE] in the US, has one item directly focusing on feedback. Roughly 40 per cent of students responding to the 2008 administration of the AUSSE said that they often or very often received feedback on their academic performance, whereas the staff perception was that this level of feedback applied to double this percentage (see ACER 2009, p.22, Figure 9: this comparison was not made in the subsequent year's report). A discrepancy of this magnitude invites further exploration.

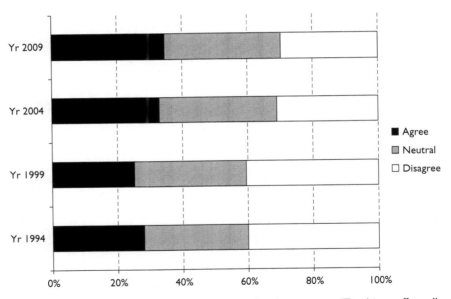

Figure 1.1 First-year Australian students' responses to the statement 'Teaching staff usually give me helpful feedback on my progress'.

Source: James *et al.* 2010, p.58.

The National Student Survey (UK)

The sector-wide results from 2006 to 2009 show that the positivity of students' responses to the items on the NSS 'assessment and feedback' scale, though gently rising, has been consistently some ten percentage points below that of both the 'organisation and management' and the 'academic support' scales (the next weakest in terms of positivity – see HEFCE 2010, p.14). If attention is focused on the three items relating to the actual provision of feedback (i.e. ignoring the two items relating to procedural aspects of assessment[3]), the level of positivity is lower still: Figure 1.2, relating to the 2009 administration of the NSS, illustrates the point.

For the purposes of this chapter, the three key NSS items are as follows:

AF7: Feedback on my work has been prompt.
AF8: I have received detailed comments on my work.
AF9: Feedback on my work has helped me clarify things I did not understand.

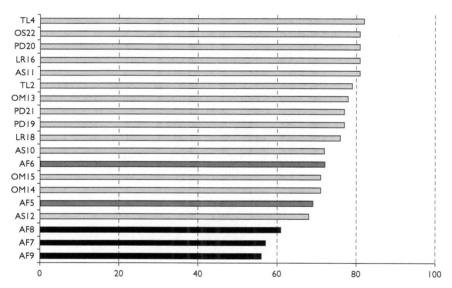

Figure 1.2 Global scores for the 2009 NSS 'core' items, in descending order of percentage agreement with the item (from HEFCE 2010, Annex D).

Notes:
AF = assessment and feedback (black shading signals that the item relates to actual feedback; mid-grey marbling signals that the item relates to assessment procedure)
AS = academic support
LR = learning resources
OM = organisation and management
OS = overall satisfaction
PD = personal development
TL = teaching and learning

The numbers indicate the particular NSS item (for the items, see HEFCE 2010, Annex A).

AF7 is open to interpretation as to what 'prompt' means. Results from the NSS have led to some institutions specifying time-limits within which feedback should be provided. AF8 is relatively unproblematic, as far as it goes – indeed, it almost invites a binary 'agree/disagree' response. However, some students might infer that the item refers to written comments on submitted work, and overlook tutors' less formal comments on work in progress (such as when conducting laboratory work or creating artefacts in a studio). AF9 is limited to the mitigation of weaknesses: there is nothing focusing on 'feedforward' (though it is possible – with perhaps a stretch of the imagination – to construe AF8 as subsuming this).

The First Year Experience survey (UK)

The sole substantial survey of students' first-year experience in the UK (Yorke and Longden 2007) drew on two of the 'feedback' items from the NSS and developed a third that sought to move away from the 'rectification' aspect of NSS AF9 towards something more constructive in intent. The levels of agreement with the provided statements were rather lower than those reported for the NSS's near-graduates (Figure 1.3: compare with Figure 1.1), but were rather

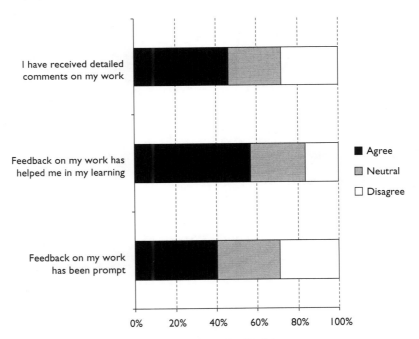

Figure 1.3 First-year students' responses to feedback items.
Source: Yorke and Longden 2007.

higher in the case of the 'helpfulness' item than on a roughly similar item in the Australian first-year experience surveys.

What inferences can be drawn from the data?

Surveys of the kind illustrated in this chapter can only give a 'broad brush' depiction of students' experience. For some purposes, this may be sufficient: a putative student may be satisfied to know that the feedback on work in a subject area in a particular institution is generally felt to be helpful, rather than be concerned about what actually makes it helpful. An institutional manager might simply need to know that responses to items reach a criterion level, only being concerned to instigate some enhancement-oriented action should that level not be attained.[4] An example of this last point is the distribution of positive responses in one UK institution to the three items specifically related to feedback in the 2010 NSS, where for each item there was a very wide range. Figure 1.4 shows the data in relation to the promptness of feedback: a similar distribution obtained in respect of the other two 'feedback' items. Any manager worthy of their post would surely be inquiring as to why feedback was perceived to be so much better in some subject areas than in others, and be prompting the worst-performing areas to give enhancement urgent attention. Managers, however, need to avoid knee-jerk reactions to NSS data since they need to get to the bottom of reasons for the outcomes in a subject area in a particular year — the disruption

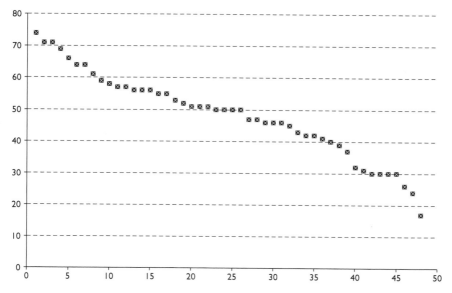

Figure 1.4 Percentage agreement with the NSS item 'Feedback on my work has been prompt', in descending order, for subject areas in a particular institution in 2010.

engendered by a move to new accommodation, for example, would be a possible cause of low ratings. One year's outcomes are not necessarily a good indicator of the general run of provision in an area – after all, economists warn of placing too much weight on a single month's national trade figures.

What published data do not tell

Useful sources of illumination of the ratings given to the NSS and the CEQ are the free-text comments of students. These comments cannot be addressed in this chapter, since they are provided for the use of individual institutions and are not generally available. Given that students may not share the interpretations given by staff to wordings, it is important to ensure that, to the best extent possible, staff understandings of the 'messages' align with what the students are seeking to convey. The free-text comments go some way towards such an alignment, but do not necessarily pick up respondents' interpretations that are different in focus from that intended in a relevant questionnaire item. The subtleties (sometimes the non-subtleties) of respondents' meanings, even when picked up by an institution, may not be fully understood.

There is some evidence that students responding to the CEQ do not always take a synoptic view in respect of their programmes but hang their responses on experiences of particular salience (Eley 2001).

Whilst the CEQ and the NSS may be sufficient to satisfy political require-ments in respect of accountability and the provision of information, they are of limited value when it comes to the enhancement of the student experience. A mere two or three items relating to feedback, limited to the issues shown earlier in this chapter, cannot do justice to the complexity inherent in providing an optimal student experience – an experience that encourages students to stretch out to progressively higher levels of achievement, and which inevitably involves an integration of the cognitive with the affective. Scores on the scales' items cannot – except in the crudest sense – be taken as proxy measures of the quality of the student experience nor of institutional effectiveness.

Unintended consequences?

The politicisation of feedback is a by-product of political desires for account-ability and the demonstration of quality in higher education. It risks institutions taking the view that 'getting the ratings right' is a sufficient solution to the problem of poor ratings. Responses to a few survey items are inadequate as pointers to improved practice, as is exemplified by the absence of 'feedforward' in the standard questionnaires. To focus solely on ratings would be to commit an institutional variant of students aiming for a grade rather than focusing on learning.

Improving feedback is not a matter of finding a magic bullet, but involves some depth of understanding of assessment as practised and of what feedback is expected to achieve (in other words, institutional learning). The politicisation (at various levels) of feedback and related issues, if insensitive, is likely to inhibit the very developments deemed desirable.

Notes

1 'Average' is represented by the second and third quartiles of scores combined, with above and below average being represented by the top and bottom quartiles, respectively.
2 Higher education in Northern Ireland was funded directly by the UK Government.
3 It is debatable whether the five items on assessment and feedback should be divided into a pair focusing on procedures and a trio focusing on actual feedback (see Marsh and Cheng 2008). This subdivision makes conceptual sense.
4 The philosophy of continuous quality improvement requires an enhancement orientation towards all aspects of 'the student experience', but a pragmatic approach to management focuses on the aspects most in need of attention whilst keeping an eye on opportunities to encourage improvement in less pressing aspects.

References

ACER (2009) *Engaging Students for Success*, Camberwell, Victoria: Australian Council for Educational Research.

AVCC/ACDP (1988) *Performance Indicators (Report of the AVCC/ACDP Working Party on Performance Indicators)*, Braddon, ACT: Australian Vice Chancellors' Committee and Australian Committee of Directors and Principals.

Bourke, P. (1986) *Quality Measures in Universities*, Belconnen, ACT: Commonwealth Tertiary Education Commission.

Brown, R., Carpenter, C., Collins, R. and Winkvist-Noble, L. (2007) 'Recent developments in information about programme quality in the UK', *Quality in Higher Education* 13(2): 173–84.

Commonwealth Tertiary Education Commission (1986) *Review of Efficiency and Effectiveness in Higher Education*, Canberra: Australian Government Publishing Service.

CVCP (Committee of Vice-Chancellors and Principals) (1985) *Report of the Steering Committee for Efficiency Studies in Universities ('The Jarratt Report')*, London: Committee of Vice-Chancellors and Principals.

CVCP (1995) *University Management Statistics and Performance Indicators in the UK*, Cheltenham: Universities Statistical Record.

CVCP and UGC (University Grants Committee) (1986) *Performance Indicators in Universities: a first statement by a joint CVCP/UGC working group*, London: Committee of Vice-Chancellors and Principals.

CVCP and UGC (1987) *Performance Indicators in Universities: a second statement by the joint CVCP/UGC working group*, London: Committee of Vice-Chancellors and Principals.

Dawkins, J.S. (1988) *Higher Education: a policy statement*, Canberra: Australian Government Publishing Service.

Eley, M. (2001) 'The Course Experience Questionnaire: altering question format and phrasing could improve the CEQ's effectiveness', *Higher Education Research and Development* 20(3): 293–312.

GCA (Graduate Careers Australia) (2010) *Graduate Course Experience 2009: the report of the Course Experience Questionnaire*, Melbourne: Graduate Careers Australia.

HEFCE (Higher Education Funding Council for England) (1999) *Performance Indicators in Higher Education: first report of the Performance Indicators Steering Group (PISG)*, Bristol: Higher Education Funding Council for England.

HEFCE (2002) *Information on Quality and Standards in Higher Education: final report of the Task Group ('The Cooke Report')*, Bristol: Higher Education Funding Council for England.

HEFCE (2006) *2006 National Student Survey: second national student survey gets under way [News item, 23 January]*. Available at: www.jiscmail.ac.uk/cgi-bin/webadmin?A2=BAKS;d747bdc3.0601 (accessed 30 January 2013).

HEFCE (2010) *National Student Survey: findings and trends 2006 to 2009*. Bristol: Higher Education Funding Council for England. Available at: www.hefce.ac.uk/pubs/hefce/2010/10_18/10_18.pdf (accessed 15 July 2011).

Hobsons (2010) *The Good Universities Guide to Universities and Private Higher Education Providers 2011*, Melbourne: Hobsons.

James, R., Krause, K.-L. and Jennings, C. (2010) *The First Year Experience in Australian Universities: findings from 1994 to 2009*, Melbourne: Centre for the Study of Higher Education, University of Melbourne.

Linke, R. (1991) *Performance Indicators in Higher Education: report of a trial evaluation study commissioned by the Commonwealth Department of Employment, Education and Training ('The Linke Report', 2 volumes)*, Canberra: Australian Government Publishing Service.

Linke, R., Birt, L., Fensham, P., Scott, R. and Smith, B. (1984) *Report of a Study Group on the Measurement of Quality and Efficiency in Australian Higher Education*, Canberra, ACT: Commonwealth Tertiary Education Commission.

Marsh, H.W. and Cheng, J. (2008) *National Student Survey of Teaching in UK Universities: dimensionality, multilevel structure, and differentiation at the level of university and discipline: preliminary results*. Available at: www.heacademy.ac.uk/assets/York/documents/ourwork/nss/NSS_herb_marsh-28.08.08.pdf (accessed 15 July 2011).

PCFC (1990) *Performance Indicators (Report of a Committee of Inquiry chaired by Mr Alfred Morris)*, London: Polytechnics and Colleges Funding Council.

Ramsden, P. (1991) 'A performance indicator of teaching quality in higher education: the course experience questionnaire', *Studies in Higher Education* 16(2): 129–50.

Richardson, J.T.E. (2004) *The National Student Survey: final report from the 2003 pilot project*, Institute of Educational Technology, Open University (mimeo).

SQW (Segal Quince Wicksteed) (1999) *Providing Public Information on the Quality and Standards of Higher Education Courses [Report by Segal Quince Wicksteed to DENI, HEFCE, HEFCW, QAA, SHEFC]*. Available at: www.hefce.ac.uk/pubs/hefce/1999/99_61.htm (accessed 15 July 2011).

Williams, B.R., Chair, (1979) *Education, Training and Employment: report of the Committee of Inquiry into Education and Training ('The Williams Report')*, Canberra: Australian Government Publishing Service.

Yorke, M. and Longden, B. (2007) *The First Year Experience of Higher Education in the UK [Report on Phase 1 of a project funded by the Higher Education Academy]*, York: The Higher Education Academy.

Chapter 2

Feedback – what students want

Alex Bols and Kate Wicklow

Introduction

There is a saying within the National Union of Students that 'feedback is the breakfast of champions'. Just as breakfast is the most important meal of the day, so feedback is one of the most important elements for learning. But if assessment feedback is the breakfast of champion scholars, then based on the meal that many students receive there are some very hungry scholars out there!

In a massified higher education system the question of how to provide effective feedback on the assessments of students, without collapsing under the burden of bureaucracy, has become ever more vexed. This chapter seeks to highlight the concerns of students about the feedback that they receive, attempt to identify what students want and highlight some of the activities that have been undertaken to tackle this by the National Union of Students (NUS) and by individual students' unions. The question of how students actually use this feedback is clearly of core importance but unfortunately there is not enough space in this chapter to look at this, but is addressed elsewhere in the book.

It is especially interesting to be writing this chapter at such a pivotal time in the higher education sector in the UK, in particular in England. With the major changes to the way in which higher education is funded and the introduction of the market there are some fundamental questions about the relationship between students and their institution. One thing we know is that on every previous occasion when the costs have been passed on to students, it has resulted in higher expectations about their experience and the quality of their course. This was seen following the 1998 introduction of full-time undergraduate fees in England and then their further increase in 2006, when we saw year on year increases in the number of students making complaints and appeals (OIA 2009), increased focus on feedback turnaround times (NUS 2010), and even protests at some universities about the number of contact hours that they receive. This focus of students becoming increasingly critical and demanding of the education that they are now contributing towards has given rise to the discourse of students as 'consumers' (Palfreyman and Warner 1998).

The NUS conducts an annual Student Experience Survey, along with HSBC, looking at various dimensions of the student experience. In the most recent version of the survey we questioned students about the way in which they saw themselves and the impact that higher fees would have on their expectations. Sixty-five per cent of students believe that if they were expected to pay more for their university experience they would have higher expectations (NUS/HSBC 2011). This could result in students that are 'more conscious of their rights and expected service standards, less tolerant of shortcomings, more demanding, more litigious' (Cuthbert 2010). The survey also asked students to plot themselves on a ten-point scale as to whether they considered themselves to be 'a student engaged in a community of learning' or whether they considered themselves to be 'a customer and expect the service I have paid for'. The results showed quite an interesting mix the whole way along the spectrum, the largest group congregated around the middle, suggesting that students might consider themselves in different ways. However, there was also some strong identification with both ends of the spectrum. Over a third of students, 37 per cent, rated themselves in the 1–3 category; in other words, they strongly agreed that they consider themselves to be a community of learning, compared to the smaller, but still significant 18 per cent that rated themselves 8–10, i.e. strongly identifying as a customer.

It will be interesting therefore to begin to tease out some of the implications that this changing attitude may have in relation to feedback. Will this more demanding relationship give rise to an attitude that 'I have paid for a service and I therefore expect it to be delivered on time' or that 'I expect the feedback to be delivered in the method most appropriate to my needs – rather than the needs of the academic'? There may also be a tension between these expectations that students themselves have and what would actually be best to facilitate their learning.

It is also important to recognise that whilst feedback is an important element in the learning process it is rightly closely linked with assessment itself in the National Student Survey due to the intertwined nature of these issues. It has been suggested that what students want in relation to assessment is FInALS (Bols, 2012). Namely that:

- Effective **F**eedback is an essential outcome of assessment.
- There are **IN**novative approaches to assessment.
- Assessment incorporates **A**nonymous marking.
- Assessment is **L**earning focused.
- **S**ubmission methods are accessible for students, especially for those studying flexibly.

NUS has been running a *Great Feedback Amnesty* for several years, gathering examples of both poor feedback and the type of feedback that is most effective. On the back of this campaign NUS developed ten principles for feedback (2008) and then a Charter for feedback and assessment (2010). Thinking about these principles within the context of student as consumer or active participant in their learning we have developed an acronym as a useful guide of student expectations relating to feedback:

T - **T**imely
A - **A**ccessible
L – **L**egible
K – **K**onstructive

This acronym identifies four broad areas, relating to the expectations that students have. We will explore these areas in more detail in this chapter. But underpinning these more mechanistic expectations is the principle of feedback that actually facilitates TALKing between students and academics. We believe that it is only through engaging in a real dialogue that students will truly reflect on, and accelerate, their learning.

T – Timely

The National Student Survey asks not just about the headline satisfaction relating to feedback and assessment but also goes on to ask whether 'the feedback on my work has been prompt'. This has consistently been the area of lowest satisfaction, with just 61 per cent satisfied in 2011. The NUS/HSBC Student Experience Report explores this question of the timeliness of the feedback in more detail, asking students how long, on average, it takes to receive feedback as well as looking at their expectations.

Feedback has been consistently identified as key to improving learning (Gibbs and Simpson 2004) but in order for this to have the maximum impact then students need to interact with the feedback, understand it and use it to reflect on their practice. This is where the question of the timeliness becomes so important. Students need to receive the feedback when the assessment is still fresh in their mind. If it is received more than a couple of weeks after the assessment the student will have forgotten about the details of their work and have moved on mentally. This will result in the feedback, however 'lovingly crafted' (Gibbs and Simpson 2002: 20) being ignored or even just left in the departmental office uncollected.

The NUS/HSBC Student Experience Report (2011) shows that whilst 23 per cent of students said that they received their feedback within two weeks there was still a sizable proportion – 24 per cent – that have to wait five or more weeks. When this is matched against their expectations there is clearly a wide gap, which is likely to explain, at least in part, the low student satisfaction in this area. Sixty-four per cent of students said that they expected feedback within two weeks, and almost all students, 98 per cent, said that they expected it within four weeks.

Many student unions over the last few years have been actively campaigning for a minimum turn around time for feedback on assessed work. Their campaigns have led to institutions changing their assessment policies to ensure feedback is given to students on average around three to four (working) weeks after the assessment has been submitted.

That said, there are also instances where a policy change has not been necessary. Instead, students have been better informed of the exact time in which they will be receiving their feedback, which has been proven by institutions like Northumbria University to increase the National Student Survey (NSS) satisfaction scores. Similarly other student unions, such as Sheffield Hallam, have been working with their institutions to ensure student are better informed about when they will receive their feedback and how it can be used effectively to improve future assessments. This information has been an essential driver in the student satisfaction with feedback, as well as ensuring that they have the skills to comprehend the feedback given and use it to progress.

When speaking with academics there are often concerns raised about the administrative burden of turning around large quantities of individualised feedback so quickly. However, it would be possible for example to give general feedback on the key learning points in the week after the assessment before delivering more personalised feedback at a slightly later date. This would be a more effective way of supporting students to learn from their assessment, especially if linked to a peer-to-peer discussion element and being able to harness that natural reaction of students coming out of an exam and instantly critiquing how they think they have done.

Finally in relation to the timeliness, it should be noted that whilst this summative feedback after the event is useful to get students to reflect on what they have done, if there was formative feedback whilst they are preparing for their assessment that will have had the most impact on improving learning. This could be in the form of looking at early drafts and a facilitated discussion for major pieces of work such as undergraduate dissertations or Masters essays. This type of feedback is already ingrained in some subjects such as art and design where there is an almost constant feedback process. However, where this more personalised formative feedback isn't possible tutors could outline some of the more general themes that have arisen from the assessment task in previous years.

NUS believes that: *Feedback should be timely*

Timely feedback is a key concern of students, with the NUS/HSBC Student Experience Report showing that almost a quarter of students have to wait more than five weeks to receive feedback. Students should usually receive personalised feedback within three weeks of the assessment submission deadline. There could also be generalised group feedback on the key learning areas that affect most students within one week of the assessment.

NUS believes that: *Formative assessment and feedback should be used throughout the programme*

Assessment should be used as part of the learning process, as well as a tool to measure understanding and application. Formative assessment and feedback is critical to the development of learning, and should be integrated into the curriculum in a strategic way. You should consider how to capture and formalise ongoing feedback in practical courses such as art and design. Wherever appropriate, there should be formative feedback before the assessment deadline for taught postgraduate students and for undergraduate dissertations.

A – Accessible

The way in which students receive feedback is also identified in the NUS/HSBC research as an area where there is a gap between expectations and experiences, the most significant gap being in relation to receiving verbal feedback provided in an individual meeting from the academic that set the assessment. Only 24 per cent of students say that they currently receive feedback in this way compared to the 67 per cent of students that would like to receive it. This was also particularly identified as being important by older students, perhaps due to transition into higher education and distance from previous educational experiences, with 72 per cent of those over 21 agreeing compared to 64 per cent of 18-year-olds. There were also some interesting differences by subject discipline, with architecture students (84 per cent), veterinary students (82 per cent) and history students (81 per cent) much more likely to cite individual verbal feedback as being important than engineering students (56 per cent), physical sciences students (59 per cent) and medicine and dentistry students (59 per cent).

Students receiving verbal feedback were also significantly more likely to agree that their feedback had made it clear how they could improve their performance, with 80 per cent of students receiving verbal feedback agreeing with this statement as opposed to only 63 per cent that received written comments. Students receiving verbal feedback are also more likely to agree with the statement that it motivates them to learn, with 69 per cent of those receiving verbal feedback agreeing compared to just 55 per cent of those receiving written comments.

It is also perhaps interesting that there is an assumption that all students want is their mark or grade. However, the research showed that not all students are quite so instrumental in their outlook, with only 66 per cent of students saying that this is the most useful way of receiving feedback compared to the 88 per cent of students that say this is how they primarily receive it at the moment. But again, looking at the data in different ways it flags up some interesting differences that could be further explored elsewhere. For example, the difference amongst students by socio-economic groups is perhaps surprising, with socio-economic groups A and B being much less likely to cite written marks as being useful, with 64 per cent and 63 per cent respectively, compared to socio-economic groups D and E of which 75 per cent and 74 per cent cite it as being useful. It would be interesting to explore the extent to which this is linked to prior expectations based on schooling. There are also, perhaps more understandably, differences by year of study with 71 per cent of first year students saying that written marks are useful compared to 61 per cent of third year students.

What we think this particularly highlights is that different students will have quite different expectations. Therefore, when considering the different methods of delivering feedback it is important to first get a clearer understanding of what students want. This is particularly true for different types of students, such as those studying part-time or through distance learning and so it is necessary to consider the accessibility of the way in which feedback is delivered.

The other issue that arises in relation to accessibility of feedback is ensuring that students receive feedback in all the different forms of assessment that they undertake. This is especially important for exams, which for some students is their primary form of assessment. Whilst 88 per cent of students say they would like to receive feedback on their exams, only half currently receive more than just a grade, with 27 per cent receiving online feedback, 13 per cent written comments and 5 per cent each receiving verbal feedback individually or in a group.

NUS believes that: *Receiving feedback should not be exclusive to certain forms of assessment*

Traditionally, summative feedback is usually only given to written essays and some forms of practical work. But students need feedback on all forms of assessment they come across in order to develop their learning. Most courses rely on exams as the summative assessment – it is therefore important that students receive feedback on these, especially in exams prior to finals.

And that: *Students should be given the choice of format for feedback*

Students want feedback in a variety of formats, including verbal, written and electronic, and at the start of the year students should be able to state their preferred form of summative feedback. This provides a useful focus for a meeting with a personal tutor, while giving students a choice in the form of feedback; and making the feedback more physically accessible to them. This should ensure that all students, no matter whether they are full-time, part-time or distance learners, will have easy access to their feedback. Regardless of format, the feedback should always be written in plain English, and be legible and clear.

L – Legible

Written grades and feedback are the most common forms of feedback, with 88 per cent and 81 per cent of students respectively receiving feedback through these methods. It is therefore essential that students can read and understand these comments. The question of legibility may seem like an obvious point but it is shocking the number of times we hear comments from students about how bad lecturers' writing is and that they can't read the feedback.

This question of the legibility of the feedback is likely to be linked to the growing desire amongst students to receive feedback online. In the first NUS/HSBC survey in 2008 only a tiny handful of students said that they wanted to receive feedback online – not even registering as a single percentage point. This has now increased to almost a third of students, 29 per cent, in the most recent version of the research. Clearly legibility isn't the only reason why students want to receive online feedback, as ICT becomes more firmly embedded within their higher education experience, but we believe that it is at least part of the explanation for the significant rise in recent years.

Looking in more depth at the desire for online feedback there were some interesting differences by subject discipline, with 40 per cent of medicine and dentistry students wanting online feedback, 38 per cent of engineering students and 36 per cent of biological sciences students compared to just 18 per cent of history students and 20 per cent of veterinary sciences students. Perhaps with the reputation that doctors have for difficult-to-read handwriting it is not surprising that they top the list, but, more seriously, it will be necessary to further explore the different expectations that different groups of students have.

In addition to simply being able to read the feedback it is important that students are able to understand the feedback so that they do not misinterpret or miss key pieces of advice. Therefore ensuring that feedback is written in plain English so it can be easily understood by all students is essential, as it can be too easy to slip into academic shorthand but the student may not have the same understanding of the feedback as the academic, potentially causing frustration on both sides.

The development of e-assessment has been a positive move for the availability of typed, electronic or video feedback. JISC have funded an array of projects over the past few years which have aimed to enhance digital innovations in assessment and feedback. What we have found from these is that although technology can play a huge part in making feedback more accessible to students, some academics are not digitally literate enough to be able to incorporate these into their daily routines.

NUS believes that feedback: *Should be legible and clear*

Feedback should be written in plain language so it can be easily understood by all students. It should also be legible so that nothing is misinterpreted or missed.

K – Konstructive

The final element of TALK is the extent to which feedback is Konstructive – yes, I know we're cheating spelling it with a K rather than a C but everyone loves a good acronym! Whilst the timeliness, accessibility and legibility of the feedback are all essential elements if the content of the feedback itself is not helpful then the whole game is lost.

The literature suggests that there are two key reasons why students want feedback: first, it helps to act as a yardstick for their progress and understanding; second, feedback can be helpful in identifying what they have done well, so that they can reproduce it next time, and where there are areas that they can learn from, so that they can focus on this area in the future (Price *et al.* 2008). It is this second aspect that the constructive dimension addresses.

However, at present there are still question marks relating to the usefulness of the feedback that students receive. The NUS/HSBC research shows that only 58 per cent of students agree with the statement that the feedback they receive 'makes it clear how to improve my performance'. This suggests that there is still a long way to go in terms of students receiving constructive feedback that actually helps to identify ways in which students can improve their performance and feedback that actually connects with the student. It is perhaps this that begins to hint at some of the underlying dissatisfaction in relation to the overall question of feedback.

This research into the usefulness of the feedback that students receive reinforces the anecdotal evidence gathered through the NUS Great Feedback Amnesty. When asked to comment on the feedback that they receive, students made comments like:

> 'All I get is a grade next to my matriculation number without any indication on how I'm actually doing.'

'I got an essay back where the only comment was "use a bigger text size" – there was nothing on how to improve my grade.'

'For a rather lengthy scientific report, the feedback I received consisted of a mere 2 ticks and a question mark.'

These quotes really articulate some of the frustrations that some students have in relation to the feedback that they receive. There are, however, some significant differences about the usefulness of the feedback by subject discipline, with 75 per cent of history and philosophy students and 73 per cent of languages students agreeing compared to 41 per cent of veterinary students and 47 per cent of students studying subjects allied to medicine. It would be interesting to further explore whether these students actually receive better feedback, or just that the departments are better at explaining it and managing their expectations.

TALK

Feedback is seen by the sector as a particularly difficult issue to crack. There has been a lot of effort invested in trying to improve student satisfaction, but with relatively limited success. Like all good puzzles the four pieces of TALK fit together as a whole to create a wider picture, namely the importance of TALKing. But it is also worth stressing that without any individual piece of the puzzle the overall picture becomes distorted.

This dialogue between students and academics is key to helping to create real understanding. The Learning Pyramid (National Training Laboratories, Bethel, Maine) makes the point that lectures, reading and audiovisual have limited impact in terms of the student's retention of information, estimating a 5 per cent, 10 per cent and 20 per cent retention rate respectively. This brings to mind the Chinese proverb that 'I hear and I forget, I see and I remember, I do and I understand'. The learning pyramid goes on to suggest that where there is a real discussion, students retain about 50 per cent of the information. Interestingly, and chiming with the Chinese proverb, it goes on to suggest that if a student has to teach others they will retain about 90 per cent of the information. It is therefore not one-way feedback that results in real understanding but rather an exchange of ideas through constructive dialogue.

The second dimension that this highlights is that there has been a lot of discussion recently surrounding contact hours. It is sometimes easy for students to revert back to the consumer approach, demanding lots of contact hours to meet their expectations surrounding value for money. However, as the learning pyramid demonstrates, it is not lots more sitting in large lectures to meet the demand for increased contact hours that will create deep learning but rather a personalised approach to learning, with the guide on the side, supported through the personal tutor system.

This begins to hint at the question of the quality of the feedback as opposed to the quantity of it. In some focus groups that we organised students commented that the best feedback is when they are taught by the same person who then really gets to know you and is therefore able to provide useful feedback that is pitched at the right level.

NUS believes that: *Students should have access to face-to-face feedback for at least the first piece of assessment each academic year*

For most students, a discussion about their work is the most productive form of feedback they can receive. At the start of each academic year, it is crucial that students are given an opportunity to discuss their work with a tutor, to enable them to set goals for the coming year. As well as helping students to develop their learning, this can act as a progression monitoring tool for the institution. If face-to-face feedback is impossible (due to distance or part-time learning, etc.), technology can be used to facilitate a discussion between tutor and student.

NUS believes that: *Students should be supported to critique their own work*

Students should not be overly reliant on feedback from tutors. One of the key skills developed in higher education is the ability to critique, and students should be supported to be able to critique their own work and that of fellow students. Developing students' abilities to peer review and self-reflect is an important skill for future employment, as well as deepening their own learning.

Conclusions

Students want feedback that meets the TALK criteria, but it is important to tailor this to respond to the different needs and expectations of students depending on how they consider themselves in relation to being a consumer or partner in their education. This will mean a mixed approach of setting clear deadlines for returning feedback and engaging students in the process of how they will receive feedback, but also making clear that less frequent but more in-depth feedback may actually be better in the long run, especially if linked to them developing their ability to critique other students' work and having the opportunity to do more of this.

It is also important to note that there are many valid reasons why students in different departments receive their feedback in different ways. However, unless the students themselves know this then they will look at friends in other departments and will not be comparing like with like. The key to effective feedback is not just the way in which it is delivered but how students are inducted into the academic community so that they are able to make the most of the feedback that they receive.

References

Bols, A. (2012) 'Student views on assessment', in L. Clouder, C. Broughan, S. Jewell and G. Steventon (eds) *Improving Student Engagement and Development through Assessment: theory and practice in higher education*, Abingdon: Routledge.

Cuthbert, R. (2010) 'Students as consumers?' *Higher Education Review* 42(3): 3–25.

Gibbs, G. and Simpson, C. (2002) 'Does your assessment support your students' learning?' Available at: http://isis.ku.dk/kurser/blob.aspx?feltid=157744 (accessed 15 December 2012).

Gibbs, G. and Simpson, C. (2004) 'Conditions under which assessment supports students' learning', *Learning and Teaching in Higher Education* 1: 3–31.

NUS (National Union of Students) (2008) 'The ten principles of good feedback practice', NUS Briefing, The Great Feedback Amnesty.

NUS (2010) 'Feedback and assessment campaign toolkit'. Available at: www.nusconnect.org.uk/campaigns/highereducation/learning-and-teaching-hub/feedback/campaigntools/ (accessed 20 June 2012).

NUS/HSBC (2011) 'Student experience report: teaching and learning'. Available at: www.nusconnect.org.uk/resourcehandler/55f67a43-e0ae-4b8f-b8fa-6735d453262e/ (accessed 20 June 2012).

OIA (Office of the Independent Adjudicator) (2009) Annual Report. Available at: www.oiahe.org.uk/media/13808/oia-annual-report-2009.pdf (accessed 20 June 2012).

Palfreyman, D. and Warner, D. (1998) *Higher Education and the Law: a guide for managers*, Buckingham: Open University Press.

Price, M., O'Donovan, B., Rust, C. And Carroll, J. (2008) 'Assessment standards: a manifesto for change', *Brookes eJournal of Learning and Teaching* 2(5). Available at: http://bejlt.brookes.ac.uk/article/assessment_standards_a_manifesto_for_change/ (accessed 20 June 2012).

Chapter 3

Feedback on feedback

Uncrossing wires across sectors

Maddalena Taras

Introduction

Traditionally, different communities of practice in the compulsory and higher education sectors and specific assessment procedures of accreditation have resulted in separation of focus, practice and research. The internationalisation of communications through publications, conferences and personal contacts has dissolved barriers across sectors, requiring an understanding of discourses and practices to maximise clarity of transfer between sectors (Taras 2008).

This chapter aims first at clarifying representations and understandings of feedback both within and across sectors. It examines three aspects of assessment: definitions of feedback; the relationship between feedback and formative assessment; and different models of self-assessment. Second, it evaluates five self-assessment models (Taras 2010) to see how dialogic understandings can be achieved and where and how the student voice is placed: without self-assessment, any dialogic understanding of formative assessment and feedback cannot take place.

Higher education (HE) and the compulsory sector (CS) have much to contribute to each other, but any movement across sectors must be understood in the original context and then learning from that transferred to the new context by taking note of the impact of the transfer. The models of self-assessment are very useful for the CS and HE as they demonstrate how useful summative assessment has been traditionally for providing feedback to students. This discourse is of interest to all educationalists and stakeholders as it provides them with choices to support student learning.

Definitions of feedback

A basic premise in current educational learner and learning centred discourses is that learners are at the epicentre of the process. This negates the concept of feedback as a product to be imposed on learners. Feedback is conceived as key to learning and by examining definitions of feedback and their relationship to formative assessment (FA), alignment between learning theories and definitions can be evaluated.

Work by Ramaprasad (1983) and Sadler (1989) is used extensively across sectors to distinguish between information and feedback: 'Feedback is information about the gap between the actual level and the reference level of a system parameter which is used to alter the gap in some way' (Ramaprasad 1983: 4).

The idea of 'gap' may be a deficit that could be linked to a value judgement. Perhaps it could be a difference in opinion or focus and not represent a gap in the sense of something missing. The idea of 'gap', if one exists, is linked to action by learners. '[Feedback] requires knowledge of the standard or goal, skills in making multicriterion comparisons, and the development of ways and means for reducing the discrepancy between what is produced and what is aimed for' (Sadler 1989: 142).

Therefore, feedback will instigate change and support student learning only if learners actually use it. This effectively takes feedback from the control of tutors and puts it firmly in the domain of learners' choices. It is convenient to call this type of feedback 'formative feedback' (the terminology in the literature) since it seems impossible to change the current espoused meaning of 'feedback' from that of information. Indeed, Sadler (2010) adopts the accepted definition that equates it to knowledge of results because it is evident that current discourse across the world uses it in this manner: 'Feedback is taken to include all communications from a teacher to a student following appraisal of a student response' (Sadler 2010: 537). This definition is an accurate representation of generally accepted perceptions and understandings, rather than a focus on whether it will have an impact on learning, as was the focus in Sadler (1989).

He chooses instead to focus on the aspects and parameters of feedback that can support learning. This definition represents feedback as being a one-way conduit from tutors to learners and fuels the behaviouristic metaphor of learning being the filling of a bucket. Sadler (2010), although keeping the same basic thinking as previous papers as to how learners can develop expertise to learn from feedback, adds a new emphasis: in addition to mandatory self-assessment, learners require training through peer-assessment to develop the same critical assessment skills as tutors require. In the 1989 paper, we could argue that exemplars performed the same function, especially if they were used to help learners judge the quality of the work presented. The dialogic, interactive aspects of current thinking on feedback, which provide the students with their voice and autonomy, are introduced through the mandatory use of peer- and self-assessment and in the process of formative feedback.

In the CS the work of Black and Wiliam has led to recent developments in assessment and can be taken as representative of many discourses and definitions. Their work will be examined in order to understand the thinking represented in their definitions. As Sadler (2010) notes, much of the empirical research on feedback has been carried out within this sector, as seen in the feedback reviews by Natriello (1987), Crooks (1988), Black and Wiliam (1998) and Hattie and Timperley (2007). In these reviews, the focus is on how feedback influences student learning and the parameters that can influence its efficacy.

The initial part of the definition of feedback provided by Black and Wiliam (1998) in their seminal article would seem to echo that of Sadler (2010) and the general understanding of the term: 'for the sake of simplicity, that the term feedback be used in its least restrictive sense, to refer to any information that is provided to the performer of any action about that performance' (Black and Wiliam 1998: 51). However, the qualifying statement that follows would seem to contradict directly Ramaprasad (1983) and Sadler (1989 and 2010) who require a standard of comparison in order to be able to assess and subsequently to provide feedback: 'This need not necessarily be from an external source . . ., nor need there necessarily be some reference standard against which the performance is measured, let alone some method of comparing the two' (Black and Wiliam 1998: 51).

The first statement indicates that feedback can be provided by learners themselves in self-assessment: this is not contentious. However, what follows could be seen as problematic: 'The actual performance can be evaluated either in its own terms, or by comparing it with a reference standard' (Black and Wiliam 1998: 51). The question arises as to what evaluating something 'in its own terms' actually means. This is not clarified in the paper since the examples that follow relate to alternative means of comparing.

Against the idea of evaluating something 'in its own terms' is Wittgenstein's problem of definitions which he states cannot be measured against themselves but require a point of comparison. Winter clarifies that it is a problem which questions the measurement metaphor in assessment and makes it technically inaccurate not to say impossible to carry out.

> Hence, all rules (and especially assessment procedures) can only operate as interpretive judgements within a knowledgeable community. Learning can never, therefore, be 'measured', as with a ruler . . . Indeed, the limitations of the ruler as a metaphor for educational judgements return us to the alternative metaphor of the 'second dimension'. . . . The mathematical principle here is that to identify a point along one dimension you need a second dimension; or, more generally: to identify a point in N dimensions, you always need N+1 dimensions.
>
> (Winter 1995: 77)

What does this mean? It means that any assessment, evaluation, judgement is a comparison. If a book is deemed 'good', then it is so because it can be compared to 'excellent' or 'bad' books. Therefore, any comparison is made either implicitly or explicitly, but it cannot be done 'in its own terms' because it does not have any.

As a possible interpretation of evaluating something 'in its own terms' it could be that learners set their own criteria and parameters making the comparison implicit. But this too would require a comparison and the evaluator would need to be aware of the learners' parameters. This is why, in most definitions of feedback, this second dimension is represented by the 'gap' or reference standard.

From their discussion, Black and Wiliam appear to be signalling that assessment, and therefore ultimately feedback which is the product of assessment, can be arrived at without explicit or implicit criteria and standards. This attempt to make FA (and assessment for learning) exempt from being rule-bound has resulted in them taking both FA and assessment for learning outside of theoretical constraints. It is beyond the scope of this chapter to delve deeper into the discussion (see Taras 2009 for a detailed discussion).

Feedback and formative assessment

As noted above, feedback is often defined in relation to how it can support learning and it has increasingly become synonymous with formative assessment (FA), whether implicitly or explicitly. 'Feedback is defined in a particular way to highlight its function in formative assessment' (Sadler 1989: 119). Sadler's feedback definition is integral to formative assessment and his definition of FA is not greatly different from Ramaprasad's definition of feedback (or formative feedback).

> Formative assessment is concerned with how judgements about the quality of student responses (performance, pieces, or works) can be used to shape and improve the students' competence by short-circuiting the randomness and inefficiency of trial-and-error learning.
>
> (Sadler 1989: 120)

Whereas feedback appeared as a conduit from tutor (also peer and self) to learner, FA is the prerogative of the learner who may use feedback to support more efficient learning.

It is sometimes difficult to make a distinction between definitions of feedback and FA, particularly when using Ramaprasad's definition of feedback (see, for example, Black *et al.* 2003: 4–15). Directly linked to this, a problem arises in terminological distinctions between diagnostic and formative assessments.

> All formative assessment is to a degree diagnostic, and the term diagnostic assessment is also used. . . . [D]iagnostic assessment is an expert and detailed enquiry into underlying difficulties, and can lead to radical re-appraisal of a pupil's needs, whereas formative assessment is more superficial in assessing problems and particular classroom work, and can lead to short-term and local changes in the learning work of a pupil.
>
> (Black and Wiliam 1998: 26)

If we compare these distinctions between diagnostic and formative assessments and Sadler's discussions of the complexities and subtleties of FA (Sadler 1989, 2010) then the most important difference between HE and CS is that the CS definitions of FA are downgraded and trivialised by comparison to accepted definitions and understandings in HE. For CS, classroom FA involving teachers and teaching is an ad hoc and informal process: if feedback comes from this FA, then the feedback too will be ad hoc and informal. It is difficult to try to understand another individual's thoughts and this may explain why the citation presents FA as 'more superficial' within the context of classroom discourse.

In HE, FA has generally been understood as complex, diagnostic and supportive feedback which is used to improve outcomes, involves learners and their understandings of the parameters. This is linked to the complex nature of learning, but also to the complex nature of assessing complex work and ultimately providing feedback which is dialogic, negotiated and understood by all concerned: feedback is ultimately controlled by learners (Price *et al.*, this volume; Alverno College, n.d.). Trivialising FA and feedback effectively deprives learners of their voice because using FA is their decision and their right to make that decision. Empowering learners is about allowing them to learn, not maintaining the illusion that we can make them learn.

Learners and feedback

Despite attempts to focus definitions of feedback on learners' understandings and uptake, most discourse still views feedback as a one-way telling. FA has taken this semantic role but feedback is still expected to be the missing link, catalyst and panacea of learning – this is why our definitions and understandings of feedback in relation to other aspects of assessment are so important. This chapter, like this book, supports the dialogic, negotiated understanding of feedback (and FA!) which is part of the student voice and therefore within the domain and control of learners.

Assessment is judging and giving a value to something (even if this is unexpressed). One can assess implicitly and not provide feedback. Feedback is just one product of assessment. Is feedback a part of assessment? No, it is the next step, which is a consequence of assessment. If ethical and transparent, we would expect that it is an articulation of the judgement in terms of specific criteria, standards and goals in order to explain and justify these. This was the basis of the rationale that supports explicit assessment parameters and refutes the possibility of assessing something 'in its own terms'.

The Osney Grange Group 'Agenda for Change' (Price *et al.*, this volume) has concluded that feedback is a 'relational process' that is integrated into learning and teaching. This is very similar to the Alverno process of supporting learning:

> Faculty and other trained assessors observe and judge a student's performance based on explicit criteria. Their diagnostic feedback as well as the reflective practice of self assessment by each student, helps to create a continuous process that improves learning and integrates it with assessment. We call this process student assessment-as-learning.
>
> (Alverno College, n.d.)

Learners amalgamate and integrate all feedback and reflections into new thinking and understandings.

Overall, much of the feedback provided by tutors is often a shot in the dark that may not be relevant or helpful to learners and learning. This vast generalisation comes from my own experience of discussing 'feedback' about their work with learners. It also comes from the National Student Survey which has demonstrated year after year that feedback and assessment fall short of desired and expected results (Yorke, this volume). My own personal reflections, observations and research lead me to believe that when we provide feedback we are often making assumptions about learners' thinking and intentions. Considering the number of learners most tutors would encounter over an academic year, there is a high potential for making errors of judgement. Only learners can really tell us if our assumptions and presumptions about their work and thinking is accurate – hence the need for dialogic and continuous interactions over time.

Getting inside others' heads to both understand and subsequently eliminate the causes of errors is a magic trick we have expected tutors to perform. But, feedback is not a freestanding piece of information; rather it forms part of a learning context where all the protagonists need to be engaged in the process (Taras 2008). In addition to understanding what caused the errors, tutors would need to be cognisant with the intentions of learners and how these errors can be transformed into positive aspects of their work.

Within the context of classroom interactions and work in the CS, teachers demonstrated the difficulty of reading the minds of learners and knowing how to advise them: 'teachers . . . found it extremely difficult, if not impossible, to offer advice to the students as to how to improve' (Black *et al.* 2003: 58). This again would confirm that it is difficult for any individual to place themselves within another's thoughts: how much more difficult for teachers to do this every day for many individuals?

Why self-assessment?

If dialogic discourse is the catalyst that can provide 'feedback' to learners, then self-assessment is the missing link which will permit learners to question, understand and integrate that feedback into their own work and thinking to permit learning. I would go further and say that the only way to make feedback and FA dialogic is through self-assessment: peer assessment and tutor discussions support this.

Self-assessment provides learners with a voice and empowers them to think for themselves. The importance of self-assessment is documented in HE, professional development: 'I judge the introduction of self-assessment . . . as the most powerful factor for change and development' (Cowan 2006: 111), and also across all ages in the CS: 'Almost all the teachers mentioned some form of self-assessment in their plans . . . the effect of the intervention can be seen to almost double the rate of student learning' (Wiliam 2007: 1059).

Despite the differences between FA and feedback definitions across sectors, there is a consensus that self-assessment is central to learning: this is in accordance with thinking on dialogic, negotiated feedback as noted above. However, the choices of self-assessment models available to support learners have been little discussed as have the implications for the student voice and institutional responsibilities.

Five models of self-assessment

The five models of self-assessment identified by Taras (2010) will be examined to see how, directly and indirectly, they require the production, understanding and use of feedback. Taras (2010) notes that all self-assessment models can vary the amount of learner involvement and that tutors can increase learner participation by providing them with greater responsibility.

The five models of self-assessment will be examined in turn and are: the standard model, self-marking, the sound standard model (Cowan 2002), the model with integrated peer/tutor feedback (Taras 2008, 2010), and learning contract design (Cowan 2006). All models were developed for adult learners and the standard model is by far the most widespread in HE and is the main model that has filtered down to the CS.

Standard model

The standard model developed in the USA in the 1930s (Boud 1995) and is the most commonly used in all sectors. It is the basic 'self-assessment' default model. It requires learners to provide their own feedback by looking to their own expertise and abilities in order to compare their work against the criteria and standards to judge how and how far this work achieves the requirements. It usually requires self-grading.

Taras (2010) signals that this cyclical process of reflection and updating should lead to the 'optimum' product within time and contextual constraints. Distance from the work and external feedback would permit a reappraisal of the quality of the work. One potential issue is that learners may convince themselves of the correctness of erroneous aspects within this introspective cycle: another is that adjustment of one aspect of the work may set off kilter the balance of the rest.

The role of tutors and peers is to provide feedback on the self-assessment in addition to the work itself. Perhaps an essential and necessary aspect, within a dialogic understanding of feedback, is to ensure discussions on how external feedback contributes to the self-assessment otherwise learners are isolated in their own preconceptions.

To summarise, a positive is that learners reflect and consider their work in order to improve it. A negative is that external feedback is usually provided after completion of the work and often no provision is made for FA to occur because updating of the work or performance is not generally part of the model. Learners are led to the fountain of knowledge but not permitted to drink, so to speak. Furthermore, there is the danger that the student voice is transformed into a confessional, which may not help their work (Taras 2010).

Self-marking

Self-marking is perhaps the most obvious manifestation of one of the primary motivators for the early development of self-assessment – reducing tutors' marking workload (Boud 1995, Taras 2010). Nevertheless, it has a number of positives for learners in that the feedback or marking sheet provided makes explicit tutors' interpretations of the task, criteria and process, enabling learners to question ambiguities. Tutors and peers may be involved in checking the self-marking and so increase dialogue. Self-marking is an active process of comparison, which is the basic tenet of feedback to support learning. If learners are part of the marking sheet production after completing their work, this further maximises their participation. From this it would seem that self-marking may be considered a more participatory and active dialogic process than the standard model (which requires 'talking to yourself').

Sound standard model

The sound standard model (Cowan 2002), like self-marking, is a means of providing students with a model with which to compare their work. It provides two exemplars that represent a 55 per cent grade (or 'sound standard') as points of comparison that can be used for them to decide their own feedback and grades. The premise is that most students will produce work in this quality band and can add or deduct marks from this baseline. One critique is that students are not being provided with exemplars of excellence to aspire to, although students with weaker work may find it less daunting and more positive. As with 'self-marking' learners are active participants in the comparison and decisions about their work. Further dialogue with peers and tutors is possible and desirable.

Model with integrated peer/tutor feedback

This model requires, as part of the process, the understanding and integration of peer and tutor feedback with the learner's own (Taras 2008, 2010). It is the interaction of peer/tutor feedback with their perceptions of their work which is the catalyst to new learning. The ideal process is presented as being participatory, dialogic and interactive, thus providing the maximum opportunity for the student voice. With modern technology, this can be achieved in many ways and does not limit learners to face-to-face real-time discourses, although this is the context where it was trialled and disseminated in HE in the UK across subject specialisms and in Sweden at secondary level in language learning (Oscarson 2009).

Learning contract design

An important premise of this learning contract design model (Cowan 2006) is that learners accept and acknowledge the central part in their own learning. Also, as responsible adults with a history of learning to draw on, they are required to make all their decisions. These will be supported and discussed with peers and tutors to help inform choices and decisions that are totally learner-led. Weekly contacts permitted individuals to decide on curriculum, timelines, learning and assessment processes and products. The final assessment is subject to endorsement of the stated parameters by tutors. Such freedom of choice requires trust and dedication from all concerned. Feedback is regular, mutual and supportive of learners and learning within a strong communication and community structure. The student voice is central at all stages of this process.

It is difficult to judge the extent to which any of the above self-assessment models are used. Outside of mainstream reports or published articles, it is often serendipitous as to whether we become cognisant with dissemination and use. Cann (2010), in response to Taras (2010), communicates the following:

> Interesting that the 'Strongest model of self-assessment, Learning contract design (LCD)' features included weekly objectives, peer feedback with a new peer each week, original, reviewed objectives and methods on display at the public notice board. This is pretty much an exact description of our Friendfolio approach.
>
> (Cann 2010)

With mass communications through the world-wide web, informal postings are an increasing source of information.

Conclusion

This chapter has raised issues that are central to the support of student learning within an institutional setting irrespective of age or context. Our epistemologies and beliefs of learning and assessment must align with practice if these issues are to be resolved. The student voice must be at the centre, but it must be conceived as a responsibility that learners will take and institutions must accord. Students cannot be at the centre of learning unless they are at the centre of assessment: making indefensible dichotomies between formative and summative assessment to maintain a status quo that marginalises and excludes learners from assessment on any pretext cannot produce an ethical, sustainable education. Muddying the waters in discussions of definitions of feedback and FA is also unhelpful. Whatever terminologies we use, the central premise and tenet that can make use of research and produce research-led teaching and learning can be simplified. We begin with learners, how they are included and become a central part of all assessment, and then the processes, practices and supporting institutional frameworks can follow.

This statement is less dramatic than it sounds and it certainly does not involve dismantling our institutional frameworks or processes of quality or quality assurance. It merely required self-assessment to be mandatory for learners – everything else has been demonstrated to accommodate easily to this central tenet of learning.

At institutional level this challenges the last and most meaningful bastion of control – assessment. Student participation in assessment as equal partners is mandatory for dialogic, meaningful feedback and hence learning: peer- and self-assessment are two necessary means for doing this. Excluding students from assessment makes a nonsense of all learning and teaching developments of the last three decades. If we can credit our students with the name of learners, then we must also make them central in the assessment processes and products. The other choice is to forget totally the words 'FA' and 'feedback' as meaningless and vacuous and superfluous to our needs and beliefs.

References

Alverno College. Available at: www.alverno.edu/for_educators/student_as_learn.html> (accessed 22 January 2009).

Black, P. and Wiliam, D. (1998) 'Assessment and classroom learning', *Assessment in Education* 5(1): 7–74.

Black, P., Harrison, C., Lee, C., Marshall, B., and Wiliam, D. (2003) *Assessment for Learning: putting it into practice*, Maidenhead: Open University Press.

Boud, D.J. (1995) *Enhancing Learning Through Self Assessment*, London: Kogan Page.

Cann, A.J. (2010) Available at: http://scienceoftheinvisible.blogspot.com/search?q= friendfolio (accessed 20 May 2010).

Cowan, J. (2002) *Plus/Minus Marking: a method of assessment worth considering?* York, UK: The Higher Education Academy.

Cowan, J. (2006) *On Becoming an Innovative University Teacher: reflection in action* (2nd edn), Oxford: Oxford University Press.

Crooks, T.J. (1988) 'The impact of classroom evaluation practices on students', *Review of Educational Research* 58: 438–81.

Hattie, J. and Timperley, H. (2007) 'The power of feedback', *Review of Educational Research* 77(1): 81–112.

Natriello, G. (1987) 'The impact of evaluation processes on students', *Educational Psychologist* 22: 155–75.

Oscarson, D. (2009) *Self-Assessment of Writing in Learning English as a Foreign Language: A Study at the Upper Secondary School Level*. Available at: http://hdl.handle.net/2077/ 19783 (accessed 10 June 2009).

Ramaprasad, A. (1983) 'On the definition of feedback', *Behavioural Sciences* 28(1): 4–13.

Sadler, D.R. (1989) 'Formative assessment and the design of instructional systems', *Instructional Science* 18: 145–65.

Sadler, D.R. (2010) 'Beyond feedback: developing student capability in complex appraisal', *Assessment and Evaluation in Higher Education* 35(5): 535–50.

Taras, M. (2008) 'Assessment for learning: sectarian divisions of terminology and concepts', *Journal of Further and Higher Education* 32(4): 389–97.

Taras, M. (2009) 'Summative assessment: the missing link for formative assessment', *Journal of Further and Higher Education* 33(1): 57–69.

Taras, M. (2010) 'Student self-assessment: processes and consequences', *Teaching in Higher Education* 15(2): 199–213.

Wiliam, D. (2007) 'Keeping learning on track: classroom assessment and the regulation of learning', in F.K. Lester (ed.) *Second Handbook of Mathematics Teaching and Learning* (pp. 1053–8), Greenwich CT: Information Age Publishing.

Winter, R. (1995) 'The assessment of professional competences: the importance of general criteria in Edwards', in A. Edwards and P. Knight (eds) *Assessing Competence in Higher Education*, London: Kogan Page.

Chapter 4

Assessment feedback

An Agenda for Change

Margaret Price, Karen Handley, Berry O'Donovan, Chris Rust and Jill Millar

Introduction

This chapter presents, explains and justifies the clauses of an Agenda for Change, which is being proposed by a group of international experts in the field of assessment feedback. This group of researchers, writers and practitioners were brought together for two days of discussion in June 2009 by ASKe, a Centre for Excellence in Teaching and Learning focused on assessment based at Oxford Brookes University, UK. The discussion critically examined the theory and practice of feedback and a strong commitment to bring about change emerged. The outcomes of the meeting were the Feedback: an Agenda for Change (see below)[1] and a number of initiatives to promote the ideas within it.

Agenda for Change

Clause 1: It needs to be acknowledged that high-level and complex learning is best developed when feedback is seen as a relational process that takes place over time, is dialogic, and is integral to learning and teaching.

Clause 2: There needs to be recognition that valuable and effective feedback can come from varied sources, but if students do not learn to evaluate their own work they will remain completely dependent upon others. The abilities to self- and peer-review are essential graduate attributes.

Clause 3: To facilitate and reinforce these changes there must be a fundamental review of policy and practice to move the focus to feedback as a process rather than a product. Catalysts for change would include revision of resourcing models, quality assurance processes and course structures, together with development of staff and student pedagogic literacies.

Clause 4: Widespread reconceptualisation of the role and purpose of feedback is only possible when stakeholders at all levels in higher education take responsibility for bringing about integrated change. In support of this reconceptualisation, there are already robust, research-informed guiding principles, and in some cases supporting materials.

Clause 5: The Agenda for Change calls on stakeholders to take steps towards bringing about necessary changes in policy and practice.

Each clause of the Agenda will be considered in turn.

Clause 1

Clause 1: It needs to be acknowledged that high-level and complex learning is best developed when feedback is seen as a relational process that takes place over time, is dialogic, and is integral to learning and teaching.

The problem

Feedback as a delivered message is a commonly held conception among stakeholders in higher education. However, we fail to see the potential value of feedback if we conceptualise it (implicitly or otherwise) as a *product* that is the culmination of an earlier assessment *process*. More seriously, we risk looking for solutions in the wrong directions. David Nicol, for example, cautions that the *feedback-as-product* discourse assumes that 'better' feedback is more detailed, more explicit, and given more quickly (Nicol 2010: 502). Implicit in that discourse is an assumption that 'knowledge', transmitted as a feedback message, will be understood by the receiver in a manner intended by the sender, irrespective of the situation and context of the recipient. The focus is on the 'object' of feedback and we see this idea embedded in the assessment and feedback questions in the UK National Student Survey. What is overlooked is what *mediates* the exchange: the interactions between sender and receiver; and the network of social relations which shape the interpretation processes and make possible the development of shared understanding.

The re-conceptualisation proposed in the Agenda

The Agenda proposes an alternative conceptualisation of feedback: as a *dialogic and relational process* that is integral to learning and teaching and thus takes place over time. Attention now shifts away from the feedback product, and towards the student and the social context in which he or she is learning.

We recognise that the key terms of 'dialogic' and 'relational' will be interpreted in multiple, and perhaps contested, ways. An important purpose of the Agenda is to encourage debate, to develop our sensitivities about similarities and differences in interpretations, but not necessarily to prescribe a single definition. What we offer below is an articulation of key terms, which we hope will resonate with readers.

Dialogic

The concepts of 'dialogue' and 'dialogic' are central to the Agenda, but the terms are understood differently depending on the level of interaction and intended outcome. For example, on some occasions, 'dialogue' implies a specific form of transaction, such as a to-and-fro exchange of words in order to correct or clarify terminology. For this chapter, however, we wish to emphasise broader educational aims, and propose a definition of dialogue as an interaction between parties *with the intention* of generating a shared understanding, i.e. something deeper than knowledge transmission. Dialogue is *through the word*, but when we speak of learning and students' education we cannot define dialogue merely by the type of interactions that manifest themselves to others: intentions are also relevant as well as how the particular interaction is embedded in ongoing conversations and processes. Our definition of dialogue draws inspiration from scholars who pursued the phenomenology of learning and meaning-making. Hans Gadamer, for example, argued that knowledge is not something 'out there' waiting to be discovered and then transmitted through an exchange of words, but instead arises out of conversations conducted in a network of social relations. We each have a 'horizon of understanding': it is through dialogue that we come to understand a horizon that is not our own, *in relation* to our own, and we appreciate that there are multiple perspectives and ways of understanding complex subjects and issues (Gadamer 1979).

The Agenda for Change proposes 'dialogue' in opposition to 'monologue' (Nicol 2010) and the transmission or cognitivist view of learning that monologue may (albeit inadvertently) promote. The cognitivist paradigm still underpins many of today's feedback practices (Askew and Lodge 2000), even though our pedagogies have moved far beyond that, conceiving learning as a socially constructed and situated practice (Vygotsky 1978; Lave and Wenger 1991). A dialogic understanding of feedback helps to redress this disjuncture, enabling us to reconceptualise feedback according to socio-constructionist principles. Whereas cognitivism carried an assumption of *knowledge-as-commodity* that could be coded and taught through transmission and error-correction techniques, socio-constructivism sees *knowing-in-practice* as an accomplishment negotiated between participants of socio-cultural communities who come to share a similar understanding of their practice and context. The focus on *knowing* and *understanding* is a subtle but important shift, and requires pedagogies that stimulate inquiry and inter-subjective understandings.

In this context, we propose 'dialogue' and 'dialogic feedback' as more appropriate for the 'high-level and complex learning' of higher education. Our aim is to help students to understand what is meant by 'quality' in their academic work as it is applied and judged by their assessors. Rather than merely copying model answer formats as recipes, we want students to understand the criteria and standards by which they are assessed so they can apply their understanding to new assessment situations. What is at stake here is students' assessment literacy and what Perry called students' intellectual and ethical development (Perry 1971). Perry observed in his college students a transition from a dualist epistemology (where the tutor is the source of knowledge, the student's role is to acquire knowledge and produce assignments according to a template, and the tutor's function is to 'correct' faulty imitation), towards a more contextual appreciation of knowing, and recognition of the contested nature of knowledge and 'quality' in some subjects. Developing such understanding takes time in a dialogic process arising from 'relational attunement' (Lock and Strong 2010: 120) to the perspectives and understanding of others. Perhaps more important, pragmatically, is that tutors expecting a dialogue on the contestability of some disciplinary concepts may 'fail' if faced by perplexed students in 'dualist' mode who expect corrective feedback that tells them 'the right answer'. The epistemological development of the student and the educational aims of the institution make a difference to the effectiveness of dialogic feedback.

What do dialogic feedback processes look like in practice? Although prescriptions and templates might be tempting here, they do not necessarily constitute dialogic feedback. Perhaps we should offer a caution instead: one-to-one conversations are not necessarily equivalent or sufficient to be called dialogic feedback. For example in a tutor/student interaction 'talking at' a student may be as ineffective as poorly written feedback if given without awareness of the student situation and epistemological development. Nor do we suggest that feedback should always be given in the style of face-to-face tutorials typical of the Oxbridge system (described in Gibbs 2006). At its most basic, the dialogic process and context is about the ease with which students can make connections to try to develop inter-subjective understanding of a subject or issue; for example, by asking questions to interpret feedback; talking through interpretations and reflections with peers to generate insights; articulating ideas as a way of testing out and clarifying arguments; and finding one's own voice and authorship among the 'webs of dialogue that shape who we are' (Lock and Strong 2010: 98, drawing on the work of Charles Taylor). Dialogue can promote dialectical processes of working through apparently conflicting ideas in a search for meaning which sees that the ideas make sense when one appreciates that they are context-dependent.

Relational

The notion of connectedness leads us into a discussion about the second key term in Tenet 1, 'relational'. Our intention here is not to suggest that a precondition for learning is that teachers and students should have or need to have close, personal relationships. Instead, we draw attention to the inherently relational nature of feedback and its role in the learning process. Feedback is 'relational' even when there is no close 'relationship' between teacher and student because it is inevitable that students will make some judgement about the quality and worthiness of the feedback based on their impressions of the teacher, the teacher's credibility, the sense of trust and psychological safety when (for example) exposing one's confusion, the institution in which the teacher is employed, and so on. In a key study on science education, Chinn and Brewer (1993) showed that students who received anomalous feedback drew on a variety of strategies to make sense of – and in some cases reject – their feedback, including their assessment of the tutor, and the degree to which the feedback challenged deeply held beliefs.

The relational aspect of feedback is most visibly seen in the social psychology of small-group interactions. Orsmond et al. (2011) have shown how students seek out advice and feedback from peers whom they trust and respect – perhaps calling on some peers for advice about interpreting feedback on 'assignment structure', and others on the disciplinary content. In this important respect, the 'dialogical context' that David Nicol refers to is also a relational context.

Less visibly, the relational aspect of feedback is also influenced by the social structures and discourses that shape the socio-cultural practices of our educational institutions. So although the discourse of the value of feedback is firmly embedded in institutions among both staff and students the reality in practice may, for example, be a focus on grades rather than feedback. We perhaps only glimpse this shaping when there are cultural clashes or 'culture shocks' (Griffiths et al. 2005) such as the introduction or increases in student fees and institutions have to make choices about how to respond to changing student expectations. Even without such dramatic change students differ in their expectations about what are normal or acceptable practices when talking to teachers, or asking for advice and clarification: some are comfortable in doing so; others less so. The power dynamics embedded in social practices in HE institutions will thus influence the potential for dialogic interactions. Furthermore, the relational atmosphere may itself shift 'through the word', i.e. through dialogue. Face-to-face dialogue – being in the presence (physically or metaphorically and emotionally) of each other in a joint effort towards understanding – may influence the conversational space, generating more psychological openness to the possibility that each person has something valuable to offer, and is worth listening to.

Finally, an aspect of 'relational' sometimes overlooked is students' relationship with the disciplinary content, and with the assignments in which they have invested time and energy. Moore (1989) calls attention to the 'learning-to-content interaction' that is just as relevant to learning as 'student-to-student' and 'student-to-teacher' interaction. Indeed, an apparently solitary action like reading feedback is embedded in relational webs which influence how students may attend, respond, judge or act on it.

Clause 2

Clause 2: There needs to be recognition that valuable and effective feedback can come from varied sources, but if students do not learn to evaluate their own work they will remain completely dependent upon others. The abilities to self- and peer-review are essential graduate attributes.

The problem

If our concept of learning relies exclusively on the 'teacher as expert', we perpetuate an assumption that helpful feedback can only ever be generated by a teacher; and a power dynamic where the student remains perennially dependent on the teacher as the font of knowledge, and the arbiter of 'quality'.

There are two rather different issues here. One (about feedback sources) was mentioned above in relation to Clause 1 and the dialogic and relational aspects of the feedback process. There, we argued that students routinely seek out feedback from various sources if only to help make sense of the tutor feedback (for example, see Orsmond *et al.* 2011), and they evaluate those sources according to judgements about credibility, trust and other relational dimensions.

The second issue, linked closely to the first, raises questions about the *purpose* of feedback in the learning process: if it is not simply to correct mistakes or explain errors, what is it? In the Agenda for Change, we echo others (for example, Boud and Falchikov 2006) in arguing that feedback can help learners to develop their own evaluative abilities, enabling them to become progressively less dependent on tutors as arbiters of quality, relying more on their own abilities to discern quality in their own and others' work. Sadler proposed that the

> indispensable conditions for improvement are that the *student* comes to hold a concept of quality roughly similar to that held by the teacher, is able to monitor continuously the quality of what is being produced *during the act of production itself*, and has a repertoire of alternative moves or strategies from which to draw at any given point.
>
> (1989: 121, emphasis in original)

The complexity of developing self- and peer-evaluative abilities is considerable, and usually under-estimated with the result that such skills are rarely well developed before students graduate. Such abilities involve skilful judgement and sensitivity to what 'quality' looks like or *could* look like, as judged by those who will assess one's work. As academics, we know only too well how difficult it is to achieve marking consistency within a teaching team, and it is no wonder that students also take time to develop an assessment 'nose' in the manner of wine connoisseurs.

For complex learning tasks, academic standards cannot be fully explicated because there is no formula for their production. This means that assignment briefs, criteria grids, 'standards' documentation are artefacts that always require interpretation. 'Exemplars' of student (or similar) work are useful because academic standards are embedded within them, but they are only as useful as the dialogue that goes with them. Exemplars as mere stand-alone *illustrations* of work are more likely to be copied without inspiring learning about what constitutes 'quality' (Handley and Williams 2011).

One could also ask, 'whose definition of quality are we talking about?' If quality is not absolute (and therefore can't be explicated), how can students navigate between possibly competing ideas about quality? Whose definition are they using when evaluating their own work and those of others? This is a problem talked about by students, such as those in our Fund for the Development of Teaching and Learning project who talked about creating assignments differently according to the requirements of the assessing tutor. Although there are serious issues here about marking consistency (see Bloxham, this volume), at one level, the students are demonstrating the very abilities that Clause 2 advocates: the ability to make judgements about their work in relation to *the context in which their work will be marked*. Just as different genres of writing require different styles, so different assessment tasks (and perhaps different tutors) may emphasise different aspects of work, such as writing, creation, analysis, criticality, presentation. Students who recognise this, who are confident in their understanding of alternative genres, and are flexible in their approach for each of them, demonstrate 'pedagogic and assessment literacy' in a similar way that authors accomplished in writing for different genres demonstrate their 'literacy'. Literacy is demonstrated by applying what one understands about styles, academic quality and so on *to the task at hand*.

As educators, we can encourage and support students in developing their evaluative skills, and their assessment literacy, by giving them practice in discussing exemplars and in other activities discussed in this book. But we should also be aware of the socio-cultural hegemony of certain 'styles' of writing or producing work that some students are familiar with, and others are not. The dominance of the 'Western analytic' model of writing essays in business schools, for example, may *not* be immediately recognised by students schooled in other writing traditions.

Clause 3

> Clause 3: To facilitate and reinforce these changes there must be a fundamental review of policy and practice to move the focus to feedback as a process rather than a product. Catalysts for change would include revision of resourcing models, quality assurance processes and course structures, together with development of staff and student pedagogic literacies.

The problem

Feedback is largely treated in isolation without recognition of the power that organisational culture and processes have to support or undermine its effectiveness. Consequently higher education institutions' responses to student surveys critical of feedback have largely focused on simple initiatives to solve a complex problem and have limited impact.

The need for a holistic view

Responses to the UK National Student Survey,[2] reflecting measures in other countries, have highlighted the lower level of satisfaction with assessment and feedback compared with other aspects of higher education provision. This has provided the impetus to search for improvement. However while the conceptualisation of feedback remains product-focused, change has been concentrated on isolated rules and processes, for example turnaround time or use of feedback templates.

As already suggested in this chapter, in order to really challenge current practice the context and situatedness of feedback must be recognised (Pryor and Crossouard 2008). Feedback, integral to assessment, takes place within a learning milieu that, while heavily influenced by the teacher, is also dependent on the learning environment and context. In turn the context is shaped by an array of factors ranging from organisational rules and regulations to requirements for staff training and beliefs about the learning process, all of which reflect and are reflected in organisational values and culture (Price *et al.* 2010). Therefore feedback as a relational, dialogic process must be enabled through a much broader base stretching as far as organisational structures, policies, systems and culture (see, for example, the approach of Alverno College, USA[3]).

Consequently, there must be an extensive review to highlight anomalies that reinforce the conceptualisation of feedback as a product and, perhaps, undermine feedback as process. For example the many workload planning systems allocate time to produce a feedback product while ignoring time required for meaningful dialogue with learners; or where an external examiner's role is framed to focus mainly on reviewing student achievement (grade distributions, marks, etc.) rather than quality of work and feedback drives staff to provide feedback that emphasises justification of the mark rather than on-going development; or assessment rules that only allow for very limited use of student self and peer assessment; or policies on anonymised marking that restrict the possibility of personalised feedback given in the context an individual's progress that could be part of an on-going dialogue.

Similarly, course structures are rarely designed with the effectiveness of feedback at their heart. The structure of a programme must enable an on-going dialogic feedback process. However, all too often programmes are created that have many demarcations that signal to students and teachers alike the segmentation of learning, ending an unfinished dialogue in order to begin another. Such signals reinforce the idea of feedback and knowledge as product rather than an integral part of the learning process as proposed in Clause 1. A segmented programme largely relies on the student to interpret feedback alone with few opportunities to establish the extent of their understanding, leaving both teachers and student dissatisfied.

Acknowledging feedback as a process presents challenges for the assurance of quality because 'objective' judgements of quality tend to rely on 'snapshots' of practice that cannot easily depict on-going processes. The quality of a feedback process will best be gauged by those involved in the dialogue, teachers and students, but the quality of their judgements will be heavily dependent on their pedagogic literacy. Pedagogic literacy leads to understanding of the complexity of the learning process, in particular the role of assessment and feedback in learning, and reduces the influence of assumptions and uninformed 'intuition' for both teachers and students. Therefore, rather than seek to regulate and monitor feedback quality using artefacts and quantitative measures it needs to be assured through greater confidence in teachers' professional prowess and students' evaluative abilities in relation to their learning.

Not only will pedagogic literacy allow continuous monitoring of quality but also the quality of a feedback dialogue will be enhanced if all parties are 'speaking the same language' about learning. Meaningful questions can be asked, responses explored, gaps in disciplinary understanding uncovered and future learning discussed. Pedagogically literate students will be in a position to judge whether their learning is progressing and what else they need to develop understanding of their subject. They will also be far better equipped to make judgements about the work of their peers. Teachers with better levels of pedagogic literacy will have a much better understanding of how best to use the limited resources available to them, using them to have greatest effect on learners.

Unfortunately in higher education little emphasis has been placed on professional development of teachers and even less on developing students' understanding of assessment and feedback processes. The culture of an organisation provides the backdrop for feedback practice while at the same time the feedback practice forms part of the culture. The prevalent learning approaches, expectations of teachers and students, standards to be reached, use of peer review, class sizes and balance between formative and summative assessment, will, among other factors, determine how the concept of integral, relational, dialogic feedback will be applied. However, for feedback processes to truly work there must be more than rhetoric (even if embodied in policy documents), the dialogue must be real and be part of the culture.

Clauses 4 and 5

Clause 4: Widespread reconceptualisation of the role and purpose of feedback is only possible when stakeholders at all levels in higher education take responsibility for bringing about integrated change. In support of this reconceptualisation, there are already robust, research-informed guiding principles, and in some cases supporting materials.[4]

Clause 5: The Agenda for Change calls on stakeholders to take steps towards bringing about necessary changes in policy and practice.

The problem

We noted when discussing Clause 1 that while the majority of stakeholders continue to focus on feedback as a product, widespread change will be very difficult and, unfortunately, evidence-based change is not well embedded in higher education.

Consistency rather than contradiction

Students, teachers, management, quality agencies, professional bodies, government and their agencies, etc., all purport to be concerned about the quality of the student experience, and feedback in particular. However, they are each pursuing subtly different agendas that have particular effects, often at odds with improving feedback. A voice for the student body, NUS, press for informed change (Bols and Wicklow, this volume) but their views are often better informed than most students on campus who are sometimes expressing contradictory opinions within institutional processes and expecting teachers to respond to them. Many teachers, overwhelmed by initiatives in the higher education sector (enacted in institutions but often driven by government), are often resistant to new requirements or initiatives. Even though they want to make feedback more effective they cannot commit to change when their performance is being measured in ways aligned with current conceptions of feedback and against their multiple roles within an increasingly complex higher education sector.

Management, driven by targets to improve ratings in league tables, can sometimes confine their actions to superficial initiatives that may improve ratings but fail to address fundamental problems with feedback. Quality agencies concerned with maintaining quality and standards often require the collection of students' work and feedback samples for quality review and this, perhaps unintentionally, emphasises the importance of product over process and certainly makes some institutions reluctant to use dialogic feedback approaches, which are seen as more difficult to evidence. Similarly, some professional bodies guard their established practices, especially in relation to assessment, which makes changes such as peer assessment a step too far. Different stakeholders make decisions that pull in different directions, and as a consequence there is not only an overall lack of coherence to improving feedback but there are moves that make it worse. Better feedback practices can only come from an understanding of what makes effective feedback and a commitment that is consistent among all stakeholders.

Considerable robust research evidence exists that supports the use of integrated relational, dialogic feedback (for example see Nicol 2009). If stakeholders could acknowledge this research evidence it may be possible to achieve coherence and co-ordination of their initiatives and actions. However, higher education stakeholders, particularly decision-makers, seem reluctant to draw on it or make significant changes despite many polices, reports, etc., attesting to the importance of the feedback process. Satisfaction surveys have provoked institutions and some national bodies to examine the nature of feedback more closely but unfortunately often the concern is with achieving improvement in the satisfaction score and how it sits with the institution's external profile rather than anything more fundamental. Consequently poor student satisfaction survey scores impel change to practice in a particular way. As clearly demonstrated in the chapter by Yorke, where the survey accords with good evidence based practice there is alignment between policy and practice. However, all too often survey questions are based on the dominant conceptualisation of feedback as a product (for example, timing, detail and clarity), thereby driving a different agenda.

As outlined in previous sections, using robust research evidence to inform the rethinking of the concept of feedback and how it is put into practice is the only way to radically improve its contribution to learning and satisfaction of learners and teachers. Better feedback practices can only come from an understanding of what makes effective feedback and a commitment, consistent among all stakeholders, to the changes necessary to support new practices. All stakeholders, especially those with national power and influence, must take the steps necessary to bring about changes in policy and practice that will enable the implementation of feedback processes that are a positive and effective contributor to the development of student learning.

Notes

1 Available at http://www.brookes.ac.uk/aske/OsneyGrangeGroup/.
2 See http://www.thestudentsurvey.com/.
3 http://www.alverno.edu/.
4 For example, see the work of David Nicol and the REAP Project http://www.reap.
   ac.uk/.

References

Askew, S. and Lodge, C. (2000) 'Gifts, ping-pong and loops: linking feedback and learning', in S. Askew (ed.) *Feedback for Learning*, London: Routledge.

Boud, D. and Falchikov, N. (2006) 'Aligning assessment with long-term learning', *Special Issue: Learning-Oriented Assessment: Principles and Practice. Assessment and Evaluation in Higher Education* 31(4): 399–413.

Chinn, C. and Brewer, W. (1993) 'The role of anomalous data in knowledge acquisition: a theoretical framework and implications for science instruction', *Review of Educational Research* 63(1): 1–49.

Gadamer, H. (1979) *Truth and Method*, London: Sheed and Ward.

Gibbs, G. (2006) 'Why assessment is changing', in C. Bryan and K. Clegg (eds) *Innovative Assessment in Higher Education*, Abingdon: Routledge.

Griffiths, D., Winstanley, D. and Gabriel, Y. (2005) 'Learning shock: the trauma of return to formal learning', *Management Learning* 36(3): 275–97.

Handley, K. and Williams, L. (2011) 'From copying to learning? Using exemplars to engage students with assessment criteria and feedback', *Assessment and Evaluation in Higher Education* 36(1): 95–108.

Lave, J. and Wenger, E. (1991) *Situated Learning*, Cambridge: Cambridge University Press.

Lock, A. and Strong, T. (2010) *Social Constructionism: sources and stirrings in theory and practice*, Cambridge: Cambridge University Press.

Moore, M.G. (1989) 'Three types of interaction', *American Journal of Distance Education* 3(2): 1–6.

Nicol, D. (2009) *Transforming Assessment and Feedback: enhancing integration and empowerment*, Glasgow: Quality Assurance Agency for Higher Education.

Nicol, D. (2010) 'From monologue to dialogue: improving written feedback processes in mass higher education', *Assessment and Evaluation in Higher Education* 35(5): 501–17.

Orsmond, P., Merry, S. and Callaghan, A. (2011) 'Communities of practice and ways to learning: charting the progress of biology undergraduates', *Studies in Higher Education*: 1–17 (iFirst article).

Perry, W. (1971) 'Cognitive and ethical growth: the making of meaning', in A. Chickering (ed.) *The Modern American College*, San Francisco: Jossey-Bass.

Price, M., Carroll, J., O'Donovan, B. and Rust, C. (2010) 'If I was going there I wouldn't start from here: a critical commentary on current assessment practices', *Assessment and Evaluation in Higher Education*, first published on 20 April 2010 (iFirst article).

Pryor, J. and Crossouard, B. (2008) 'A socio-cultural theorisation of formative assessment', *Oxford Review of Education* 34(1): 1–20.

Sadler, D.R. (1989) 'Formative assessment and the design of instructional systems', *Instructional Science* 18: 119–44.

Vygotsky, L. S. (1978) *Mind in Society: the development of higher mental processes*, Cambridge: Harvard University Press.

Chapter 5

Opening up feedback

Teaching learners to see

D. Royce Sadler

The context

Assessment tasks that require students to produce complex responses provide the context for this chapter. Such tasks are typically labelled 'divergent', because no uniquely correct response exists. Examples include: extended solutions to non-routine problems; literary, artistic, musical or other creative performances and works; critical and analytical investigations and reviews; theories and abstract syntheses; computer software; technological, engineering and architectural plans; industrial and product designs; medical and other health-related procedures; project reports; social and other policies; financial, administrative and management schemes; and sophisticated models of interactive systems. Responses may require high levels of technical or procedural skill; high levels of intellectualization, cognitive activity or aesthetic appreciation; or all of these. Some require special abilities that are not easily categorized.

Graduated complex tasks provide settings and practice sites for students to develop their knowledge and skills. Student responses provide the bases for inferring the depth of their learning. The quality of each response is judged by making a refined qualitative appraisal using multiple criteria. After graduation, complex works typically serve specific professional or discipline-related purposes or ends. Because the focus here is on complex works in general rather than works in specific disciplines, fields or professions, the following terms are used interchangeably: achievement, attainment, performance, accomplishment, capability, proficiency and competence.

Learning for complex outcomes

Three basic requirements for learners to become proficient in a given domain are that: they acquire a concept of high quality and can recognize it when they see it; they can with considerable accuracy judge the quality of their works-in-progress and connect this overall appraisal with particular weaknesses and strengths; and they can choose from their own inventories of potential moves those that merit further exploration for improving quality (Sadler 1989). Judging one's own work accurately and dispassionately requires substantial personal detachment from it. Furthermore, in order to develop and become competent and confident in self-assessment, students need experience in doing it independently of their teachers and peers.

The task of teachers is not to coach students through the production of particular complex responses by offering ongoing judgements about quality together with advice on how to improve them. It is to teach students how to judge quality and modify their own work during production. In practice, this involves attending simultaneously to dual agendas: the large scale (how the work is coming together as a whole) and the small scale (aspects that require further attention). For all of this, learners need to have acquired the relevant skills, know-how, and knowledge. Developing this capability normally requires repeated practice on a range of tasks and, in many cases, considerable experimentation to and fro during the work's production. In developing an essay, for example, students may revise their work many times. Even experienced academics often do the same when writing journal articles. However, in certain professions practitioners must attain a very high level of proficiency so they can perform given procedures correctly the first time; recovery or salvage may be impossible afterwards. In such cases, learning with practice typically takes place in non-critical situations first.

Key questions are: How do accomplished producers engage, cognitively and procedurally, in consistently creating complex works of high quality? What knowledge and skills are necessary and how are these applied in practice? The design of learning environments needs to be influenced by answers to questions such as these if students are to eventually master what is required. Students can then carry that capability forward to new situations in more advanced courses or outside formal education. In all of this, where does feedback fit in?

Feedback is often regarded as the most critical element in enabling learning from an assessment event. In practice, it often seems to have no or minimal effect. Whenever creating good feedback is resource intensive, this produces a low return on investment. What can be done? Merely improving the quality of feedback and how it is communicated to learners may not be enough. The proposition argued in Sadler (2010) is that the major problem with feedback is that it has been to date, and is virtually by definition, largely about telling. Research into human learning shows there is only so much a person typically learns purely from being told. Most parents know that already. Put bluntly, too much contemporary assessment practice is focused on communicating better with students.

Teaching by telling is commonly dubbed the transmission model of teaching. It portrays teachers as repositories of knowledge, the act of teaching being to dispense, communicate or 'impart' knowledge for students to learn. Consistent with that was an early conception of feedback as 'knowledge of results' – simply telling students whether their responses to test items were correct or not. Telling is limited in what it can accomplish unless certain key conditions (touched upon later) are satisfied. By itself, it is inadequate for complex learning. Being able to use, apply, and adapt knowledge, or to use it to create new knowledge, requires more than merely absorbing information and reproducing it on demand. Educational research over the past few decades has recognized the need for students to interact with information and skills, to make these their own, to incorporate them into their existing knowledge bases and structures, and to 'construct' or build knowledge that will serve them as adaptable personal capital. This emphasis may be relatively recent, but the process itself is what humans have always done. What has changed is the perspective.

To the extent that the traditional feedback model operates under transmission-model thinking, it reinforces the assessor's role in providing judgements, explanations and advice as new information (formal knowledge) for students to appropriate. In so doing, it largely misses the point. The knowledge base of learners has to be appropriately organized and sufficiently extensive for learners to be able to convert feedback into deeper knowledge and, ultimately, improved proficiency. If a student's knowledge foundation is deficient, personal appropri-ation of feedback simply cannot occur. Evidence for this comes from research on the development of expertise (Bereiter and Scardamalia 1993). An important goal should be to avoid treating feedback as a homogeneous commodity con-veyed from assessors to learners, one-way telling being the main vehicle. Activities involving peer assessment (Boud *et al.* 1999) and recent work on dialogic feedback by Nicol (2010) represent substantial improvements on that. However, the focus needs to shift away from the narrow issue of how feedback can be improved and communicated, and towards the wider issue of how *assess-ment* (rather than feedback) can enhance student learning. The problem can then be framed differently. Any assumption that feedback must remain the primary assessment-related tool inhibits opening up the agenda.

Competent producers of complex works

For many complex works, no precise blueprints exist. There are no algorithms or production formulas for getting to the end product, and no optimal path to it. Indeed, the nature of the end product is not necessarily known beforehand. However, during productive activity or the process of solution, its nature develops or is clarified as it emerges progressively. Producers may start with what they think are more or less clear ideas of the problem and only tentative ideas of solutions or strategies. As their work proceeds, both the full character of the problem and potential ways to solve it take concrete form as trial moves are made and their effects analyzed. Amendments are made and, at various stages, overall designs modified, the whole activity being directed towards the develop-ment of works of consistently high quality. Producers know when and how to adjust provisional plans and which alternative moves to try next when some do not work out. They notice things that matter and must be attended to, and pay no or relatively little attention to minor aspects that do not matter. They recognize why and how the organisation of each work may need to be revised as it starts to take shape. As all this is going on, they may – or may not – verbalize and reason out parts of it.

Depending on the nature of the end product, competent practitioners can identify features which require protection, elaboration or relocation as necessary. The knowledge and thinking of producers grows as they engage in sophisticated contingency management. They perceive certain aspects as salient in the circumstances and know to make local adjustments for the benefit of the overall quality or effectiveness of the work. They identify their own mistakes, recognizing weakness or incompleteness. They know that some changes will necessitate compensatory moves or decisions elsewhere, and draw elements and tactics from their repertoires to make them. They may find it difficult to explain to themselves or to others the reasons for all their actions, but they know when changes are needed. Throughout, they project themselves into specific situations: the perspective or position of the subjects of their attention (in certain human service fields and professions); or into the role of audience, consumer or observer (if they produce live or artefactual works). In short, they possess a refined sensitivity to contextual cues as these occur on the run, including shortcomings of their own creation.

The concept of 'knowing to'

To the extent that this is a reasonable portrayal of what competent producers do, the issue for academic teachers is to figure out how learners can acquire the types of competence required. As indicated earlier, feedback as traditionally conceptualized largely involves the assessor running with dual agendas (overall quality and matters of detail) but the most problematic aspect of the classical feedback model is that assessors (whether academics or student peers) are the ones who do the noticing, the thinking about repair and modification, and the generation of ways to improve. Learners need to develop awareness and responsiveness so they can detect anomalies or problems for themselves. They need to know when something matters in and of itself, and when exactly the same thing matters in one context but not at all in another. This is a significant contextualized figure–ground skill that must be developed. It constitutes a distinct form of knowing, 'knowing to', which involves detecting, 'sensing' without necessarily using the standard five senses. It begins with a feeling of unease or discomfort that something is not as it could be, and that a change would improve correctness, efficiency, flow or elegance. This type of knowledge cannot necessarily be made explicit, that is, expressed in words. It nevertheless exists, even when a person cannot define it in concrete terms or otherwise explain it.

'Knowing to' accounts for some of what Polanyi (1962) called 'tacit knowing'. Wittgenstein (1953: XI, 93) observed: 'I contemplate a face, and then suddenly notice its likeness to another. I see that it has not changed; and yet I see it differently. I call this experience "noticing an aspect"'. Abercrombie (1969) in her seminal work on judgement captured some of the same essence in her discussion of the influence and intricacies of perception and prior expectations on what is noticed and deemed to count as data in a particular context. Consistent with the work of Polanyi, Wittgenstein and Abercrombie is that of Dreyfus and Dreyfus (1984: 225): '[E]xperience-based similarity recognition produces the deep situational understanding of the proficient performer.' Simultaneously with the apprehension or understanding of a complex situation, the 'associated decision, action or tactic presents itself.'

The knowledge and skills students require do not, and cannot, come about by being told about them or by any form of explicit teaching. How can one person explain to another what they should notice in a particular context (including those of their own making) but is not worth noticing in other contexts if the possible occurrence or existence is not known in advance, and a multitude of things (features, aspects, properties, characteristics) are at least potentially worth noticing? Then, once something is noticed, knowing to do something or at least try. Learners must develop know-to knowledge directly through experience if they are eventually to become self-monitoring.

Educators can provide open assessment environments in which learners grasp the subtle skills required, at the same time ensuring that the process does not become unduly labour intensive for either party. Such environments immerse learners in decision spaces that are similar to those inhabited by the already competent, the closest of whom is presumably the teacher. It involves understanding the macro-level determinants of quality through taking evaluative action in contexts where configural (rather than componential) judgements are demanded. Equally, it involves understanding the micro-level determinants and knowing how to shape the work as a whole through small-scale tactics. This type of 'seeing' typically goes unrecognized in most of the research on assessment for learning, where the focus has been on feedback. It is not esoteric seeing, because perceptive and selective noticing are everyday activities.

The substantial literature on the nature of expertise and how it is developed is an important resource for further thinking. As well as the authors listed above, this literature includes contributions relating to the development of competence by medical and health practitioners, airline pilots and many other professionals involved in complex decision contexts. It turns out that a great deal of what experts do cannot be expressed completely in words and thus codified; it must be learned by experience. Progress on an alternative strategy can be made by seeking answers to questions such as these: What do competent producers do? How does their expertise manifest itself? How did they get that way? How can higher education teachers enable students to develop that type of capability? How can students be launched on trajectories towards sophisticated professional capability by the time they graduate? This is an important thrust of Bereiter and Scardamalia's (1993) research.

Another question remains: Are there any circumstances in which external feedback regularly leads to improvement? The answer is emphatically affirmative, but only when certain conditions are met. The most crucial condition is that the producer already possesses enough explicit and tacit knowledge to understand the full implications of the feedback. Only then can appropriate action be taken. To illustrate, consider manuscripts being evaluated for publication. Some authors do not know enough about academic writing and publishing for the reviewers' feedback to be understood and utilized except as a recipe to be followed blindly. The feedback is situated outside their 'zone of proximal development' (Vygotsky 1986). Other authors understand that something they happened not to initially 'see' when they produced their work has been subsequently 'seen' or 'noticed' by a reviewer. Its significance is then grasped immediately. External feedback can be a powerful tool for improvement, but can have this impact only when the requisite knowledge base has been established.

Case account

This account is of an approach to inducting undergraduate students into the types of processes outlined above and represents but one way to provide students with appropriate evaluative experience (Sadler 1989). I have used a similar process in professional development for academics. It is based on my own attempts, but includes some refinements I now recommend in retrospect. The aim was to provide an evaluative environment in which students could develop their ability to:

- make realistic, honest holistic judgements focused exclusively on the quality of academic works similar to those they produce themselves;
- distinguish between aspects of works that were germane to the judgement and pass over aspects that were routine, normally expected and not deserving of special mention;
- construct sound rationales for their judgements; and
- develop their personal repertoires of tactics and moves for improvement.

An additional aim was to provide students with a sufficiently positive experience of learning to motivate them to participate fully, even though none of the work produced would be credited towards the course grade.

The approach adopted was a form of peer assessment with a specific agenda in mind. Inter-scorer reliability was put to one side as secondary to the main exercise. For each tutorial, students had to create a short work of about 300 words in response to a specified academic task and bring three identical de-identified copies to the session. High quality responses required substantial cognitive activity and engagement to address a novel and previously unseen issue. Students had to distil, process, apply and integrate material from different sources (course lectures, notes, websites, textbooks and discussions) rather than reproduce, adapt or compile existing content.

Tutorial groups, each of about 20 students, met with me for one-hour sessions. The activities replaced the tutorial exercises and discussions used previously. Close engagement with the new processes became a primary pedagogical approach, and were billed as such to the students. In the first round of a tutorial session, one copy of each student response was put into a pool and then randomly allocated to another student. Two or three appraisals could be completed in a one-hour session. Students without completed 300-word papers would have nothing to do during the tutorials. As it turned out, attendance remained high.

The evaluative exercise ran along the following lines. The first step was to make a judgement: 'What is the quality of the work you have just received to appraise?' Students' initial concerns followed a fairly consistent pattern: 'Where are the criteria? How can I make an appraisal without criteria or a rubric?' Most of the students' earlier peer assessment activities had employed preset criteria. My response was that they should look closely at the quality of the work, think hard and analyze their reactions. I urged them to be patient, despite their sense of insecurity, and reiterated: 'The aim here is to learn about overall quality, to recognize it when you see it. What is the quality of the work you have before you? What do you react or respond to as you read it? How does it come over?'

Initially I had asked students to record their judgements on a numerical scale, because I wanted them to commit to a definite representation of their considered holistic judgement. However, some students put as much or more effort into deciding the number as into making the judgement. This clouded the issue, as would the use of any familiar symbols or scales. Interpretations of marks, letters or grade division points are invariably loaded towards past marking practices and habits. For example, a mark of 75 on a 100-point scale may have traditionally been the cut-off for a particular designation of quality (an A, or First Class). I now recommend that students represent their judgement of overall quality by the placement of X on a fixed-length line segment without scale points of any kind, 'low quality' being on the left and 'excellent' on the right.

The second step required students to justify their appraisals in 50 words or fewer, sticking to the qualities and properties of the work itself and avoiding praise or censure. Students necessarily invoked whatever criteria were necessary to explain their judgements. This step provided raw material for analysis in later whole-group discussion: the criteria invoked, the terms used, and the necessity to make judgements and provide rationales that would be tailored to each work individually but in all probability be different from one work to another. The third step was to provide written advice to the author as to how either the appraised work could be improved, or future similar works made better.

The concreteness of the three steps was important. People often think they know something thoroughly in the abstract. However, expressing it in material form and thus externalizing it makes the structure of the 'held' knowledge fuller and tidier. Furthermore, a certain seriousness of purpose enters into the exercise from knowing that an appraisal, its justification and suggestions for improvement will be later accessed by the producer of the work, especially if the activity design includes discussion (Abercrombie 1969).

On several occasions, students observed that the work being appraised did not actually address the specified issue at all. It consisted simply of material obviously garnered from different sources, technically relevant to the subject-matter mentioned in the task specifications, but not directed towards addressing the issue, solving the problem or answering the question. How could its overall quality be assessed if it was not what it was supposed to be? These students had made clear distinctions between the subject-matter content itself, and operations to be performed on that content to address the issue specified. Teachers commonly encounter this phenomenon, but many students do not recognize this as a potential problem. Yet this recognition is crucial for students who have not previously made connections between a task as it is specified, their submitted responses, and the feedback they subsequently receive.

As would be expected, not all students discovered this for themselves. I now recommend that a fourth step be added: 'Did the response actually attempt to address the issue stated?' This should be implemented only after students have had some experience with the original three steps to allow room for individual discovery. However, it should then become the first step to be attempted, because it is pre-emptive: unless the student work can be recognized as an attempt to address the task as it is specified, the question of how well it does so makes no sense. I also recommend that student authors and critics engage in forthright discussion about the works they appraise without becoming sensitive or defensive. My goal was to provide students with practice at being objective, which is why only the characteristics of each actual work were relevant.

As to the quality of feedback provided by other students, it could range from strong and on target to weak and misguided. An explicit point was made with students that this could happen, and that part of their responsibility was to learn to evaluate the quality of feedback. However, if students received essentially the same message from various sources, they should take it seriously. A related issue was this: What should be done if the overall level of student appraisal capability is low, so that they simply share their ignorance or inexperience? In each randomized pool of responses I included my own de-identified attempt at the same task (which also provided me with a check on the adequacy of my task description). In exchange, I received one student response that I appraised exactly as the students did. By the end of each session, at least some students in each round became aware of what my high-quality response looked like. But I had also received feedback on my work from several students. This informed me about their interpretations and misunderstandings. Putting my own work into the pool helped to allay fears and promote trust. After several sessions, I distributed to every student a copy of my own attempt at the task then current, they assessed it, provided their rationales and we engaged in group discussion. These activities constituted my attempt to calibrate students against a level of quality that was not limited to the ideas of students within a particular tutorial group.

Two key features of the assessment environment outlined were deliberate. First, students mutually appraised multiple works that were all responses to the same assessment task. As explained in Sadler (2010), for students to develop a concept of quality, they need to see as extensive a range of quality as possible, and also to see and appreciate how quite different works can be legitimately judged to be of about the same quality. Second, the identification of criteria followed (rather than led) the making of a judgement so that the role of criteria would remain important but subordinated to the main task of holistic appraisal (Sadler 2009a, 2009b). Peer assessment protocols that employ the same criteria for all works are foreign to this process. That somewhat different criteria are typically invoked for different works, including those of the same quality, is not an aberration; it is precisely the point.

Taken together, the four steps require students to focus intensively on the characteristics of the actual works as they stand, to look – and see – without the strictures of any standardized appraisal template. The main intended benefit was for students as budding assessors, not as constructors of feedback for peers or as consumers of feedback from peers. Students need to develop the practical ability to make both macro and micro appraisals, initially of works other than their own. This should improve the likelihood of later transfer and application of that knowledge to self-monitoring the quality of their own works during production.

Conclusion

Much more than we give credit for, students can recognize, or learn to recognize, both big picture quality and individual features that contribute to or detract from it. They can decompose judgements and provide (generally) sound reasons for them. That is the foundation platform for learning from an assessment event, not the assumption that students learn best from being told. They need to learn to discover what quality looks and feels like situationally. They need to understand what constitutes quality generally, and specifically for particular works. Equally, students need to be able to detect aspects that affect overall quality, whether large or small, and understand how and why they interact. Students need a vocabulary for expressing and communicating both what they find and how they judge, at the least for that part of their evaluative knowledge they can express in words. Only after students have acquired a sufficient basis of appropriate tacit knowledge can they can understand the content and implications of a marker's feedback. At that point, feedback can be effective as learners become more discerning, more intuitive, more analytical, and generally more able to create, independently, productions of high quality on demand.

References

Abercrombie, M.L.J. (1969) *The Anatomy of Judgement: an investigation into the processes of perception and reasoning*, Harmondsworth, Middlesex: Penguin.

Bereiter, C. and Scardamalia, M. (1993) *Surpassing Ourselves: an inquiry into the nature and implications of expertise*, Chicago: Open Court.

Boud, D., Cohen, R. and Sampson, J. (1999) 'Peer learning and assessment', *Assessment and Evaluation in Higher Education* 24: 413–26.

Dreyfus, H.L. and Dreyfus, S.E. (1984) 'From Socrates to expert systems: the limits of calculative rationality', *Technology in Society* 6: 217–33.

Nicol, D. (2010) 'From monologue to dialogue: improving written feedback processes in mass higher education', *Assessment and Evaluation in Higher Education* 35: 501–17.

Polanyi, M. (1962) *Personal Knowledge*, London: Routledge & Kegan Paul.

Sadler, D.R. (1989) 'Formative assessment and the design of instructional systems', *Instructional Science* 18: 119–44.

—— (2009a) 'Indeterminacy in the use of preset criteria for assessment and grading in higher education', *Assessment and Evaluation in Higher Education* 34: 159–79.

—— (2009b) 'Transforming holistic assessment and grading into a vehicle for complex learning', in G. Joughin (ed.) *Assessment, Learning and Judgement in Higher Education*, Dordrecht: Springer 4: 45–63.

—— (2010) 'Beyond feedback: developing student capability in complex appraisal', *Assessment and Evaluation in Higher Education* 35: 535–50.

Vygotsky, L.S. (1986) *Thought and Language*, revised and edited by A. Kozulin, Cambridge, Mass: MIT Press. (Originally published in Russian as *Myshlenie i rech*, 1934.)

Wittgenstein, L. (1953) *Philosophical Investigations*, translated by G.E.M. Anscombe, Oxford: Basil Blackwell.

Chapter 6

Building 'standards' frameworks

The role of guidance and feedback in supporting the achievement of learners

Sue Bloxham

Introduction

> I know this isn't quite what they want and I know this isn't quite the right standard and I'm like, I'm at degree level, what kind of do I need to, what is degree level . . .
>
> (Jane from Bloxham and Campbell 2010)

The quotation is an illustration of student confusion regarding what is expected of them at University. The student is struggling to grasp their teachers' concept of quality, one of the 'indispensible conditions for improvement' (Sadler, 1989: 121); yet without that understanding, they will have difficulty making sense of the guidance and feedback that is offered. This chapter will examine this challenge for teachers. It will argue that, far from helping reduce students' confusion, typical guidance and feedback approaches may encourage students to perceive standards differently from their teachers and strategies to improve student performance need to address these differences in staff and student views. The concept of individual *standards frameworks*, that is, the unique grasp of academic standards that each teacher uses in grading student work, will be used to explore barriers to, and potential strategies for, fostering student understanding of guidance and feedback.

The argument will not distinguish feedback from broader guidance about academic work, recognising that comments on students' summative work are only one form of feedback in the overall 'guidance and feedback loop' (Hounsell *et al.*, 2006). In this model, feedback on work acts as guidance, and ongoing guidance about an assignment acts as feedback on work completed and work in hand. Consequently, the development of students' perception of good performance is something that should be integrated into the whole assessment cycle. In addition, the text conflates the distinction between criteria and standards. *Criteria* signal the qualities that are being assessed (for example, quality of argument) whereas *standard* indicates levels of achievement (for example, pass, merit). A typical rubric combines the two in indicating the standards required to achieve different grades for each criterion. The terms are often conflated in practice (Bloxham *et al.*, 2011) with both concepts reflecting teachers' sense of quality in academic work. Therefore, for the purposes of this chapter, 'standards' will be used as shorthand to represent teachers' broad idea of quality in assessment tasks. The chapter refers chiefly to assessment in UK higher education but the principles are relevant to student learning in other national systems.

Transparent approaches to guidance and feedback

The importance of students grasping assessment standards has been recognised in recent quality assurance and enhancement measures. In particular, there has been an effort to make standards 'transparent' through explicit information such as assessment criteria, rubrics (marking schemes), and learning outcomes. For the purposes of this chapter, we will refer globally to these artefacts as 'assessment information'. These strategies have been a genuine attempt to make assessment less mysterious (Orr, 2010) and university policies now frequently require such information to be published to students. With respect to feedback, teachers have been encouraged to frame feedback in relation to this information, for example writing comments in relation to specific learning outcomes and criteria.

However, this simple proposition of transparency has not been borne out in practice and understanding of expectations and standards does not appear to be better for students who are provided with these 'transparent' criteria (Gibbs and Dunbar-Goddet, 2007). Why has this explicit approach failed to deliver transparency for students? An explanation may be found in the failure of such 'assessment information' to clearly represent the standards we use to mark – standards that are only really given expression, implicitly, in the act of grading and moderating students' performance. In attempting to make these standards transparent, we have implied that teacher judgement is analytical, can be made explicit and is fixed whereas the evidence suggests that it is holistic, tacit and variable between tutors. The following sections will explore this misalignment in more detail.

Holistic

A key feature of our efforts to make standards transparent to students has been to represent them in an analytical form as in a typical set of assessment criteria or learning outcomes. However, studies are emphasising the extent to which grading decisions are holistic (Sadler, 2009) and Brooks (2009), in her review of research on judgement in marking, identifies a range of reasons why published criteria do not reflect the 'ways in which judgement are actually enacted', which is 'intuitive and increasingly independent of rules and routines' (Brooks, 2009: 6). Empirical studies support these assertions. Grainger *et al.*

(2008) found that staff work backwards from an holistic judgement, awarding marks to individual criteria afterwards. Likewise, Bloxham *et al.* (2011) observed that assessment criteria were only used to check or confirm holistic judgement at the end of the marking sequence and Orr (2010) noticed that criteria were used more for adjudication in difficult cases rather than as guidance to the marker.

It is important to note that presenting judgement as analytical may also have damaging consequences for student learning. Written criteria encourage students to focus on individual aspects of their work rather than its overall coherence, leading to the view that too much guidance prevents students from engaging properly with the task (Bloxham and West, 2007; O'Donovan *et al.*, 2008). Indeed, when explicit assessment guidance is not provided, there may be an unintentional benefit of getting students to focus on the whole rather than the parts. Certainly, Gibbs and Dunbar-Goddet (2007) found that students operating in an explicit assessment environment had less of a grasp of standards than those learning in a more ill defined context.

Tacit

The tacit nature of academic standards makes it 'difficult for teachers to describe exactly what they are looking (or hoping) for, although they may have little difficulty in recognizing a fine performance when it occurs' (Sadler, 1989: 126). This tacit knowledge is, by definition, difficult to make transparent (Eraut, 2000) in the way that UK and other universities have attempted to do, for example through explicit learning outcomes and assessment criteria. Furthermore, as markers become more 'expert' and their judgement becomes increasingly intuitive, they are less able to articulate the tacit knowledge they are using in marking.

As O'Donovan *et al.* (2008) suggest, past and more homogenous cohorts of students may have come to know tacit academic standards through interaction with their teachers. However, recent evidence suggests that staff and students develop contrasting perceptions of an assignment and grading. In particular, international students and those from under-represented groups may be particularly disadvantaged because they do not bring with them the same tacit knowledge of the system as their more privileged peers. Thus, it could be argued that whilst assessment information creates an illusion of more equal opportunity in assessment, in practice the advantages of prior cultural and social capital will shine through in an easier grasp of tacit standards.

Differentiated by teacher

The tacit nature of standards means that they are largely learned through an informal process involving participation in relevant communities and practices (Orr, 2010; Shay, 2005). This mutual engagement creates 'a shared repertoire of terms, knowledge, understanding, tacit conventions and practices' (Crisp, 2008: 249). Nevertheless, the socially situated nature of this learning creates the potential for some individual differences in marking judgements as each teacher's unique experience influences their knowledge of standards. Whilst processes such as moderation act to maintain the standards of the community, studies suggest that individual teachers are influenced by their values, specialist knowledge, engagement with student work, history and previous experience (Orr, 2010; Shay, 2005).

This unique set of influences combine to create a personalised lens for each assessor through which they read and judge student performance, and this has been conceptualised as an individual's *standards framework* (Bloxham and Boyd, 2011) or *interpretive framework* (Shay, 2005). As Shay (2005) explains, the standards framework that each examiner holds combines objective elements learnt from participation in the relevant field, and subjective elements arising from the local context and dependent on the assessor. The concept of the standards framework helps explain tutor differences in complex marking judgements at this level and why students sometimes complain that assessors appear to be using different assessment criteria or mark to different standards.

In a period of anxiety about standards (Brown, 2010), it is important to consider how the safeguarding of standards through academic communities can be made more systematic and demonstrable, maintaining trust in teachers' accurate and consistent judgement. On the other hand, recognition by students that professional judgement will always involve the potential for legitimate individual difference is important in successfully engaging with guidance and feedback.

Summary

The research suggests three important aspects of marking, which are all characteristics of complex professional judgement: first, that teachers make holistic judgements despite the impression of analytical assessment given by much guidance; second, that the standards used by teachers are not easily accessible to students and staff; and third, that teachers hold personalised *standards frameworks* that can influence their marking. When we consider these conclusions in comparison with the 'transparency' drive discussed above, we can see that there is a potential disjunction between current guidance and feedback mechanisms and how judgements are made in practice.

Undoubtedly, an understanding of the difficulty of communicating tacit knowledge has underpinned recent efforts to help students understand assessment, including an emphasis on developing students' understanding of standards (O'Donovan *et al.*, 2008). However, in general, our efforts to do this have not acknowledged either the holistic nature of that judgement nor the importance of teachers' individualised sense of standards. There has been a growth in activities such as using criteria to mark exemplars, asking students to write their own criteria, peer assessing against criteria and providing feedback against learning outcomes or assessment criteria; what O'Donovan *et al.* (2008: 207) have referred to as the *social constructivist model*. Yet these approaches imply judgement is analytical and the same for all tutors, and therefore there may be limits to their usefulness.

The implications for guidance and feedback

How, then, can we help students to develop an emerging *standards framework* that matches that of their teachers and, ultimately, that of their subject community? This is no simple matter. We need to help students to develop a general grasp of the standards in their discipline, what Shay (2005: 676) describes as 'universal criteria', at the same time as acknowledging that students may face different expectations from teachers and from multi-disciplinary courses where they often find varying protocols, for example, for evidence, structure or citation. Helping students to understand our standards is unlikely to be sufficient unless they also have a grasp of the nature of the assessment process, particularly the nature of professional judgement. Understanding the complexity involved, the tacit nature of standards and the subjective/objective nature of professional judgement may help assuage the frustrations implicit in complaints about inconsistent marking and difficulty in grasping teacher expectations.

In attempting to achieve this, we need to draw on our understanding of professional learning as referred to above in relation to learning to mark. We need to create similar *social* learning opportunities for students to help them perceive standards in the same way as their teachers. Teacher learning about marking and standards is inductive, arising from the practice. It is a social, participative, informal and lengthy process. An attempt to replicate this for students forms the basis for the principles outlined below. These principles for designing more effective guidance and feedback aim to help students both to develop a *standards framework* closer to their teachers and to acquire a better understanding of professional judgement. The principles are that guidance and feedback should:

1 emphasise holistic judgement processes;
2 be embodied in real judgements;
3 involve dialogue with 'experts';
4 take place over time;
5 be open about the variable nature of complex judgement and explain university assessment processes.

Let us look at each of these in turn.

Principle 1: Holistic

Analytic assessment is a poor representation of professional judgement (Brooks, 2009) and therefore we should help students to make holistic appraisals of their work in progress rather than criterion by criterion. Institutional requirements for analytic criteria should be more flexible and encourage other forms of guidance as outlined below. However, for students raised on a diet of criteria, they are unlikely to renounce their attachment to this approach easily. For this reason, helping students to understand the nature of professional judgement is important (see principle 5 below). We will need to be explicit about how we are using a range of activities to help them acquire a broad understanding of academic expectations.

The consequences of this principle are that whilst teachers may need to communicate views on specific aspects of a student's writing, this feedback should be given in the context of *what the piece was aiming to do* – its overall purpose and meaning – rather than implying that these aspects are independently assessed criteria. In relation to guidance, the focus should also be on the purpose of the assessment task and how it relates to the overall aim of the module or course. Principles 2 and 3 develop this further.

Principle 2: Embodied in real judgements

Our strategies for providing feedback and guidance to students have tradition-ally taken a deductive approach, assuming that students can learn how to complete assessments in practice from the principles that we provide them with. Whilst this may be entirely appropriate for elements of their work (for example, referencing protocols), tacit knowledge is learned in a more inductive way, from the concrete to the abstract. Therefore, we should place greater emphasis in our guidance and feedback on helping students to draw learning about standards from real examples.

There has been limited research on the use of exemplars in higher educa-tion, although there have been very positive outcomes from exemplar-based workshops with students, and evidence that they help students to grasp the 'basic structural elements' of writing (Handley and Williams, 2011: 103), improve examination results and are a useful addition to traditional assessment information. Sadler (1987) suggests that exemplars convey levels of quality, argu-ing that they embody implicit standards in 'concrete' form. Several different exemplars of the same standard are needed in order to recognise that there are multiple ways of achieving the expected quality. Emerging work suggests that exemplars need to be accompanied by dialogue in order to help students to achieve a better understanding of the way teachers make their holistic marking decisions, for example by posting exemplars on a virtual learning environment (VLE) with a recorded commentary by the teacher that the student can play during or after reading the extract. The potential to ask questions anonymously about exemplars, with answers given in class or posted on the VLE, may be another means to creating clarificatory dialogue. As a form of guidance, such feedback on completed work means that the teacher is not explaining to students in a disembodied way what they are looking for in student work.

There are some concerns regarding exemplars, such as students perceiving that feedback on an exemplar covers all problematic aspects (Handley and Williams, 2011), although the risks may be outweighed by the benefits gained. Handley and Williams suggest that constructed and short exemplars may be more useful than exemplars drawn from complete student work.

Principle 3: Dialogue with 'experts'

Recent developments in feedback theory have emphasised the need for more dialogic approaches, to allow tacit assumptions of teachers to be made more visible. Students value dialogue, seeing it as crucial to their understanding of both assessment tasks and feedback (Bloxham and West, 2007; Carless, 2006). Studies show that black and minority ethnic students and international students particularly seek dialogue in order to help them understand what teachers are looking for, as dialogue provides the opportunity for students to clarify feedback and identify the particular expectations of individual teachers.

A key aspect of professional judgement is that it is learned through repeated participation in activities in conjunction with experts. Indeed, Gibbs and Dunbar-Goddet (2007) found that students were most likely to state that they understood the expected academic standards if they had participated in repeated formative assessment with oral feedback. Therefore, in thinking about dialogue in relation to guidance and feedback, we need to consider what format will be most useful to students. Northedge (2003) argues that student-to-student dialogue may be too low level, principally because it is not dialogue in the company of someone with 'expertise'. This would suggest that dialogical opportunities should involve engagement with those who already have a grasp of the standards (teachers, peer advisers, postgraduates) and comprise opportunities to ask questions to make explanations and judgements clearer. These latter components may provide a better window into the teacher's sense of standards as they describe things in different ways, provide different examples of what they are looking for, use more everyday language, and overall give a richer and more accessible picture of their expectations than mere statements of outcomes and criteria can manage. But how do we do this in a mass higher education system? Some possible ways:

- Teachers outline their expectations in a dialogical arena (in class or online) where the students have the opportunity to ask questions.
- When assignments are set, perhaps formal guidance should be limited but students are given the opportunity to pose questions that the teacher answers on the VLE for all the students to use.

- Adaptations of Rust et al.'s (2003) intervention, which used a combination of students assessing exemplar assignments coupled with input from the teacher to explain the criteria used. In this way, the dialogue about real work is informed by an expert view.
- Feedback dialogue is inbuilt in seminar sessions. Work is returned to students and they are asked to read the feedback and bring it to the next seminar. During the seminar, students work in groups on a prepared task whilst the teacher meets each student for 3–5 minutes to check their understanding of feedback on the returned work and clarify or emphasise the main elements they need to pay attention to in further work.
- Working with drafts: the teacher describes what they are looking for in a piece of work (possibly using exemplars) and then asks the students to review each others' drafts in the context of the teacher's explanation of the requirements. The students are encouraged to give each other feedback and to ask questions that are generated by looking at the drafts.

Struggling students are often reluctant to seek tutorials with their teachers regarding assessment. An implication of this is that dialogical activities regarding guidance and feedback need to be structured into course delivery rather than left to the initiative of individual students.

Principle 4: Takes place over time

It is clear from analysis of how teachers learn standards that the development of students' perception of standards needs to take place over time and be embedded in their programmes. Gibbs and Dunbar-Goddet (2007) argue that for students to really understand the standards of their discipline they need to go through repeated cycles of formative assessment, each involving attempts at a task and feedback on progress. Handley and Williams (2011) suggest that we will improve students' engagement if we shift feedback to earlier in the assessment cycle so that students find it more useful for the work in hand. This links closely with Sadler's (1989) view that an essential condition for improvement is that students should be able to regulate their own work whilst they are in the process of doing it. The current interval often found between when the work is carried out and when students receive feedback works against this condition, whereas feedback delivered during the completion of work is more likely to help the student get a sense of their own progress against standards. The feedback arrives at a point where it is really useful and therefore becomes part of the guidance. Two ways of staging this more timely feedback according to Handley and Williams (2011) is through feedback on drafts and using exemplars. The latter has been discussed above.

In relation to the former, many teachers are reluctant to provide feedback on drafts despite the obvious advantages and the fact that students find feedback on drafts to be much more useful (Carless, 2006). It is felt that such assignments are no longer the student's own work or the teacher is providing too much information or, merely, that the additional feedback load is too onerous for teachers. Methods for integrating feedback into the learning process in this way without significantly increasing teacher workload have been identified by researchers (Handley *et al.*, 2008). It is also important to relax institutional or departmental rules against feedback on drafts in undergraduate study.

Principle 5: Open about the nature of complex judgement and assessment processes

The content of this chapter reinforces the importance of inducting students into 'the dilemmas encountered in judgement processes' (Morgan and Wyatt-Smith, 2000: 139). How well do students understand the tacit and socially constructed nature of professional judgement in marking? Research on students' perspective on assessment has produced mixed results. Whilst some students believe that teachers know the expected standards and are objective in their use of them, other research has found that students think that different teachers may be looking for different qualities and can mean something different by the same terms (Bloxham and West, 2007; Hunter and Docherty, 2011).

The means to helping students understand marking judgements is surely to involve them as partners in assessment, including the judgment process. In an effort to provide better assessment information, we have bureaucratised it, giving it a 'truth' and 'solidity' beyond that ever envisaged when we first attempted to describe how we think we should evaluate student work. It has taken on a technocratic life of its own, more substantial than that which can be supported by empirical data. Consequently, we should help students to understand that explicit assessment information is only a guide, an honest effort to help; but that the process of judgement is far more complex than can be represented in a short list of criteria or a marking scheme matrix.

In addition, Sadler (1989: 135) argues that involvement in assessment helps students to understand the difficulties teachers face in making assessments. It positions them as 'insiders rather than consumers'. In a later paper, Sadler (1998: 83) suggests that part of the curriculum must not just be teacher-supplied feedback on work in hand but the induction of students into the processes of making sound judgements, 'in other words, the processes and resources that are accepted as natural and normal for the professional teacher need to be replicated for the students and built into their learning environment'. Therefore, just as Handley and Williams (2011) suggest that teachers should try to 'stand in the shoes' of their students, this chapter advocates that students should be helped to 'stand in the shoes' of the marker, to help them understand the marker's perspective. Being involved in peer review of other students' work starts the process of having to think about and recognise the complexity of judgement that is taking place.

Furthermore, students need to understand the assessment processes within the university, including the safeguards that are put in place to counteract potential teacher subjectivity, such as second marking, moderation and external examining.

Concluding comments

Whilst this chapter has focused on developing students' understanding of standards, it is unclear how well teachers recognise that they hold a personal *standards framework*. Language is often seen as transparent by teachers and it is not unusual for staff in training workshops to claim, naively, that students should know what is expected because it is in the handbook or guidance. Therefore, it is probably the case that we also need to help teachers to become more assessment literate; to have more conscious access to their standards' frameworks; and to be aware of how they might influence and be influenced. We need to help assessors to see the potential bias in judgement, or at least to understand their own perspectives better. Undoubtedly, then, we are working in difficult and controversial terrain when we ask for a clearer alignment between teacher standards and their guidance and feedback. Nevertheless, it is surely a challenge worth pursuing!

References

Bloxham, S. and Boyd, P. (2012) 'Accountability in grading student work: securing academic standards in a twenty-first century quality assurance context', *British Educational Research Journal* 38(4): 615–34.

Bloxham, S. and Campbell, L. (2010) 'Generating dialogue in assessment feedback: exploring the use of interactive cover sheets', *Assessment and Evaluation in Higher Education* 35(3): 291–300.

Bloxham, S. and West, A. (2007) 'Learning to write in higher education: students' perceptions of an intervention in developing understanding of assessment criteria', *Teaching in Higher Education* 12 (1): 77–89.

Bloxham, S., Boyd, P. and Orr, S. (2011) 'Mark my words: the role of assessment criteria in UK higher education grading practices', *Studies in Higher Education* 36: 655–70.

Brooks, V. (2009) 'Marking as judgement', *Research Papers in Education* 27 (1): 63–80.

Brown, R. (2010) 'The current brouhaha about standards in England', *Quality in Higher Education* 16 (2): 129–37.

Carless, D. (2006) 'Differing Perceptions in the Feedback Process', *Studies in Higher Education* 31(2): 219–33.

Crisp, V. (2008) 'Exploring the nature of examiner thinking during the process of examination marking', *Cambridge Journal of Education* 38(2): 247–64.

Eraut, M. (2000) 'Non-formal learning and tacit knowledge in professional work', *British Journal of Educational Psychology* 70 (1): 113–36.

Gibbs, G. and Dunbar-Goddet, H. (2007) *The Effects of Programme Assessment Environments on Student Learning*. Available at: www.heacademy.ac.uk/projects/detail/projectfinder/projects/pf2656lr (accessed 10 February 2013).

Grainger, P., Purnell, K. and Zipf, R. (2008) 'Judging quality through substantive conversations between markers', *Assessment and Evaluation in Higher Education* 33(2): 133–42.

Handley, K. and Williams, L. (2011) 'From copying to learning: using exemplars to engage students with assessment criteria and feedback', *Assessment and Evaluation in Higher Education* 36(1): 95–108.

Handley, K., Price, M. and Millar, J. (2008) *Engaging Students with Assessment Feedback: Final Report for FDTL5 Project 144/03*. Available at: https://mw.brookes.ac.uk/display/eswaf/Home.

Hounsell, D., McCune, V., Hounsell, J. and Litjens, J. (2006) 'The quality of guidance and feedback', paper presented to the Northumbria EARLI SIG Assessment Conference, 30 August–1 September.

Hunter, K. and Docherty, P. (2011) 'Reducing variation in the assessment of student writing', *Assessment and Evaluation in Higher Education* 36(1): 109–24.

Morgan, W. and Wyatt-Smith, C.M. (2000) 'Im/proper accountability: towards a theory of critical literacy and assessment', *Assessment in Education* 7(1): 123–42.

Northedge, A. (2003) 'Rethinking teaching in the context of diversity', *Teaching in Higher Education* 8(1): 17–32.

O'Donovan, B., Price, M. and Rust, C. (2008) 'Developing student understanding of assessment standards: a nested hierarchy of approaches', *Teaching in Higher Education* 13(2): 205–17.

Orr, S. (2010) '"We kind of try to merge our own experience with the objectivity of the criteria": the role of connoisseurship and tacit practice in undergraduate fine art assessment', *Art, Design and Communication in Higher Education* 9(1): 5–19.

Rust, C., O'Donovan, B. and Price, M. (2003) 'Improving students' learning by developing their understanding of assessment criteria and processes', *Assessment and Evaluation in Higher Education* 28(2): 147–64.

Sadler, D.R. (1987) 'Specifying and promulgating achievement standards', *Oxford Review of Education* 13(2): 191–209.

Sadler, D.R. (1989) 'Formative assessment and the design of instructional systems', *Instructional Science* 18(2): 119–44.

Sadler, D.R. (1998) 'Formative assessment: revisiting the territory', *Assessment in Education* 5(1): 77–84.

Sadler, D.R. (2009) 'Indeterminacy in the use of preset criteria for assessment and grading', *Assessment and Evaluation in Higher Education* 34(2): 159–79.

Shay, S. (2005) 'The assessment of complex tasks: A double reading', *Studies in Higher Education* 30(6): 663–79.

Part II

Enhancing the student role in the feedback process

Overview

David Carless

A key message of this volume is that feedback in whatever form needs to be a process in which active engagement from the learner promotes improved student learning. The focus of Part II is on the student role in the feedback process and how teaching and learning activities organised by tutors can enhance student involvement through, for example, engagement with standards and criteria. The contribution of this part to the volume as a whole is to discuss various teacher and student activities that can promote engagement, reflection and student learning. Major themes of the section include: student involvement with feedback and assessment; dialogic feedback; student self-assessment; and peer feedback.

Kay Sambell's chapter concerns student input into the agenda for change on assessment and feedback. It concerns an undergraduate elective course in which students developed guides on assessment for learning. What students included and did not include in the guides provides an indication of what they felt was important for incoming first-year students to know about assessment and feedback. How students learn was an important dimension and the social dimension of learning was emphasised, for example, through peer dialogue and peer-mediated learning. In relation to this, Sambell touches on the notion of student communities of assessment practice, foregrounding an issue taken up in the chapter by Orsmond and colleagues. Whilst as a point of comparison with the chapter by Hendry, working with exemplars was not a topic featuring in student guides.

The chapter by McArthur and Huxham is about dialogue in feedback. They develop links between the social nature of learning, the social nature of dialogue and the role of feedback as dialogue in a broader transformative learning process, and not merely as an adjunct to assessment. Their conception of feedback as dialogue implies its integration throughout the learning process, not just as part of formal assessment. In the first half of the chapter they sketch the essence of dialogue, drawing particularly on Paulo Freire's work. In the second half, they give some practical examples of how dialogic feedback can be implemented. A particular example they call 'boot grit feedback', which focuses on identifying and discussing concepts that students find difficult.

Walker's chapter is about how students respond to common types of written feedback comments. The chapter focuses on conventional written feedback to students on completed assignments. Three main types of comment are identified: content comments, skills–development comments and motivational comments. The evidence shows that content comments are often not understood unless an element of explanation is included and that students find generic skills-development comments to be the most useful. The chapter concludes by discussing how departmental strategies might promote change and improvement in feedback practice, including a focus on developing generic skills across the curriculum.

The chapter by Carless is about what he calls sustainable feedback, in other words enhancing the student role in generating and using feedback so as to reduce their reliance on tutor guidance. Dialogic teaching and the use of oral presentations as learning and assessment tools are key themes in the chapter. Dialogue is central to sustainable feedback in that it emphasises the students' role in making sense of feedback and using it to develop their own self-evaluative capacities. The chapter also touches upon the importance of trust as an important dimension in assessment and feedback, yet something which is often in short supply. Trusting 'virtues' such as openness, empathy and genuine interest in the ideas of others may facilitate student engagement with feedback.

Orsmond, Merry and Handley place the delivery and utilisation of feedback within the theoretical parameters of social learning models. The chapter places emphasis upon feedback being integrated into the practice of student communities and illustrates how students' self-awareness of their individual community practice is a necessary condition for learning to occur from tutor feedback. A key theme of the chapter is how students might use peer feedback and self-evaluation as part of the feedback process. A framework for modeling the development of self-assessment practices is discussed and its implications for the curriculum noted.

The chapter by Hendry is about using exemplars. The chapter draws on work in Australian universities, some conducted by the author and some by other colleagues. The re-orientation to feedback in the chapter is to see it as comprising guidance or scaffolding integrated with teachers' instruction *before* assessment tasks are carried out. Dialogic cycles of interaction in relation to exemplars are a major theme of the chapter. A practical point is a suggestion that a small number of purposeful comments may be more effective at promoting student uptake of feedback than a larger number of less focused responses. This is an important issue that prompts us to question views of feedback as something to be delivered to students.

These chapters reinforce key messages in the volume concerning the importance of how students react to, activate or generate feedback. Effective feedback is predicated on student response and uptake. The student voice is the major theme of the chapter by Sambell and is also a prominent feature of all the other chapters. Student uptake of feedback is at the heart of the chapter by Walker and is a recurrent sub-theme in all the others. Consistent with this emphasis on the student is the notion of dialogic feedback. Dialogic feedback is central to the chapter by McArthur and Huxham; is a major feature of the chapter by Carless; and is an undercurrent of the other four chapters of the section. Features of dialogue include: its relational nature; its integration within the learning process; and its focus, not merely on exchanging information but on developing new knowledge and understanding.

A variety of different terms are used in the chapters to encapsulate the importance of student participation in identifying standards and using criteria. Peer feedback, peer interaction, peer critique and peer assessment interact with student self-assessment, self-evaluation or self-regulation. Social learning and self-assessment are emphasised in the chapters by Sambell and Orsmond, Merry and Handley. Carless discusses the development of enhanced self-evaluative capacities amongst students. Hendry talks about self-monitoring, self-regulation and self-efficacy. Taken as a whole the chapters reinforce messages that tutor feedback needs to interact with student opportunities to provide feedback on the work of peers as a means to enhance their own self-evaluative capacities.

Chapter 7

Involving students in the scholarship of assessment

Student voices on the feedback agenda for change

Kay Sambell

Introduction

This chapter focuses on an initiative designed to promote students' awareness, reflection and conceptual development of assessment for learning (AfL) in higher education (McDowell *et al.* 2006). It involved the creation of an optional module that explicitly invited undergraduates to engage with, and contribute their voices to, recent research and development work on assessment and feedback. Having studied and discussed the growing literature on AfL in higher education, students subsequently authored guides to AfL. These were, on the whole, collaboratively created and were targeted at lecturers or first-year students. Many of the guides that students produced explicitly encouraged their readers to rethink and improve their own feedback and learning practices.

The chapter highlights the concepts and situations that students chose to prioritise as they sought to position readers' views of feedback within their understandings of the scholarship of assessment (Rust 2007). It particularly focuses on the analysis of the guides, with a view to identifying some of the key insights about the feedback 'agenda for change' (Osney Grange Group 2009) that these students developed and sought to communicate to others.

The scholarship of assessment in higher education

Rust (2007) makes a powerful case that given what we know about the central importance of assessment and its power to positively or negatively affect students' learning, it is vital that the scholarship of assessment is placed at the centre of the activity of the growing Scholarship of Teaching and Learning (SoTL) community. Aggregations of the existing literature have generated widely accepted principles in which assessment supports deep approaches to learning (Gibbs and Simpson 2004; Nicol 2009). These have led to strong philosophically and empirically based arguments that staff should rethink and change their assessment practices to bring about a new 'assessment culture' that focuses on learning rather than simply measurement (Birenbaum 2003). This essentially requires a radical reappraisal of the fundamental purpose of assessment, and the development of key concepts about the links between assessment and learning, so that assessment can be seen afresh through a new lens (Boud *et al*. 2010).

Whilst recognising the challenge that assessment has to fulfil multiple purposes simultaneously, the aim has been to encourage academics to promote 'learning-oriented assessment' (Carless *et al*. 2006) or 'assessment for learning' (McDowell *et al*. 2006). The ideological and transformative nature of this agenda for change prompted Boud and Falchikov (2007) to dub it an 'assessment-for-learning counter-movement.' In line with the philosophy of the SoTL movement, many have set out not only to explore and improve their own assessment practices, but also to advance the larger profession of university teaching by rendering their work public, subjecting it to critical evaluation and allowing it to be useable by others in the field (Hutchings and Shulman 1999).

The principle of student involvement in assessment and feedback

Importantly, Rust (2007) identifies the student experience of feedback as a central issue in the scholarship of assessment. Of most salience for this chapter is the recognition that feedback should help students understand more about the learning goals, their own achievement status in relation to that goal, and how to bridge the 'gap' (Sadler 1989). Importantly, this conceptually links feedback to the issue of student involvement in the assessment process.

A substantial element of the emergent literature has tended to focus attention sharply on students' direct responses to teacher-led AfL interventions. Innovators have built on the presupposition that student involvement in assessment (Falchikov 2005) is vital, so students explicitly learn to *become* assessors, not just to be assessed by others. From academics' perspectives, student involvement in making (rather than simply receiving) judgments are viewed as key to 'epistemic apprenticeship' (Claxton 2011), enabling access to the body of unseen, unheralded and unarticulated know how (Sadler 2010) of subject domains. Accordingly the notions of subject-lecturers 'seeding' communities of assessment practice (Price *et al*. 2007), promoting social learning and dialogue (Nicol 2010) around specific assessment episodes, and designing interventions which help students learn to make evaluative judgements within the specific domain (Price *et al*. 2010) have gained momentum and prominence.

In practice, higher education practitioners have tended to mobilise the resources of self- and peer assessment to increase student participation in assessment practice (Black and McCormick 2010). This, too, is a prominent aspect of the literature, and focuses on strategies academics often employ to initiate the productive staff–student dialogues that need to occur to improve learning and to support students in generating and/or making sense of assessment criteria and applying them, either to exemplars, or to their own work and that of their peers. Considerable emphasis has also been placed on designing and researching practices that activate students as generators and processors of feedback 'messages', by promoting, for example, 'peer feedback as the learning element of peer assessment' (Liu and Carless 2006). Additionally, to minimise the gap that can occur between teachers' feedback and students' appreciation of its practical significance, there is growing awareness that students need direct access to, and dialogue about, a range of examples of student work. To this end innovators have created explicit opportunities for their students to model appraisal experiences in the way that staff do. An increasing body of work explores involving students with exemplars to enhance achievement and induct them within the context of specific curricula (Handley and Williams 2011; Hendry this volume; Sambell 2011).

The case study: engaging students in the scholarship of AfL

To date most of this scholarly enterprise has, understandably, been conducted and disseminated exclusively by subject-teachers and educational developers. This chapter focuses, however, on an initiative that adopted a somewhat different, albeit complementary, tack. Rather than focusing on students' direct responses to teacher-led assessment and feedback designs in the local assessment practices associated with specific course-content, it explicitly sought to engage students on a more general level, by raising their awareness of the critical debates and relevant scholarly activity surrounding the AfL agenda itself.

A module for students was designed and delivered by the author as part of a suite of enhancement activities developed within Northumbria University's Centre for Excellence in AfL. This was done because it seemed apparent that while novice and experienced staff across the university were offered many formal and informal opportunities to engage with literature and practice around AfL, students were rarely targeted. So, in common with analogous staff development opportunities, a student-facing AfL credit-bearing course was designed to help promote awareness, reflection, conceptual development and change.

The course was developed and delivered by academics that were keen to promote and debate the burgeoning scholarly literature in this area. For a number of years it was offered annually to students on a large Joint Honours programme in the School of Health, Social Work and Education Studies, where undergraduates could elect to take it as a second-year option. These students were all studying courses within an applied social focus (such as Disability Studies, Childhood Studies). None of the course-routes offered students licence to practice: each was being studied as an academic area of enquiry. This meant that students taking the optional module (about twenty each year) were not Education students and had little or no previous experience of education-related study. Some chose the option because they had ambitions to do a postgraduate course in teaching; however, many had no such aspirations. Moreover, while it seems reasonable to anticipate that students choosing the module might engage with the topic in a more positive way than in core compulsory courses, in practice several admitted selecting the module predominantly on pragmatic grounds (for instance, because it was timetabled at a convenient time) rather than because of a high level of inherent enthusiasm for the topic. This meant that the students producing the guides actually represented a diverse mix of motivations and academic attainment.

The course explicitly offered students the chance to learn about, and engage with, the scholarship of assessment. Over a twelve-week period undergraduates studied the philosophy and principles of AfL. They were introduced to the Centre for Excellence's model of AfL and the evidence and principles upon which it was founded. They became conversant with published scholarly work, reading and discussing publications about: the desirability of innovation and change in assessment practice (Brown and Knight 1994); the importance of students' perspectives of assessment; models of feedback (Nicol and MacFarlane-Dick 2006) and work promoting student involvement in assessment and feedback processes, especially via self- and peer assessment (Rust et al. 2003).

The course was organised around a series of interactive lectures, workshops and project-based learning. Learners could choose to work individually or in groups to produce guides that might help first-year students or lecturers to perceive the relevance of contemporary scholarly work on AfL. Students chose a variety of creative, lively and accessible formats, including booklets, magazines, DVDs and leaflets. The guides, many of which explicitly encouraged their readers to rethink and improve their own approaches to feedback, took shape gradually. As the module progressed, 'teaching' sessions were given over to their design and development, with ample opportunity for student–student and staff–student dialogue. The guides were submitted for summative assessment, together with a reflective commentary explaining the student's rationale. It was agreed that, with relevant permissions, selected student guides might be edited and used in future staff or student development activities. Indeed, several have been utilised and a number were formally published.

The following analysis briefly explores themes and issues students highlighted as a result of their engagement with the scholarship of AfL. These were derived from two sources. First, content analysis of the student-authored guides from two different years was carried out. This focused particularly on guides that focused on feedback and that were specifically directed at first-year students. Analysis aimed to identify the key insights about the feedback agenda for change that their authors developed and sought to communicate to less experienced students. This analysis was also supplemented with data from interviews undertaken with nine student-volunteers recruited from two of the cohorts who took the module. These interviews sought to illuminate student views of the material and the impact of engaging with this form of scholarship.

Student voices on the feedback agenda for change

The need to redefine learning

The first extremely striking thing to emerge was the extent to which these second-year students felt that, in order to position first years' views of feedback within the context of AfL, readers needed to redefine the term 'learning'. Student authors commonly advised readers to see learning afresh. Often, as in the following extract from a guide, advice was couched in terms of the personal revelations the author had gained by engaging formally with the scholarship of assessment:

> I had never learnt about or understood that there might be contrasting ways of approaching learning. By looking at it I started to see learning differently. This provided me with a chance to approach my own studies in a new light. You can, too!

Many others similarly referred explicitly to the reader's 'approach to learning' to explain and try to reframe other students' conceptions of feedback, as this extract illustrates:

> Discovering what type of approach to learning you have will change your attitude towards feedback. You can't effectively know how to use feedback if you don't understand the basics about learning.

In fact, almost all student guides we analysed were found to devote substantial time and space to explanations that were designed to enlighten readers about constructivist views of learning. Most drew heavily on the approaches to learning literature and explained the differences between 'deep' and 'surface' approaches. The following extract typifies the way in which the scholarly literature on *learning* (rather than assessment per se) was frequently employed to encourage readers to take a new look at learning and move beyond a surface approach. It was written as a satirical piece entitled 'How to spot a surface learner':

Only does the bare minimum to get by.
('Well that's *me* off to the pub.')

Just memorises, when more is needed.
('Yeah, just cram, don't think.')

Loves to 'cut corners'.
('A few lists to pad out that essay will do the job.')

Most student authors explicitly foregrounded general discussions of learning and learnership (the role or position of being a learner). Their guides not only painstakingly explained the features of a deep approach, but also placed emphasis on trying to offer readers a new way of seeing their roles as learners as follows:

> The idea of surface learning helped me to understand what's important. You must take a more active role – not just sit in the classroom and get fed information by teachers.

Readers were exhorted to appreciate that active learning was a matter of individual sense-making and something for which learners and staff were jointly responsible. This was done with the conviction, it seemed, that in order to promote the feedback agenda, student-readers urgently needed to view themselves as active participants in learning.

In one sense, the heavy emphasis these students paid to the student learning literature might seem unsurprising. The demonstrable link between students' approaches to learning and their perceptions of the (often tacit) requirements or demands of assessment regimes actually underpinned relatively early calls for assessment reform. Consequently any engagement with the literature on AfL and the development of emergent agendas demands that SoTL scholars become conceptually familiar with constructivist and student-centred paradigms.

However, for some of these participating second-years, the metaphors of deep and surface approaches to learning appeared startlingly potent and new. They seemed to afford them personally with new insights about learning, with which they appeared unfamiliar. Interviews revealed, for example, that thinking about learning in this way was a revelatory experience:

> That was a real eye-opener to me, it was suddenly: 'Hey! This is the way you should be looking at it!'

Another said:

> I wished I'd known all that about deep and surface in my first year. That's been one of the best kept secrets of university, I must say!

Engaging with the AfL literature raised their awareness of some of the tacit values, attitudes and assumptions about university learning, teaching and feedback processes that had hitherto remained invisible to them.

The need to redefine effective teaching and learning environments

Concomitantly, again rather than focusing on assessment and the sorts of interventions that were prominent in the literature they were reading, most student publications exhorted their imaginary first year reader to move away from a transmission-based, content-driven view of teaching. Instead, they urged readers to redefine the term 'teaching' to raise awareness of the formative value of engagement with directed study or group-discussion tasks as the way to derive useful feedback:

> You need to realise that assessment tasks that are not marked, but which encourage meaningful interaction, are being used.

In this way, and in contrast with the dominant preoccupations and emphases of the literature, the student guides heavily promoted the developmental nature of informal classroom dialogue, social learning and active participation. The extent to which the student guides focused on convincing the reader of the value of social interactions with peers, both within and beyond formal classroom settings, was an extremely striking phenomenon.

Further, most guides firmly sought to 'normalise' feedback by recasting it in the context of dialogue within the student community, as exemplified here:

> You can get feedback from a wide range of places, but sometimes you don't even realise you're doing it. Working in groups and talking to your friends is a main way of learning. You can learn where you are up to with a partic-ular subject by listening and talking to your peers. Giving comments and chatting about each other's work or even having to defend your own work will often highlight any misunderstandings or reveal any gaps.

Once more, it is interesting to note that concepts from the student learning literature, especially the idea of constructive alignment, became a powerful con-ceptual driver in the way these student authors made their case for participating actively in classroom dialogue. It is also interesting to acknowledge how feedback here becomes positioned informally: as a 'chat' with friends. This tendency to 'naturalise' assessment language, and render it in everyday, informal terms, was a frequent and prominent feature of the guides. For example, authors seemed to anticipate that certain assessment-related terminology would cause alarm, which they took pains to neutralise, as the following extract suggests. At this point in her guide, the author was trying to persuade readers to approach lectures and seminars actively:

> AfL is all about including the student. You, too, can learn to self-assess. But don't worry! If you think about it, you do the process of self-assessing every day. Just with simple things, like assessing how you look.

In fact, in interviews, some claimed that in personal terms discovering more about approaching classes effectively was the most beneficial aspect of the module. They felt strongly these ideas should be introduced to the first-year experience:

I've got so much out of it, it's going to change the way I do things next year: big time! It made me do my assignments earlier: go to classes with the idea of building up steadily and trying to see the links. I wish they'd covered this stuff in the first year!

The need to redefine feedback

As indicated earlier, the course paid considerable attention to published scholarly work that questions the way in which feedback is conceptualised and which examines the role of students in the assessment process. It focused extensively on literature that views feedback as 'a dialogic and contingent two way process' involving 'teacher–student and peer-to-peer interaction' (Nicol 2010) and flagged up arguments and case studies about the importance of recasting students as active agents with regard to feedback information via participation in teacher-led self- and peer assessment activities and the discussion of exemplars.

To drive home their perceptions of the implications of this feedback agenda, many student authors sought to help their readers rethink the term 'feedback'. Often they highlighted 'limited' views of feedback by offering illustrative quotes from fellow students they had interviewed. They typically used these to point out the need for readers to redefine and reposition feedback as a process, not a product, as the following extract exemplifies:

'Feedback is the written comments, which I only ever get after I get an assignment back, which is then too late to improve.'

A lot of students see feedback this way. But you as a student need to start thinking about all the other times you receive feedback and how you can use this effectively. As a student you actually gain feedback from many sources throughout everyday of your lives: this can be from peers, lecturers, tutor comments and self-assessing.

It was noticeable though, once more, how far the student guides tended to emphasise ongoing engagement, typically situated in everyday learning and teaching situations:

As a student you need to know how you are doing, and not just at the end of the module. All too often we find out we're 'not up to scratch' when it's too late to do anything about it . . . In assessment for learning, feedback plays a significant part in helping to extend your understanding. As Race describes it, feedback can be thought of as 'ripples on a pond'. The ripples represent your learning and the feedback increases the intensity of the ripples and keeps them going . . . but when we talk of feedback, don't expect continuous marks and grades. With assessment for learning the feedback is much more . . . than the % in the bottom corner (Race 2005). It's not just your lecturer who can provide feedback.

Student authors tended to position feedback as a matter of deepening their sense of subject material, predominantly in negotiation with peers and as part of the normal flow of teaching and learning, in order to understand the goals of the work and regulate their own progress accordingly.

It is interesting, too, to consider what the guides did *not* choose to talk about. They appeared curiously reluctant to focus on teacher-led interventions or strategies that staff might use to involve their students in, say, discussions about standards, criteria and assessment processes. In fact, the students' publications remained virtually silent about teacher-initiated peer and self-evaluation processes, despite this kind of activity being routinely used in the students' own classroom experiences, and despite the course discussions focusing strongly on such strategies, as reported in the literature. Furthermore, teacher-led interventions (such as the use of exemplars) that were being studied in the literature in relation to the feedback agenda were also directly employed in the students' own experience of the course. There was, however, a conspicuous absence of any reference to such assessment practices in the guides. Moreover, few guides talked about discussing the work students were preparing for written assignments and, surprisingly, dialogue with tutors seldom featured in the guides.

Instead, while the student guides focused heavily on the principles of interaction and dialogue, and used the literature and its terminology to substantiate their claims, their arguments were almost exclusively focused on the formative nature of *peer* interaction about subject matter. Time and again the guides highlighted extremely informal feedback situations, with feedback represented as occurring quite naturally from social contact with students who are also working in a given area, as the following extract exemplifies:

> You should not just rely on assessment feedback. By sharing ideas and working with peers you create your own feedback to one another and create an environment which is relaxed, but you learn at the same time, without even feeling that you are learning!

Implications

Whilst admittedly these student voices on the feedback agenda for change come from a small and rather particular sample of students, they offer some useful and important insights into the key messages students derived from their introduction to the scholarship of assessment. Interestingly, although these students recognised, appreciated and seemed to endorse the philosophical principles of AfL they discerned in the literature, they tended to interpret and reframe the AfL agenda in different ways and with noticeably different emphases than the ones that are foregrounded in texts written by and for staff.

There are a range of possible reasons for the ways in which these students chose to represent assessment and feedback in their guides. Maybe their interpretations of the AfL literature simply stem from their relative inexperience of learning and teaching in higher education. Some, however, probably relate to perceptions of power. For instance, the guides showed that the students received a clear message from the literature as emphasising the student's responsibility for playing an active part in the feedback process. Perhaps students decided to emphasise peer dialogue and peer-mediated learning as the principal context for feedback because this offers a situation in which the locus of control and potential for change lies with the student, rather than the teacher. Further, their relative silence about interventions designed to stimulate staff–student dialogue might also relate to students' perceptions of the unequal power-relations between students and staff, which students find 'unsafe', for fear of exposing their inadequacies to an assessor (Carless 2006). Such perceptions understandably function as barriers to effective dialogic feedback practices involving staff. Handley (2007) importantly suggests that there is an issue about encouraging students to feel that they are members of an academic community where the norm is to discuss one's work in a relatively open, informed and scholarly manner. It is worth remembering that this ideal, of course, is difficult given the power differentials of assessment. So whilst a major goal of AfL is to minimise hierarchical relationships, in practice this is challenging to achieve. It could be that the guides acknowledge this and indicate a student tendency to discuss assessment issues in what are essentially student communities of assessment practice that exist beyond the gaze of the assessor (Orsmond *et al.* 2011). After all, we know that students often show resistance to innovations designed to involve them in assessment, especially if they see assessment predominantly through the lens of measurement culture (Race 2010).

Of course, it is also important to acknowledge that because the guides were submitted for grading, student authors indubitably felt some pressure to conform to the teaching team's expectations, and might simply be saying what they felt their teachers wanted to hear. Were that simply the case, it fails to explain why so much of the scholarship highlighted and 'legitimated' by the module teaching team did not feature in the guides. Instead, it is tempting to view these student voices as framing the debates and terms they encountered in the scholarly literature in ways that reveal their particular priorities and preoccupations. Their responses seem to suggest that the students were more concerned with learning *in general*, rather than focusing on engagement with particular disciplinary material, which tends to feature powerfully in academics' standpoints.

Overall, these students' engagement with the scholarship of assessment predominantly appeared to prompt them to explore and promote reflection on the tacit rules of academic practice at a deep-seated and general level. From their viewpoint, the concepts of 'approaches to learning' and 'constructive alignment' appeared to function as essential prerequisites for an appreciation of AfL. These concepts cannot, from what these students are saying, be taken-for-granted or assumed. Indeed, there are strong indications that some students, well into their courses, may remain disconcertingly unaware of them. One implication might be that more could be done to raise students' awareness of such elements. In practice, this might entail reviewing and redesigning traditional introductory Study Skills or Learning to Learn programmes or sharing examples of the student publications, so that students are formally introduced to the foundational concepts that were promoted so heavily in the student guides. Explicit efforts to develop students' pedagogical awareness, as an essential aspect of their assessment literacy, might be productive ways forward with the feedback agenda, to render the values positions implicit in higher education's conceptions of learning more visible to those outside its discourse community. This is important because, as Haggis (2006) notes, the inherent value positions of terms like 'deep approaches' and 'learner responsibility' are often only implicit in assessment instructions and assumptions about the structuring of assignments. Without an understanding of these value positions, some students may be disadvantaged.

References

Birenbaum, M. (2003) 'New insights into learning and teaching: their implications for assessment', in M. Segers, F. Dochy and E. Cascaller (eds) *Optimising New Modes of Assessment: in search of qualities and standards*, Dordrecht: Kluwer Academic Publishers (pp. 13–36).

Black, P. and McCormick, R. (2010) 'Reflections and new directions', *Assessment and Evaluation in Higher Education* 35(5): 493–9.

Boud, D. and Associates (2010) *Assessment 2020: seven propositions for assessment reform in higher education*, Sydney: Australian Learning and Teaching Council.

Boud, D. and Falchikov, N. (2007) *Rethinking Assessment in Higher Education: learning for the longer term*, London: Routledge.

Brown, S. and Knight, P. (1994) *Assessing Learners in Higher Education*, London: Kogan Page.

Carless, D. (2006) 'Differing perceptions in the feedback process', *Studies in Higher Education* 31(2): 219–33.

Carless, D., Joughin, G. and Mok, M. (2006) 'Learning-oriented assessment: principles and practice', *Assessment and Evaluation in Higher Education* 31(4): 395–8.

Claxton, G. (2011) 'Higher education as epistemic apprenticeship', keynote speech to the NAIRTL 5th Annual Conference on Higher Education, 9–10 June, Galway, Ireland.

Falchikov, N. (2005) *Improving Assessment through Student Involvement: practical solutions for aiding learning in higher and further education*, New York: RoutledgeFalmer.

Gibbs, G. and Simpson, C. (2004) 'Conditions under which assessment supports students' learning', *Learning and Teaching in Higher Education* 1(1): 3–31.

Haggis, T. 2006. 'Pedagogies for diversity: retaining critical challenge amidst fears of "dumbing down"', *Studies in Higher Education* 31(5): 521–35.

Handley K. (2007) 'When less is more: students' experiences of assessment feedback', Higher Education Academy Annual Conference, 3–5 July, Harrogate.

Handley, K. and Williams, L. (2011) 'From copying to learning: using exemplars to engage students with assessment criteria and feedback', *Assessment and Evaluation in Higher Education* 36(1): 95–108.

Hutchings, P. and Shulman, L. (1999), 'The scholarship of teaching: new elaborations, new developments', *Change* 31(5): 11–15.

Liu, N.F. and Carless, D. (2006), 'Peer feedback: the learning element of peer assessment', *Teaching in Higher Education* 11(3): 279–90.

McDowell, L., Sambell, K., Bazin, V., Penlington, R., Wakelin, D., Wickes, H. and Smailes, J. (2006) 'Assessment for learning exemplars: the foundations of CETL AfL', Occasional Paper 3, Newcastle: Northumbria University. Available at: http://www.northumbria.ac.uk/static/5007/cetlpdf/exemplars.pdf (accessed 17 December 2012).

Nicol, D. (2009) *Transforming Assessment and Feedback: enhancing integration and empowerment in the first year*, Glasgow: Quality Assurance Agency for Higher Education.

Nicol, D. (2010) 'From monologue to dialogue: improving written feedback processes in mass higher education', *Assessment and Evaluation in Higher Education* 35(5): 501–17.

Nicol, D. and MacFarlane-Dick, D. (2006) 'Formative assessment and self-regulated learning: a model and seven principles of good feedback', *Studies in Higher Education* 31(2): 199–218.

Orsmond, P., Merry, S. and Callaghan, A.A. (2011) 'Communities of practice and ways to learning: charting the progress of biology undergraduates', *Studies in Higher Education*, iFirst Article DOI: 10.1080/03075079.2011.606364.

Osney Grange Group (2009) *Feedback: an agenda for change*, Oxford: Oxford Brookes University. Available at: www.brookes.ac.uk/aske/documents/OGG%20agenda%20for%20change.pdf (accessed 18 July 2012).

Price, M., Handley, K., Millar, J. and O'Donovan, B. (2010) 'Feedback: all that effort, but what is the effect?' *Assessment and Evaluation in Higher Education* 35(3): 277–89.

Price, M., O'Donovan, B. and Rust, C. (2007) 'Putting a social-constructivist assessment process model into practice: building the feedback loop into the assessment process through peer review', *Innovations in Education and Teaching International* 44(2): 143–52.

Race, P. (2010) *Making Learning Happen: a guide for post-compulsory education*, 2nd edn, London: SAGE Publications.

Race, P., Brown, S. and Smith, B. (2005) *500 Tips on Assessment*, 2nd edn, London: RoutledgeFalmer.

Rust, C. (2007) 'Towards a scholarship of assessment', *Assessment and Evaluation in Higher Education* 32(2): 229–37.

Rust, C., Price, M. and O'Donovan, B. (2003) 'Improving students' learning by developing their understanding of assessment criteria and processes', *Assessment and Evaluation in Higher Education* 28(2): 147–64.

Sadler, D.R. (1989) 'Formative assessment and the design of instructional systems', *Instructional Science* 18(2): 119–44.

Sadler, D.R. (2010) 'Beyond feedback: developing student capability in complex appraisal', *Assessment and Evaluation in Higher Education* 35(5): 535–50.

Sambell, K. (2011) *Rethinking feedback in higher education: an assessment for learning perspective*, Bristol: ESCalate.

Chapter 8

Feedback unbound

From master to usher

Jan McArthur and Mark Huxham

Introduction

> Be on your guard;
> *Unmanageable oaf* cuts both ways.
> *Finds the subject difficult,*
> Acquitting you, converts
> Oaf into idiot, usher to master.
> ('Reports' by U.A. Fanthorpe 2005)

A major theme of this book is that feedback should encourage dialogue; between students and lecturers, amongst peers and individually, as a form of self-critique and reflection. Here we endorse that theme but also propose an understanding of dialogue that goes beyond simple exchange or the presence of two or more voices. Inspired by Freire's (1996) critical pedagogy, we seek to make a link between the social nature of learning, the social nature of dialogue and the role of *feedback as dialogue* in a broader transformative learning process and not merely as an adjunct to assessment.

Our analysis is informed by our commitments to the social justice purposes of higher education. Our aim is to consider how feedback can become embedded in the learning experience through the notion of 'feedback as dialogue' in ways that promote critical and transformative learning. Our conception of feedback as dialogue does not simply focus on the way in which information about a student's work is conveyed to them, but on the fundamental aspects of the relationship between student and teacher, and the relationship of both to the act of learning. This radical promise of dialogue is betrayed by superficial uses of the term that employ it as a trite acknowledgement of the student voice rather than a complex and uncertain educational relationship.

This conception of feedback as dialogue implies its integration throughout the learning process. Shackled to formal assessment, feedback is like great art hung in a dark corner; in contrast, it needs to be illuminated, displayed and discussed. Nicol and Macfarlane-Dick (2006: 199) define feedback as 'information about how the student's present state (of learning and performance) relates to

. . . goals and standards' where the goals and standards referred to could include 'specific targets, criteria, standards and other external reference points (e.g. exemplars)'. There is nothing in this definition that limits feedback to assessment tasks as usually construed. Rather, feedback can illuminate multiple moments of learning, which crucially may include many identified by the student rather than the tutor. For example, when engaging with a concept in class, a student might worry about their 'present state of learning' with respect to it; they might be confused, or concerned that their peers understand it better. Feedback – from tutors or from peers – will make the difference here, but only if there are mechanisms to allow it. Tutors and students need to work together to cultivate these. Hence the teacher acts not as *master* (proclaiming what should be done) but as *usher*, accompanying the student on their path towards learning.

Another illustrative concept we find useful is that of the feedback spiral (derived from the 'feedback and guidance cycle' in Hounsell *et al.* 2008). This emphasises the importance of timing to effective feedback and illustrates the multitude of points at which feedback, in its many forms, can be introduced within and between individual courses. Such a spiral can start with early advice building on students' prior knowledge, incorporating 'standard' feedback after a task and involving 'feedforward' to the next task (at the next level of the spiral). That such a conception blurs the distinction between 'feedback' and 'teaching' is one of its attractions.

In this chapter we refer to these multiple points as 'moments' for feedback as dialogue. Our use of the term moments seeks to capture the following qualities: part of something larger and ongoing; embracing initiatives that may be small and specific, but nonetheless significant to learning; recognising many different potential forms of feedback; and emphasising the dynamic aspect of movement and the possibilities of such moments acting as 'fertilizer' to boost feedback as dialogue and enhance student learning. The actual moments themselves generally involve quite modest interventions; however, their pedagogical value can be profound as part of a broader commitment to dialogical teaching. Our examples, discussed in the final section of this chapter, are chosen to be illustrative of how the idea of feedback as dialogue can be implemented at different points in the feedback spiral, and of how the context of their use – such as early or late in a module – will influence their effects. For example, feedback may be used to establish trust and to build a relationship early in the spiral, may help clarify criteria and context for summative assessments in the middle or may be used to give very specific guidance on academic tasks later on.

Several of our examples draw on our experiences using what we term *boot grit* feedback (McArthur *et al.* 2011) in which students are given the chance to ask confidentially for further information or clarification of key concepts that remain unclear at the end of class. Students engage with feedback by depositing written comments into a 'boot grit box', or electronically by texting comments to a 'text-wall' (a website that displays the comments). In either case a fast response from the tutor is essential; with paper comments this can come within an hour or two as a posting to the course VLE, with the text-wall they can be instantaneous (since the wall can be projected during the lecture). The idea is to resolve misunderstandings or knowledge gaps that might not initially seem serious, but if left unresolved could 'worry away' at the students' learning in a negative way – like a bit of grit in a boot. As such, boot grit resonates with similar approaches such as minute papers (Angelo and Cross 1993) or short 'review discussions' (Hollingsworth 1995).

Before turning to these practical examples, the next section develops our concept of feedback as dialogue, with particular emphasis on the social nature of both learning and dialogue and how these work together in our understanding of feedback as dialogue.

Feedback as dialogue

The concept of dialogue that informs this chapter is both simple and complex. It is simple because it is grounded in a sense of the essential humanness of dialogical activity: a sense that we flourish as humans and best achieve our potential through social immersion in, and engagement with, diverse perspectives and ideas. As Freire (1996: 69) explains: 'Dialogue imposes itself as the way by which they [people] achieve significance as human beings. Dialogue is thus an existential necessity'. But it is also complex because, within institutions such as universities, this can be far harder to achieve than might seem reasonable. Any dialogical encounter may be distorted by the domination of one view or person over another; there is therefore no room for the sentimentality sometimes associated with notions of dialogue (Freire 1996). The achievement of feedback as dialogue within a course is therefore no easy matter; it is usually easier to avoid such aspirations:

> Set them no riddles, just
> Echo the common-room cliché:
> *Must make more effort.*
> ('Reports' by U.A. Fanthorpe 2005)

Our understanding of dialogue rests not on the number of participants, but on the relationships between participants and/or their relationships with the focus of their dialogue (both feedback and the knowledge they engage with studying a course). We thus reject assumptions that written feedback is necessarily monological (Carless *et al.* 2011) or that a verbal exchange is always dialogical. A student and teacher may talk face-to-face about a piece of work, but unless the student is moved to reconsider the work in light of the teacher's comments, then no dialogue has occurred. Note that we stress the student should reconsider the work, not that they should simply accept the teacher's suggestions. For in this case the student's behaviour is passive; they are receiving instructions. That is not what we mean by feedback as dialogue: our conception requires active engagement with the feedback, rather than passive acceptance.

It is useful here to consider the distinction between knowledge and information (Brown and Duguid 2000). Knowledge is complex, contested and dynamic; there is a relationship between the knowledge and the knower and engagement with the knowledge is essential. In contrast, information can be simpler: it can be passed over from one person to another with very little, if any, active engagement.

We must therefore understand feedback as a piece of knowledge, with all the attendant virtues and respect that deserves. If students are to be able to actively engage with feedback, to be part of a dialogue, then that feedback cannot be presented, or regarded, as a static canonical statement. By thinking of it in terms of knowledge to be discussed and interacted with by both parties, we also introduce the notion that it is dynamic and contested: not only do students have a right to challenge the feedback; they have a responsibility to determine for themselves its validity, usefulness and implications.

This responsibility extends through all forms of feedback, albeit in different ways. It is crucial to students actively engaging with knowledge (feedback) rather than receiving it through transmission, or what Freire (1996) describes as 'bankable' approaches to teaching in which information is deposited into an empty vessel – the student. Many of the examples of boot grit feedback in the next section deal with technical concepts (McArthur et al. 2011). In asking for further clarification of such concepts students are acknowledging that they have not understood them when explained in the lecture. If the problem was just a failure of transmission, if the message was somehow dropped en route from lecturer to the recipient (student), then simply repeating the same words would rectify the problem. But this is rarely the case; students often misunderstand the feedback provided (Carless 2006; Hounsell 2003; Scoles et al. 2012).

Even technical pieces of knowledge need to be actively engaged with if they are to be truly understood in meaningful ways that can form the basis of further learning. The point, therefore, is not necessarily to encourage students to dispute every concept or definition, which could prove incredibly burdensome. However, passive student acceptance implies a teaching approach informed more by frustrated parenting experiences than pedagogical reasoning: 'because I say so'.

In providing feedback as dialogue a teacher thus acts to *usher* the student through to new thoughts and understandings: the usher acts as informed companion, but should not dictate the route or outcome, because both of these will differ from student to student. The student should simultaneously gain greater control and responsibility for their own learning and enjoy a learning *relationship* with the person who provides feedback and the knowledge with which they are engaging. The goal is therefore to allow: 'Participants to have thoughts they could not have had on their own, yet to recognise these thoughts as developments of their own thinking' (Game and Metcalfe 2009).

In emphasising the contribution students must make to the path and outcomes of their own learning, we again touch on some of the problems involved in the tight coupling of feedback with formal assessment. Surely all students on a course are required to achieve the same outcomes, if not also follow the same route? But this confuses the artefact produced for a piece of assessment, or any other learning task, with the actual engagement with knowledge experienced by each individual student. All students may produce an essay, but the learning processes for each – including their dialogical engagement with feedback – are necessarily unique. Feedback, as with any dialogic contribution, must be understood in terms of what has come before and also the future understandings likely to arise from it (Wegerif 2008). This is easily forgotten, especially when feedback is tightly coupled with assessment:

> The good have no history,
> So don't bother. *Satisfactory*
> Should satisfy them.
> ('Reports' by U.A. Fanthorpe 2005)

As Parker (2005) notes, there is something 'improper' in pre-determining what a student will learn: learning is always about more than an artefact of assessment. Hence our concept of feedback as dialogue, resting on critical pedagogy, emphasises the active role students have – through feedback as dialogue – in determining their own path; *making the path by walking* (Bell *et al.* 1990).

Feedback as dialogue should enable students to escape pre-set paths and find their own way – with all the attendant joys, surprises and achievement that comes with that. But it also has important implications for the role of the teacher who must also engage in a learning process. As Freire (1996: 78) pointedly asks: 'How can I dialogue if I always project ignorance onto others and never perceive my own?' To achieve feedback as dialogue, teachers need to find ways to let students know that they too are open to learn through the relationship. This is a relationship that is undeniably between people in very different roles – student and teacher – with all the attendant differences in experience, knowledge, power and authority. Genuine dialogue is not reached by ignoring these differences, but rather by acknowledging and, in the case of some, celebrating them. This approach is further enhanced when the teacher is open about the fact that they still have much to learn.

To summarise, the essence of feedback as dialogue is how we (students and teachers) regard the feedback provided. Is it a static, canonical statement that students should pick up and follow? Or is it a dynamic piece of knowledge, which students must engage with and take responsibility for using in their own learning? To achieve the latter requires a commitment to feedback as dialogue on the part of both student and teacher. If feedback is not given in the spirit of dynamic and contestable knowledge, then there is little chance for dialogue, no matter how many face-to-face conversations or the like occur. If students are unable to realise that they are active partners in the feedback process, then the best intentions of teachers will get nowhere.

To walk together: practical moments for feedback as dialogue

We turn now to the different moments at which feedback as dialogue can be introduced into a course. Most importantly, it must be introduced in ways that recognise that students actively interpret their own learning environments (Maclellan 2005) and this leads to a great variety of experiences. As Giroux (1992), argues, students read the world differently to academics, and to each other. Students must be able to express themselves in voices that are genuinely their own if their participation in the feedback dialogue is to be effective (McArthur 2009).

In deciding how and where to introduce feedback moments into a course we suggest two factors are essential to the realisation of the dialogue explored in the previous section: these are clarity and control. Clarity refers to attempts to explicate feedback and allow students to construct their own understandings of it. To achieve this, students must be able to contextualise feedback and to understand the aims of the provider. Treating students as partners in learning implies sharing control with them, in feedback as in other areas. This control dimension acknowledges that feedback includes emotional, moral and political issues. Rather than a simple transfer of knowledge, it can enhance or undermine self-esteem, generate trust or suspicion, subvert or buttress hierarchies of power. Hence students look to feedback for messages (such as personal attention or support) distinct from (and at times at odds with) simple information transfer (Huxham 2007).

A third dimension that informs the examples of feedback moments outlined below is that of timeliness (McArthur et al. 2011). The achievement of both clarity and control in students' experiences of feedback is influenced by the moments along the feedback spiral at which different forms of feedback are introduced. The following examples are illustrative, rather than prescriptive, of moments in which feedback as dialogue can be realised.

Moment one: establishing feedback as dialogue before a course begins

The idea of feedback as dialogue can be encouraged even before a course begins. Course handbooks may contain statements about 'feedback expectations', often with a commitment to provide feedback on assessed work within a certain period of time. While commendable to make such a commitment, the narrowness of the way in which feedback is presented can reinforce the tight coupling of feedback and assessment, and thus work against the day-to-day fostering of feedback as dialogue.

Used differently these course handbook statements on feedback can provide a strong foundation for feedback as dialogue. Consider the following extract from a handbook within the School of Philosophy, Psychology and Language

Studies at the University of Edinburgh, which has led an explicit initiative to encourage more dialogical approaches to feedback:

> Feedback for the majority of the topics for the short weekly assignments will be provided by discussion in the seminar, where you can compare your ideas with those of other students, and the way some of the topics have been developed in the literature.

Feedback is emphasised as something to be talked about, and even generated through discussion, rather than merely received by a certain date. An expectation of informal dialogue between the student and teacher, and between peers, is encouraged.

Moment two: the first lecture of a course

Dialogue should be encouraged and normalised in the very first lecture or tutorial. In our work with boot grit feedback we found that giving students opportunities to ask questions in the first lecture was both welcomed and important to the general learning culture that then developed (McArthur *et al.* 2011). Early use of boot grit establishes the two-way relationship crucial to feedback as dialogue: students ask a question and find that their lecturer, as promised, provides a timely response, normally within a couple of hours of the class. Then in the next class the lecturer is able to ask if students found the feedback useful, thus demonstrating that it is not simply a transmission process. If the explanation provided did not help, the lecturer knows to try again, to explain differently.

This feedback moment also helps to induct students into the norms and expectations of a new course. In a modularized system students may face a number of complex learning contexts as they move between subjects (Higgins *et al.* 2002), each with their own unfamiliar norms and expectations.

Moment three: introducing the teacher as learner

We use another variation on the boot grit idea to reinforce the sense that the teacher is also a learner. Timed normally around the fourth week of a new course, in which students have already become familiar with the boot grit idea, we ask students to provide boot grit feedback *for the lecturer*. While this is a piece of in-course evaluation, not feedback, it can function powerfully as dialogical fertilizer that feeds into, nourishes and improves the other moments. To achieve this, such an intervention must be sensitive to our third dimension of time by coming early enough to make a difference.

This can be achieved in simple ways, such as puzzling out loud while teaching, or bouncing ideas off students. In written feedback the teacher can acknowledge that they have learned something new or been challenged, intrigued, surprised by what the student has written. In doing so, the teacher demonstrates that they too are a learner in this dialogical exchange and demonstrate the humility that Freire (1996) also regarded as important to achieving dialogue.

Moment four: establishing the course as a safe learning space

Feedback as dialogue can contribute to the fertile learning environment within a course by minimising some of the pressures that can seem threatening to students. A key feature of boot grit is that students ask their questions anonymously but are also able to see the questions and answers from the entire class. Boot grit feedback encourages dialogue with those students who may not feel comfortable contributing in the 'bear pit' of a large lecture class (McArthur et al. 2011).

We found that students were greatly reassured to see that they were not alone in failing to grasp certain aspects of the course; indeed, it is a perfectly normal part of any learning process. Being able to study the feedback outside the class that elicited it can also allow for more timely engagement with a particular concept (unlike a busy lecture) and thus more chance of understanding it.

Using text-walls allowed students to participate in the very familiar medium of texting, and they therefore tended to express themselves freely and informally. The resulting exchanges were indicative of the spontaneity and risk inherent in any genuine dialogue, while also encouraging the development of an atmosphere of playful trust.

Moment five: large classes – bursting with potential for feedback as dialogue

The large lecture is often regarded as an evil necessity in higher education. However, it can also offer a breadth of alternative experiences for students in a safe and accessible way. Game and Metcalfe (2009: 50) describe the particular way in which large classes can form a dynamic presence in which 'students learn to appreciate and respect their own possibilities when they are surprised by hearing their shy and private inklings enunciated by others'.

Peers are important partners in the establishment of a culture of feedback as dialogue within a course. Here we refer not to the assessment context but the everyday course exchanges with peers that can flow into feedback as dialogue; thus providing an abundant source of ideas, questions, alternatives, challenges and positive reinforcements that students can harness to improve their engagement with a given subject. Although such moments occur spontaneously there are many ways in which they can be fostered and encouraged. Within large classes text-walls can illuminate a critical mass of the different perspectives of everyone involved. Used in carefully considered short slots within a longer lecture, text-walls can reinforce the complex nature of a subject, in which dialogue based on different perspectives is legitimate, without setting the whole thing off course and introducing unhelpful confusion.

Moment six: looking beyond the course

The end of a course or module provides a particular challenge in applying notions of feedback as dialogue; the conversation with one tutor may have reached an end and it can be difficult for students to see how learning during one module applies to another. But we can use dialogue to encourage students to link learning between modules and carry it forward with them. For example, in one module the second author uses a one-to-one oral interview as a final assessment (Huxham *et al.* 2010). The feedback from this interview is emailed to students, who are asked to respond with their thoughts on the feedback, on their performance and on what the experience of the interview has taught them. Although optional, students are encouraged to take part before they receive their actual grade. Most students take up this opportunity for self-generated feedback that we hope will prove useful throughout life.

Conclusion

> Strikes the right note:
> Encouraging, but dull.
> Don't give them anything
> To take hold of. Even
> Pronouns are dangerous.
> ('Reports' by U.A. Fanthorpe 2005)

Feedback as dialogue celebrates the uncertain nature of learning. It recognises the way in which learning occurs at an intersection between shared knowledge and individual perspectives. To realise their potential students need the freedom and space to make their own path through a shared course. Policies to improve the quality of learning experienced in our universities therefore need to move away from standardisation and audit-based approaches towards a greater acceptance, even celebration, of uncertainty and difference. Such approaches should not neglect quality, but redefine it in ways that truly acknowledge the social nature of learning.

Feedback as dialogue can contribute to this process by nurturing a ubiquitous sense of dialogue with the ideas of others. This cannot be achieved when feedback is bound to formal assessment because the latter inevitably involves parameters and certainties that restrict the unbounded dialogue we seek to nourish. There are, therefore, few examples of feedback linked to formal assessment (formative or summative) in this chapter, but this does not mean that feedback as dialogue has no relevance to assessment: quite the reverse. Our intention is to show the background to learning upon which any individual task or event (including assessment) occurs. Feedback as dialogue emphasises the social nature of learning and its temporal qualities. Learning occurs within contexts informed by past experiences and future aspirations: to make sense of these requires a constant act of dialogue, with ourselves, with the knowledge we engage with and with the ideas of others.

Acknowledgements

Thanks to the Higher Education Academy subject centres for Education (ESCalate) and Geography, Earth and Environmental Sciences (GEES) for funding that enabled the development of these ideas.

References

Angelo, T.A. and Cross, K.P. (1993) *Classroom Assessment Techniques: a handbook for college teachers* (2nd edn), San Francisco: Jossey-Bass.

Bell, B., Gaventa, J. and Peters, J. (1990) *We Make the Road by Walking: conversations on education and social change*. Myles Horton and Paulo Freire, Philadelphia: Temple University Press.

Brown, J.S. and Duguid, P. (2000) *The Social Life of Information*, Boston MA: Harvard Business School Press.

Carless, D. (2006) 'Differing perceptions in the feedback process', *Studies in Higher Education* 31(2): 219–33.

Carless, D., Salter, D., Yang, M. and Lam, J. (2011) 'Developing sustainable feedback practices', *Studies in Higher Education* 36(4): 395–407.

Fanthorpe, U.A. (2005) *Collected Poems 1978–2003*, Calstock: Peterloo Poets.

Freire, P. (1996) *Pedagogy of the Oppressed*, London: Penguin.

Game, A. and Metcalfe, A. (2009) 'Dialogue and team teaching', *Higher Education Research and Development* 28(1): 45–57.

Giroux, H.A. (1992) *Border Crossings: cultural workers and the politics of education*, New York: Routledge.

Higgins, R., Hartley, P. and Skelton, A. (2002) 'The conscientious consumer: reconsidering the role of assessment feedback in student learning', *Studies in Higher Education*, 27(1): 53–64.

Hollingsworth, P.M. (1995) 'Enhancing listening retention: the two minute discussion', *College Student Journal* 29(1): 116–17.

Hounsell, D. (2003) 'Student feedback, learning and development', in M. Slowey and D. Watson (eds) *Higher Education and the Lifecourse*, Maidenhead: Society for Research into Higher Education and Open University Press (pp. 67–78).

Hounsell, D., McCune, V., Hounsell, J. and Litjens, J. (2008) 'The quality of guidance and feedback to students', *Higher Education Research and Development* 27(1): 55–67.

Huxham, M. (2007) 'Fast and effective feedback: are model answers the answer?' *Assessment and Evaluation in Higher Education* 32(6): 601–11.

Huxham, M., Campbell, F. and Westwood, J. (2010) 'Oral versus written assessments: a test of student performance and attitudes', *Assessment and Evaluation in Higher Education* 37(1): 125–36.

Maclellan, E. (2005) 'Conceptual learning: the priority for higher education', *British Journal of Educational Studies* 53(2): 129–47.

McArthur, J. (2009) 'Diverse student voices in disciplinary discourses', in C. Kreber (ed.) *The University and its Disciplines*, New York: Routledge (pp. 119–28).

McArthur, J., Huxham, M., Hounsell, J. and Warsop, C. (2011) 'Tipping out the boot grit: the use of on-going feedback devices to enhance feedback dialogue', ESCalate, Higher Education Academy Subject Centre Education.

Nicol, D.J. and Macfarlane-Dick, D. (2006) 'Formative assessment and self-regulated learning: a model and seven principles of good feedback practice', *Studies in Higher Education* 31(2): 199–218.

Parker, J. (2005) 'A mise-en-scène for the theatrical university', in R. Barnett (ed.) *Reshaping the University*, Maidenhead: Open University Press.

Scoles, J., Huxham, M. and McArthur, J. (2012) 'No longer exempt from good practice: using exemplars to close the feedback gap for exams', *Assessment and Evaluation in Higher Education*, DOI: 10.1080/02602938.2012.674485.

Wegerif, R. (2008) 'Dialogic or dialectic? The significance of ontological assumptions in research on educational dialogue', *British Educational Research Journal* 34(3): 347–61.

Chapter 9

Feedback and feedforward

Student responses and their implications

Mirabelle Walker

Introduction

This chapter examines what students' responses to three common types of written feedback comments tell us about the usability of the comments, and indicates how this information can be used to enhance feedback practice.

Research into student response to written feedback comments in a variety of higher education establishments and academic subjects has shown that:

- Positive comments are valued. For example, Weaver found that over 90 per cent of students agreed with the statement: 'positive comments have boosted my confidence' (2006).
- Comments can be helpful to students in improving their work (Carless 2006; Wingate 2010).
- Comments are sometimes not understood by students. This may be because the language used by the tutors lies within the academic discourse of the subject and is only partially, if at all, understood by the students (Lea and Street 1998), or because the linking of comments to criteria makes them harder to grasp (Higgins *et al.* 2002; Carless 2006), or because students need explanations rather than brief indications of a shortcoming (Walker 2009).

It is natural to ask whether these different responses arise from different types of feedback, and the research to be described here showed that this is indeed the case and that students find some types of feedback more usable than others.

Students' response to written comments

The research (Walker 2009) categorised the written feedback comments given to 43 distance-learning technology students in summative assignments. These students were studying one of three course modules at levels equivalent to first or second year of a three-year university course. Because of the distance-learning situation, comments were made individually to students in writing. There was no formal process for discussing comments, although students were encouraged to contact their tutors if they wished to discuss the comments they received.

The comments were categorised according to a scheme suggested by Brown and Glover (2006). Three categories of comment were found to be most used in practice, namely content comments, skills-development comments and motivational comments. Since these three categories are important in what follows, a brief description of each follows.

Content comments relate to the substance of the student's answer. Depending on the subject, they will cover such matters as: the appropriateness of what has been included; any omissions; the balance of the material; the quality of the examples or evidence used; the quality of the argument; and accuracy. An example relating to an omission is, 'You should also have included some mention of cost/benefit analysis.' An example relating to balance and appropriateness is, 'You seemed to be dealing with the more exceptional areas of Web 2.0 without giving a good sense of mainstream usage.'

Skills-development comments relate to more generic matters, such as: addressing the question set; structuring the answer appropriately; the style and clarity of the writing; correct use of English; and referencing. An example relating to structure is, 'As this is a short formal report, you need to have an introduction section before launching into what you are reporting.'

Motivational comments relate to praise and encouragement. They range from a simple 'Good' or 'Well done!' to a more elaborate comment such as 'I was particularly pleased with your approach to designing the network for question 2. It was clear that you understood the practicalities of the task.'

In the research, the 43 students were interviewed by telephone regarding the written feedback comments they had received on the assignment whose feedback comments had been analysed. During each interview both the student and the interviewer had a copy of the marked and commented assignment with them, and the student was asked to look at a small number of pre-selected comments and state how they had responded to each. They were not prompted in any way as to how they might reply. Approximately equal numbers from each of the categories content, skills development and motivational were used during the interviews.

A thematic analysis of the responses was carried out, and the response themes that emerged were then matched to the category of comment that had elicited them. The thematic analysis showed (see Table 9.1) that the three strongest themes emerging were consistent with those found in other research, as mentioned at the start of this chapter.

Further examination of the 'useful/helpful' theme, however, showed that it was made up of two distinct sub-themes: the comment was useful or helpful to the student *in seeing where they had gone wrong* and the comment was useful or helpful to the student *for future work*. This distinction turned out to be important when the responses were matched to the category of comment that elicited them, so Table 9.2 shows the response themes with this distinction made.

Table 9.1 The most frequently occurring response themes

Response theme	Percentage of comments eliciting this theme
Comment useful/helpful	30.4
Lack of understanding of comment and/or need for more explanation or detail	27.2
Student pleased/encouraged by comment	23.2

Table 9.2 The most frequently occurring response themes, with the two types of 'useful/helpful' response separated out

Response theme	Percentage of comments eliciting this theme
Lack of understanding of comment and/or need for more explanation or detail	27.2
Comment useful/helpful for future work	24.0
Student pleased/encouraged by comment	23.2
Comment useful/helpful in showing student where they had gone wrong	6.4

When the response themes shown in Table 9.2 were matched to the category of comment that had elicited them, it became clear that:

- the response 'lack of understanding of comment and/or need for more explanation or detail' was mostly elicited by content comments;
- the response 'comment useful/helpful for future work' was mostly elicited by skills-development comments;
- the response 'student pleased/encouraged by comment' was elicited only by motivational comments;
- the response 'comment useful/helpful in showing student where they had gone wrong' was elicited by both content and skills-development comments, but more by the former than by the latter.

A closer examination of responses to content comments showed that the response 'lack of understanding of comment and/or need for more explanation or detail' was given to slightly over half (51 per cent) of the comments in this category. This is a surprisingly, indeed worryingly, high proportion. An additional cause for concern was that the response 'comment useful/helpful in showing student where they had gone wrong' was given to only 16 per cent of the content comments, even though it was clear that the majority of the content comments used in the interviews were intended to show the student where they had gone wrong. It became obvious that many content comments were of little or no help to the students, and this was the case across the three different modules and the 43 different tutors who had made the comments. However, when a further examination of the content comments that elicited the response 'lack of understanding of comment and/or need for more explanation or detail' was made, it became clear that they fell into one of three types:

- comments that merely indicated a problem, such as 'Not enough detail';
- comments that indicated a problem and offered a correction or improvement, such as 'You also needed to mention the effect of distance on data rate';
- comments that indicated a problem, offered a correction or improvement and explained the correction or improvement, such as 'You also needed to mention the fact that data rate decreases with distance, because users who are at the edge of the range may not in fact experience the required data rate'.

The response 'lack of understanding and/or need for more explanation or detail' was found with the first two types of comment, but it was never found with the third type of comment, the one that incorporated an element of explanation. This significant finding is discussed later in the chapter.

In the case of skills-development comments, the response 'comment useful/helpful for future work' was given to nearly two-thirds (64 per cent) of the comments in this category, indicating that skills-development comments have a usefulness to students beyond the immediate assignment. Again, the 'lack of understanding of comment and/or need for more explanation or detail' response occurred, but this time it was elicited by only 13 per cent of the comments. And again, this response did not occur if the comment contained an element of explanation.

Motivational comments were well received by students: 73 per cent of comments in this category elicited the response 'student pleased/encouraged by comment'. There was some slight evidence that for first-year students motivational comments were an important factor in inhibiting drop-out. Rather surprisingly, however, 15 per cent of motivational comments elicited the response 'lack of understanding of comment and/or need for more explanation or detail'. Further examination of the data from the interviews showed that either the student did not understand why a praise comment was written alongside a mark that the student themself judged not particularly praiseworthy, or the student wanted to know more about why they were being praised or for exactly what they were being praised. For motivational comments, this response did not occur if the comment included an element of explanation for the praise.

The foregoing results were obtained in the context of the subject discipline of Technology. In a further study in the same university to investigate how robust these results might be across disciplines, Fernández-Toro and Truman set out to replicate the work in a very different discipline: Spanish. They found similar but not identical results (Fernández-Toro *et al.*, 2012). The most striking similarity was that again the three most common response themes were, in descending order, 'comment useful/helpful', 'lack of understanding of comment and/or need for more explanation or detail' and 'student pleased/encouraged by comment'. Further, the response to motivational comments was very similar across the two subjects. There were, however, differences of detail. In particular, a higher proportion of 'comment useful/helpful' responses were of the 'comment useful/helpful in showing student where they had gone wrong' type. This occurred because language students were considerably more likely to give this response to skills-development comments than were Technology students, perhaps as a consequence of the fact that a high proportion of the skills-development comments given to language students related to inaccurate use of the target language.

The broad similarity between the responses of language and technology students suggests that, while there are likely to be specific subject-related differences at the detailed level, in general the responses found with technology students are likely to be found with students from other academic disciplines.

Feedback and feedforward

The process of matching students' responses to the category of comment that elicited them showed that students tend to respond differently to content comments as compared with skills-development comments. To understand why this is the case, it is useful to examine some fundamental ideas about feedback, starting with Ramaprasad's definition of the term, which is: 'Feedback is information about a gap between the actual level and the reference level of a system parameter which is used to alter the gap in some way' (1983: 4). We can think of the 'actual level' as the student's current understanding and skill, as demonstrated in the piece of work just completed, and the 'reference level' as the understanding and skill we would like to see. With most pieces of student work there is a gap, and in their authoritative papers on feedback, both Sadler (1989) and Black and Wiliam (1998) indicate that, to be usable, feedback must enable students to bridge such a gap.

Gap-bridging comments can, however, be of two types (Walker 2009). One type is designed to close retrospective gaps, gaps that occur in work that a student has now completed and is unlikely to return to. Such comments truly feed *back*; they give information about something that is finished for the student and unlikely to be repeated. The other type of gap-bridging comment is designed to close future gaps, gaps in the more generic elements of a student's work that may occur again and again without intervention. Such comments have the potential to help students to do better work in the future and so feed *forward*.

It is worth noting here that while the metaphor of bridging gaps is a useful one in relation to comments in the categories of content and skills development, it should not be equated with an 'ideal minus' (Chetwynd and Dobbyn 2011: 68) approach, where each student's work is judged against a well-nigh unachievable standard. In particular, the 'reference level' is not perfection, but the standard towards which we wish students to be working and which the most able will achieve.

Comments on content usually relate only to one particular piece of work. In the main, therefore, they feed back. By contrast, comments on skills development generally, though not universally, refer to generic aspects of students' work, and so feed forward. Therefore content comments mainly address retrospective gaps whereas skills-development comments address future gaps. This difference can be used to explain the differing student responses to the two categories of comment identified in the research. It seems that students need help in the form of an explanation in order to bridge retrospective gaps, and if that help is not forthcoming then they are liable to say that they do not understand the comment. But for future gaps it seems that students can often see for themselves that a comment could apply in the future, and so they are liable to say that the comment is useful for future work.

Comments designed to help students to bridge future gaps – that is, feedforward comments – provide more and better opportunities for ongoing student–tutor dialogue than do other forms of comment. They also provide better opportunities for students to adjust their future performance in response to comments received. They therefore come closer to what Hounsell (2007) calls 'sustainable feedback', subsequently defined by Carless *et al.* as 'dialogic processes and activities which can support and inform the student on the current task, whilst also developing the ability to self-regulate performance on future tasks' (2011: 397). This makes feedforward a particularly valuable form of comment.

Finally in this section, it is important to emphasise an often-overlooked aspect of Ramaprasad's definition of feedback, which is: 'information [. . .] which is used to alter the gap in some way' (1983). Feedback involves both a product (the information that is used) and a process (the actual use of this information). Students need to be actively involved in the feedback process – they need to be using the information provided in order to 'alter the gap' by improving their work. As Nicol says, 'While the quality of the comments is important, the quality of the students' interaction with those comments is equally, and perhaps more, important' (2010: 503). So the comments that students receive should not only be usable, which was the focus of the research described in this chapter, they should also be *used*. The implications of this are discussed in the next section.

Practical implications

The findings relating to the usability of comments can help to shape practice, both at the level of individual academics crafting comments on their students' work and at the level of a department or other academic unit planning its assessment and feedback practices.

At the individual level three recommendations for improved practice emerge:

- include motivational comments;
- include more skills-development comments relating to generic skills;
- when making comments on content, consider including some form of explanation.

Motivational comments are important to students. These comments take little effort to write and clearly improve the student experience of receiving feedback on their work. Although motivational comments may not move students forward in their knowledge or skills, they have an important part to play in the affective domain. Indeed, it was noticeable that during the telephone interviews some students' tone of voice warmed while they were giving their positive response to such comments.

Students find generic skills-development comments, with their feedforward potential, the most usable, so it is important to provide such comments. Many students need help and support to reach an appropriate standard in generic skills and are grateful for tutor comments that show them how to do better.

When the tutors on the three Technology modules in the research described earlier were told about the results of the research and asked to increase the proportion of skills-development comments they gave, they found doing so relatively straightforward, and a follow-up investigation in the next academic year showed a statistically significant increase in the proportion of skills development comments made (Walker 2008). This is therefore a change in practice that tutors can learn to make relatively easily.

The research showed clearly that comments on content are the ones that cause students the most problems, but that an explanation within the comment relieves the problems. As an illustration of a comment that includes an explanation, the following comment was made in connection with a computer program where the tutor had indicated an error in a temperature test:

> It is a really bad idea to have a test that looks for an exact value of something that changes with time (like temperature). Even if this program module is running continually, there is a chance that the sampling of values may miss the exact value and after that the action taken may be wrong, possibly leading to 'thermal runaway'.

This comment not only points out that the student should not have written a program that tests for an exact temperature value, but explains clearly why this is bad practice by indicating what the unfortunate consequences of doing so could be. It therefore helps to bridge the gap between the student's understanding, as displayed in the relevant portion of the program submitted, and the expected answer.

The recommendation to consider including some form of explanation when making content comments can, however, be a challenge for tutors. Writing such comments involves more work, and this is a deterrent for many. A further point is that when the tutors on the three Technology modules were asked to write content comments of this type, many of them only explained the improvement or correction. While this can be a useful component of the needed explanation, it is not in itself sufficient. In helping a student to bridge a gap, it is necessary to consider *both* sides of the gap – that is, the improvement or correction aspect and what the student has revealed about their understanding in the answer they gave. Only then can an explanation be crafted that helps that particular student to bridge their individual gap. This, of course, means that there is more work involved in writing such comments than might at first appear. Nevertheless, these are the comments that students actually understand, as opposed to explanation-free comments, or even explanatory comments designed to be copied and pasted and so not tailored to the individual. Such comments may, in fact, have been a waste of time to write because they are simply not understood. In practice, therefore, it may be more effective to identify just a small number of more serious problems with a student's work and address them with full explanatory comments than to put in an equal amount of effort pointing out every problem briefly. The student is more likely to understand the comments in the former case than in the latter. This is, of course, a matter for departments to discuss at a policy level, since students may well become confused if some departmental teaching staff focus on just a few problems while others deal with all points.

A departmental approach to the provision of feedback comments is, in fact, an important practical aspect of improving feedback, and particularly feedforward. There is a limit to what an individual tutor working alone can accomplish in this area.

For example, it is important at both the individual and departmental level to consider how students can be encouraged and supported in using the feedforward comments they receive, thus making the process more dialogic in nature. It is all too easy to assume that students know how to use feedback effectively, but in practice this is not necessarily the case. The following comment about feedback, made by a student after studying a module that supported students in using it, indicates one problem that students may initially have: 'I actually did make use of it [the feedback] instead of viewing it as unjust criticism.' A view of feedback as 'unjust criticism' is not the only obstacle to effective student use of feedforward. Another is a difficulty in seeing how a comment made in one context on one assignment can be transferred to another (albeit similar) context on another assignment. And a third is appreciating what needs to be done but not knowing how to set about doing it. It can be necessary to work with students in order to overcome obstacles such as these so that they can use feedforward effectively to improve their performance.

There are two further components of a departmental approach to improved feedforward. The first is the need for careful planning of the development of generic skills across the curriculum. While individual tutors can and do help students to develop such skills through the feedforward comments they write, the provision of skills-development comments will be much more effective if a department has designed a programme-wide skills-development thread that runs through the individual modules. This is of particular importance in those programmes where the modules are of short duration, as there may be little opportunity for much skills development within each individual module. Indeed, the whole issue of feedforward becomes more problematic where there is heavy modularisation, and so it becomes particularly important for departments to clarify how feedforward can be made to work in their programmes.

The second component in a departmental approach to feedforward is the need to consider the nature of the assignments, especially in those subject areas that are content-heavy such as science and engineering. If the questions are wholly about content, and the marking guides assign most of the marks for content, then there is little encouragement to tutors to provide feedforward on generic skills and no reason for grade-conscious students to pay attention to skills that carry no explicit marks. Here an adjustment to either the questions or marking guides or both is needed to facilitate feedforward comments.

Conclusion

This chapter has examined students' response to the feedback comments they receive, with a particular focus on whether they find the comments usable. It has shown that students appreciate motivational comments on their work, and that therefore these comments have a use in the affective domain. It has also shown that students are more likely to understand feed*back* comments – that is, comments that look retrospectively at their work – if the comments include an element of explanation designed to help the student bridge the gap between the knowledge and understanding they displayed and what was expected. In addition, it has shown that students find the feed*forward* nature of skills-development comments useful for future work. Such comments can be thought of as future gap-bridging, in that they can help students not to exhibit the same gaps in their generic skills in the future and thus support students in learning to improve their work.

The implications of these findings for individual and departmental practice have been discussed. At an individual level this involves including motivational comments, giving skills-development comments that relate to generic skills and offering gap-bridging explanations when pointing out problems. At the departmental level, this involves a holistic approach to providing feedforward across a whole programme of study, as well as to ensuring there are feedforward opportunities in individual assignments. Finally, attention needs to be given at both individual and departmental levels to the issue of how to help students use the feedforward that they receive.

Maclellan warns that 'if students are not actually monitoring and regulating the quality of their own learning, feedback of itself, regardless of its degree of detail, will not cause improvement in learning' (2001: 316). Changes at both an individual and a departmental level, not just to provide more usable comments but also to support and encourage students in learning to use them, are therefore an important element of improved learning and pay dividends in sustainable feedback that engenders enhanced student self-regulation.

References

Black, P. and Wiliam, D. (1998) 'Assessment and classroom learning', *Assessment in Education: Principles, Policy and Practice* 5(1): 7–74.

Brown, E. and Glover, C. (2006) 'Evaluating written feedback', in C. Bryan, and K. Clegg (eds) *Innovative assessment in Higher Education*, London: Routledge (pp. 81–91).

Carless, D. (2006) 'Differing perceptions in the feedback process', *Studies in Higher Education* 31(2): 219–33.

Carless, D., Salter, D., Yang, M. and Lam, J. (2011) 'Developing sustainable feedback practices', *Studies in Higher Education* 36(4): 395–407.

Chetwynd, F. and Dobbyn, C. (2011) 'Assessment, feedback and marking guides in distance education', *Open Learning* 26(1): 67–78.

Fernández-Toro, M., Truman, M. and Walker, M. (2012) 'Are the principles of effective feedback transferable across the disciplines? A comparative study of written assignment feedback in Languages and Technology', *Assessment and Evaluation in Higher Education*, iFirst Article DOI 10.1080/02602938.2012.724381.

Higgins, R., Hartley, P. and Skelton, A. (2002) 'The conscientious consumer: reconsidering the role of assessment feedback in student learning', *Studies in Higher Education* 27(1): 53–64.

Hounsell, D. (2007) 'Towards more sustainable feedback to students', in D. Boud and N. Falchikov (eds) *Rethinking Assessment in Higher Education*, London: Routledge (pp. 101–13).

Lea, M.R. and Street, B.V. (1998) 'Student writing in higher education: an academic literacies approach', *Studies in Higher Education* 23(2): 157–72.

Maclellan, E. (2001) 'Assessment for learning: the differing perceptions of tutors and students', *Assessment and Evaluation in Higher Education* 26(4): 307–18.

Nicol, D. (2010) 'From monologue to dialogue: improving written feedback processes in mass higher education', *Assessment and Evaluation in Higher Education* 35(5): 501–17.

Ramaprasad, A. (1983) 'On the definition of feedback', *Behavioural Science* 28(1): 4–13.

Sadler, D.R. (1989) 'Formative assessment and the design of instructional systems', *Instructional Science* 18(2): 119–44.

Walker, M. (2008) 'Feedback, assessment and skills development', in C. Rust (ed.) *Improving Student Learning – For What?* Oxford: The Oxford Centre for Staff and Learning Development (pp. 228–40).

Walker, M. (2009) 'An investigation into written comments on assignments: do students find them usable?' *Assessment and Evaluation in Higher Education* 34(1): 67–78.

Weaver, M.R. (2006) 'Do students value feedback? Student perceptions of tutors' written responses', *Assessment and Evaluation in Higher Education* 31(3): 379–94.

Wingate, U. (2010) 'The impact of formative feedback on the development of academic writing', *Assessment and Evaluation in Higher Education* 35(5): 519–33.

Chapter 10

Sustainable feedback and the development of student self-evaluative capacities

David Carless

Introduction

The re-conceptualisation of feedback envisaged in this volume takes at its heart a dialogic approach to feedback. Dialogue is more than conversation or exchange of ideas, it involves relationships in which participants think and reason together (Gravett and Petersen 2002). Dialogic feedback is defined as interactive exchanges in which interpretations are shared, meanings negotiated and expectations clarified. It seeks to provide opportunities for students to interact around notions of quality and standards in the discipline. Without an evolving understanding of quality, it is difficult for students to make sense of comments on their work and improve performance; and in such cases feedback becomes unproductive and unsustainable. The emphasis on dialogue is an explicit attempt to address the limitations of those forms of feedback that are largely one-way transmissive processes. These uni-directional modes of feedback largely arise because of the institutional constraint of written feedback on end of course assignments. Generating dialogue thus requires some re-engineering of the feedback process.

Within the realities of mass higher education, limited resourcing and multiple demands on teachers, does dialogic feedback appear to be a feasible aspiration? How can we hold meaningful dialogues if faced with a large class of students of widely differing motivations and abilities? The position taken in this chapter is that feedback needs to be 'sustainable'. In other words, it should not and cannot rely solely on the tutor to provide comments, but instead it requires an enhanced student role in generating and using feedback. Sustainability in feedback lies in the ability of students to improve the quality of their work independently of the tutor (Carless *et al.* 2011). Our work as educators is sustainable when students have learnt with us, and are able to continue improving without us. As part of this process, students need to be developing their self-evaluative capacities at increasingly high levels.

For the purposes of this chapter, I define sustainable feedback as:

> active student participation in dialogic activities in which students generate and use feedback from peers, self or others as part of an ongoing process of developing capacities as autonomous self-regulating learners.

The aims of the chapter are to explore sustainable feedback through discussing its theoretical underpinnings and analysing relevant classroom practices. Its significance lies partly in the use of data from a classroom case study of an award-winning teacher to exemplify features of sustainable feedback. The chapter also contributes to the volume as a whole, by its focus on re-conceptualising feedback, not as something that takes place at the end of a course or task, but as embedded within the curriculum. In this way, sustainable feedback practices facilitate efficient use of staff time by re-directing post-task comments towards dialogic interaction within regular classroom activities.

Framework for sustainable feedback

The conceptual origins of sustainable feedback lie in Boud's (2000) notion of sustainable assessment: practices that meet immediate assessment needs whilst not compromising the knowledge, skills and dispositions required to support lifelong learning activities. At the heart of sustainable assessment is the notion of students as active consumers of assessment information, using it to self-regulate their own performance. Drawing on this notion of sustainable assessment, Hounsell (2007) introduces the concept of sustainable feedback and addresses three strands: a focus on the provision of 'high-value' feedback carrying impact beyond the task to which it relates; enhancing the student role to generate, interpret and engage with feedback; and developing congruence between guidance and feedback, by orchestrating teaching and learning environments in which productive dialogue arises from course learning activities.

Sustainable feedback is also consistent with key ideas in other significant literature on feedback: a model of feedback and self-regulated learning (Nicol and Macfarlane-Dick 2006); a dialogic model of feedback (Beaumont *et al.* 2011); and a focus on student engagement with feedback (Price *et al.* 2011). Feedback needs to focus less on providing information to the student, and more on guiding them to understand the nature of quality and develop personal capability in making complex judgements (Sadler 2010). An aspect of students developing their judgement relates to what Sadler (2009: 57) refers to as connoisseurship which he defines as 'a highly developed form of competence in qualitative appraisal'. Sadler's interest, congruent with the development of sustainable feedback practices, is in how students develop expertise in making judgements about their work and that of peers.

Building on this literature, sustainable feedback is viewed as encompassing the following core characteristics (Carless *et al.* 2011):

- involving students in dialogues around learning to raise their understanding of quality work;
- facilitating feedback processes through which students are stimulated to develop capacities in monitoring and evaluating their own learning;

- enhancing student capacities for ongoing lifelong learning and supporting student development of skills for goal-setting and planning their learning.

What are some of the teaching, learning and assessment tasks through which sustainable feedback can be promoted? A key issue is the design of assessment tasks as they impact on how students organise their study time (Gibbs 2006). Here I briefly review a task utilised by the case study teacher featured in this chapter: oral presentations.

Oral presentations are common assessment tools in higher education. Through their relationship to professional communication skills, they are a relatively 'authentic' mode of assessment (Doherty et al. 2011). When an oral presentation is conceived as a position to be argued, it can facilitate a powerful student learning experience, with students perceiving it as being more demanding than written assignments, more personal, requiring deeper understanding, and leading to better learning (Joughin 2007). Oral presentations also carry opportunities for classroom dialogue through peer assessment or peer feedback. In fact, given that the audience of an oral presentation is usually a group of classmates and a single teacher, a valid assessment of the presentation should take into account its degree of success in communicating to fellow students (Magin and Helmore 2001). Engaging with the communication of peers is also a way in which students develop skills in making informed judgements, and using observation of classmates to enhance their own performance. Such processes are most likely to be productive if there are trusting relationships between all classroom participants (Carless 2009).

In summary, sustainable feedback is co-constructed by tutors and students, with an emphasis on student engagement with feedback as part of their development as self-regulating learners. It can be facilitated through dialogic interaction, which aims to enhance student understandings of quality work. Oral presentations are noted as an example of an assessment task that can facilitate dialogues between peers.

The context of the case study

The chapter uses data from a case study of a teacher in a Faculty of Business who was a recipient of a university teaching excellence award. His potential for implementing practices congruent with sustainable feedback emerged from an interview study of ten winners of teaching awards in the university (Carless et al. 2011). The rationale for studying award-winning teachers is not that they necessarily represent 'best practice', but that analysis of their pedagogy has potential to provide meaningful insights into the teaching, learning and assessment process. A single case is sufficient for the purposes of the chapter, as its aim is not to generalise but to theorise and suggest implications for practice.

The research was guided by the following questions:

What sustainable feedback practices were observable in the practice of an award-winning teacher?
What was the teacher's rationale for the practices that he adopted?
What were the student perceptions of the teacher's practices?

The research methods were interviews and classroom observations. Individual semi-structured interviews were carried out with the teacher to elicit his views of issues relevant to the research focus; and with eleven students, focusing on issues arising from the observations and the teacher interviews. Fifteen hours of classroom observations were conducted and detailed field notes were collected from two different elective courses. The discussion in this chapter draws mainly on a course on Creativity and Business Innovation.

The assessment for the course was through three components with the following weighting:

1.   Case, class and blog discussion   40 per cent
2.   Individual written case assignment   30 per cent
3.   Final project   30 per cent

The first component is essentially an assessment of student participation in the class in three aspects: their contribution to general class interaction; discussions related to business cases, which were a core feature of the module; and the course blog. The second assessment task is a more traditional written task. The third is a group project that involves an oral presentation and a related written report. Some tensions in the assessment design are apparent. Rather than placing a main emphasis on reliability in measuring student performance, there appears to be greater stress on the development of productive student learning experience. For example, the grade for student participation is useful in motivating them to contribute actively to course activities, but is hard to assess reliably.

Key themes

The case study teacher's orientation towards teaching was articulated in terms of providing challenging interactive learning activities for students; and stimulating them to make connections between different elements of their learning and experience. Various classroom activities and assessment tasks created an environment for practices congruent with sustainable feedback. I focus here on two elements: interactive dialogic whole-class teaching and the use of student oral presentations as a site for peer feedback.

Interactive dialogic teaching

The teacher's espoused philosophy is to engage students in various activities that enhance their thinking skills. His view of education is as follows:

Education is an experience of thinking, feeling and doing. For students to grow intellectually, the idea is to be able to think independently. Independence comes from mastering the art of thinking . . . I put the students at the centre of a dynamic process where they can holistically learn to think, learn to change, and hopefully learn to learn.

His courses prioritise the development of learning to learn and analytic skills over content, which he believes can easily be found through other sources and may also quickly become outdated.

Classroom observations revealed a strong undercurrent of dialogue in his teaching. For example, it was common for him to begin a class with a seemingly mundane question, 'What did you learn in the class last week?' In early observations of the course, students sometimes replied with a recount of the content of the previous class. The teacher used such responses as a stimulus to probe more deeply into what new knowledge had been generated. For example, the teacher responded:

It's better to say I learned . . . What did you learn that you didn't know before? Come on guys, make some connections.

Description is not good enough; it is too easy to forget. You have to go deeper. If you understand why, you usually won't forget. Try to understand things more deeply.

Both classroom observation and interview data suggested that this opening gambit was impacting on student learning behaviours. In later observations, it was noticeable that students were becoming better prepared to reflect on their learning from previous classes. A student referred specifically to this aspect as follows:

Before taking this course, I do not have the habit of reviewing the previous lesson. But in this course, he always asks us what we learnt from the previous lesson. So before I go to class, I always review what I have learnt and I am starting to do this now in my other courses.

The teacher also devotes some class time to focus explicitly on how students learn. For example, he concluded one classroom segment by saying: 'Learning requires a little bit of repetition. Remember things you want to learn, make connections and then some re-organisation of your understandings. That's how you learn'.

In terms of feedback, the teacher intersperses within the classroom dialogue encouraging comments – 'This is really good, fantastic . . . that's a beautiful idea' – with more critical comments. An example of the latter occurred when a student gave a rather long-winded comment, and before its conclusion the teacher interrupted and said, 'We didn't understand what you just said. Summarise it one short sentence.' This kind of direct feedback also exemplifies challenges of class participation at both cognitive and social-affective levels.

From the interview data, some student comments on the dialogic interaction are as follows:

> He challenges us to bring our thinking to a higher level. He wants to know whether you can apply your knowledge at a sophisticated level. So if I want to answer his question, I would need to think in depth because he would ask challenging follow-up questions.

> His way of interacting is that there is not one right answer, but many good answers. So you can mention an idea and then we will discuss how to improve it and that's one of the reasons why students want to speak more.

In order to participate willingly in such dialogues, students need to invest a certain amount of trust in their teacher's and peers' willingness to respond sincerely to their contributions.

The amount of class time devoted to dialogic interaction also leads to a tension in relation to the balance between process and content. Some critical student comments on this aspect:

> The course is good for critical and creative thinking but we did not get much practical knowledge from it. He has a free style and we explore some ideas further and we may forget what we are talking about in the course . . . and then time is up. It's a kind of paradox. Do we have to learn some practical knowledge in every course?

> Sometimes I don't know what we are learning because he is talking about very psychological or philosophical things. Sometimes I don't really know what that has to do with the topic of the course.

These comments relate to a common dilemma experienced by teachers, in terms of achieving a balance between the process of learning and delivering disciplinary content.

An issue I raised with the teacher was how participation is assessed in the course, and the extent to which this is articulated explicitly to students. He responded as follows:

> It's intentional that I don't articulate in detail how the mark for class participation is awarded. In the course outline, it states that success in the course depends on *effective* participation in class. It's not the quantity of participation. I would say good students know exactly what a good contribution is. Part of education is for them to become assessors themselves to know what good learning is.

My interpretation from the classroom observations is that he uses various techniques to try to model and encourage high quality-participation by guiding the students to improve their contributions to discussions. He is not explicit about how participation is graded, but he is showing during class what good contributions are like. He seems to be trying to resolve the tension between being so explicit as to constrain student creativity and impede emergent outcomes, whilst supporting students to understand what quality participation involves. This focus on interaction around the notion of quality is at the heart of sustainable feedback.

Oral presentations

One of the features of the classes was that students are regularly required to present their thoughts verbally at the front of the class through oral presentations. The teacher believes that developing the ability to carry out a convincing oral presentation is a key tool of business personnel. The presentations are always done in groups, usually involving three to five participants. They can vary from short informal sharing involving just a few minutes per group, to longer more structured presentations of fifteen to twenty minutes. The former were often related to the cases which were central to course content, whereas the latter were as part of the assessed final project, involving an oral presentation and a related written report handed in two weeks later. In other words, the oral presentations feed in to both the course participation grade and the final project grade.

I have suggested earlier that a key element of sustainable feedback is that it involves students in dialogues that raise awareness of quality performance. A major way in which the teacher does this is through one of his favoured activities involving a structured process of oral presentations and feedback. Students are video-taped when presenting in groups. Immediately after the presentation, the teacher shows one or two short extracts from each presentation. He first invites the presenter to self-evaluate their performance and then opens up the floor to suggestions and interactive discussion. His stated rationale for this activity is to use the reality of the video to heighten student awareness of the strengths and weaknesses of their own presentations, and by commenting on other students' talks developing a stronger sense of characteristics of good business presentations. He comments on the role of student peer- and self-evaluation in this activity as follows:

> Self-assessment is a big part of learning. I think every course should encourage the students to assess other students so that they know the meaning of quality. You increase their sense of empathy because you break the artificial barriers between teacher and students by reversing the roles; they do the assessing and see how tough it is. Some of them are struggling to decide which oral presentation project is good because they are learning how to assess.

Some student viewpoints on this oral presentation activity now follow:

> The video activity was really useful. I have been videoed before, but this was the first time I got feedback. It gives me more confidence because I think my presentation looked okay. I could also look closely at others presenting and I know some things to avoid, like some annoying gestures. The only problem is that the presentations and discussions are quite time-consuming

> I think the course kept on being interesting because we had the presentations, and so at each class, we had something new to do or something different to learn. But then there is less course content, so maybe the content could be expanded

The oral presentations stimulated 'time on task' often identified as a feature of productive learning. The students were involved in a lot of discussion, preparation and planning for the presentations. For example, one student reported to me that his group spent around six hours preparing for a presentation that only lasted a few minutes. They brainstormed and debated the topic of their presentation for around four hours, and then they focused more directly on the content and the roles of participants. My inference was that students were engaged in potentially valuable out of class dialogues about content through this active involvement in preparation of the oral presentation.

Oral presentations seem to be a particularly promising site for peer feedback and this was facilitated in the case under discussion by the positive classroom atmosphere and trusting relationships between classmates. Peer interaction around what makes a quality oral presentation may be even more promising than peer assessment involving marks, as the latter can carry unwanted side-effects of concerns about awarding grades to friends, and distract from the collaborative learning climate that is being established (Liu and Carless 2006).

Conclusions and implications

Feedback is too often based on what the teacher wants to say rather than on what the student is interested in hearing. This is one of the contributing factors to students' expressions of dissatisfaction with feedback, and one of the reasons why it needs re-engineering. Dialogic interaction can bridge this gap in student–staff preferences by involving participants in exchanging insights on topics of shared interest. Dialogue is central to sustainable feedback in that it emphasises the students' role in making sense of feedback and using it to develop their own self-evaluative capacities. Sustainable feedback also reconfigures the teacher role from someone who mainly provides comments on student progress, to a position of supporting students to make their own professional judgements. The example from the case study of reflective discussion of oral presentations has illustrated how peer feedback can assist students in developing a better understanding of the nature of quality.

I suggest that a facilitating factor for the development of sustainable feedback is trust of students in their teacher and classmates (see also Carless 2013). Trust is an important dimension in assessment and feedback, yet something that is often in short supply (Carless 2009). The development of trusting relationships among participants has particular implications for developing sustainable feedback. Relevant dimensions include 'competence trust' or confidence in teachers' and classmates' capacities to provide useful feedback; and 'communication trust' as evidenced by qualities of openness, empathy and genuine interest in the ideas of others. We are clearly more likely to engage with feedback from an individual who possesses 'trusting virtues': transparency, integrity and our best interests at heart (Carless 2013).

Finally, I turn briefly to the institutional level to discuss wider prospects for the promotion of sustainable feedback practices. The teacher featured in this chapter viewed the primary purpose of teaching as facilitation of learning so as to develop students' capabilities of critical thinking, self-reflection and self-improvement. He was less concerned with transmission of subject matter. This was part of the rationale for both his pedagogy and his design of assessment tasks; and a facilitating factor for sustainable feedback practices. Research shows that teachers holding beliefs focused on facilitating learning, rather than delivering disciplinary content, are but a small minority among academics (Prosser *et al.* 2005). Following from this, an issue for further exploration is the prospect of scaling up the implementation of sustainable feedback at an institutional level, so that rather than being a minority pursuit it becomes part of the pedagogic repertoire of a greater number of teachers. As noted elsewhere (Carless *et al.* 2011), incentives and resourced commitments at institutional and department levels would be useful ways of encouraging the development of sustainable feedback practices. A key challenge is the belief systems of teachers, which are obviously difficult to change. Two ways forward emerge. The first is the dissemination of good practices, and hopefully this is a contribution of the current chapter. The second is to engage teachers in critical open discussions of tacit beliefs and approaches to assessment and teaching. For feedback to be re-engineered on a wide scale, it needs to engage with or even confront the belief systems and existing practices of staff.

References

Beaumont, C., O'Doherty, M. and Shannon, L. (2011) 'Reconceptualising assessment feedback: a key to improving student learning?' *Studies in Higher Education* 36(6): 1–17.

Boud, D. (2000) 'Sustainable assessment: rethinking assessment for the learning society', *Studies in Continuing Education* 22(2): 151–67.

Carless, D. (2009) 'Trust, distrust and their impact on assessment reform', *Assessment and Evaluation in Higher Education* 34(1): 79–89.

Carless, D. (2013) 'Trust and its role in facilitating dialogic feedback', in D. Boud and L. Molloy (eds) *Effective Feedback in Higher and Professional Education*, London: Routledge (pp. 90–103).

Carless, D., Salter, D., Yang, M. and Lam, J. (2011) 'Developing sustainable feedback practices', *Studies in Higher Education* 36(4): 395–407.

Doherty, C., Kettle, M., May, L. and Caukill, E. (2011) 'Talking the talk: oracy demands in first year university assessment tasks', *Assessment in Education* 18(1): 27–39.

Gibbs, G. (2006) 'How assessment frames student learning', in C. Bryan and K. Clegg (eds) *Innovative Assessment in Higher Education*, London: Routledge (pp. 23–36).

Gravett, S. and Petersen, N. (2002) 'Structuring dialogue with students via learning tasks', *Innovative Higher Education*, 26(4): 281–91.

Hounsell, D. (2007) 'Towards more sustainable feedback to students', in D. Boud and N. Falchikov (eds) *Rethinking Assessment in Higher Education: learning for the longer term*, London: Routledge (pp. 104–13).

Joughin, G. (2007) 'Student conceptions of oral presentations', *Studies in Higher Education* 32(3): 323–36.

Liu, N.F. and Carless, D. (2006) 'Peer feedback: the learning element of peer assessment', *Teaching in Higher Education* 11(3): 279–90.

Magin, D. and Helmore, P. (2001) 'Peer and teacher assessments of oral presentation skills: how reliable are they?' *Studies in Higher Education* 26(3): 289–98.

Nicol, D. and Macfarlane-Dick, D. (2006) 'Formative assessment and self-regulated learning', *Studies in Higher Education* 31(2): 199–218.

Price, M., Handley, K. and Millar, J. (2011) 'Feedback: focusing attention on engagement', *Studies in Higher Education* 36(8): 879–96.

Prosser, M., Martin, E., Trigwell, K., Ramsden, P. and Lueckenhausen, G. (2005) 'Academics' experiences of understanding of their subject matter and the relationship of this to their experiences of teaching and learning', *Instructional Science* 33(2): 137–57.

Sadler, D.R. (2009) 'Transforming holistic assessment and grading into a vehicle for complex learning', in G. Joughin (ed.) *Assessment, Learning and Judgement in Higher Education*, Dordrecht: Springer (pp. 45–63).

Sadler, D.R. (2010) 'Beyond feedback: developing student capability in complex appraisal', *Assessment and Evaluation in Higher Education* 35(5): 535–50.

Chapter 11

Students' social learning practice as a way of learning from tutor feedback

Paul Orsmond, Stephen Merry and Karen Handley

Introduction

The primary purpose of tutor feedback in higher education is to assist students in their learning. That is the overriding aim. It is an aim that many tutors hope to achieve by spending time writing carefully constructed feedback on course-work and examination scripts. This particular tutor practice is one that has been carried out for many years in a relatively unchanging fashion. It is a practice that is handed down from experienced members of staff to new recruits and intu-itively it seems the right thing to do. The tutor, the expert, feeds back aspects of that expertise to students. Students then, in theory, assimilate that feedback and their understanding develops. However, little is known as to the process by which learning from tutor feedback occurs and the purpose of this chapter is to explore more closely that student learner process focusing on:

- the role of social learning; and
- the importance of self-assessment.

Situated learning and communities of practice

With the publication of *Situated Learning*, Lave and Wenger (1991) explored the nature of learning, taking as their focus the relationship between learning and the social situations in which it occurs. Lave and Wenger's work followed in the tradition of Vygotsky (1978), who drew attention to the socially constructed nature of learning, and also the tradition of the Russian and Scandinavian psychologists (Engeström 1987) advocating an orientation to activity and praxis. Lave and Wenger (1991) emphasised that *all* activity, including learning, is inevitably situated. But 'situated' does not mean that learning 'needs' to be located in a particular location; instead, 'situated' refers to the webs of social relationships that influence how we attend to, value and interpret communications (e.g. feedback) that we get. Lave and Wenger (1991: 34) argued that situated learning is a 'transitory concept bridge, between . . . cognitive processes and thus learning . . . and a view according to which social practice is the primary, generative phenomenon'.

Wenger (1998) subsequently developed the concept of communities of practice by defining them as having three separate attributes. These are: (1) mutual engagement, (2) joint enterprise, and (3) a shared repertoire. Communities also have key characteristics of practice. These include 'absence of introductory preambles as if conversations and interaction were merely the continuation of an ongoing process' and the 'ability to assess the appropriateness of actions and products' (Wenger 1998). Orsmond et al. (2011) showed that biology students develop communities of practice outside the overt curriculum that function in accordance with Wenger's conceptual framework. Students' forms of participation in these communities change as their identities and practices evolve, and as they become accepted by others in the community. Communities of practice are not formal institutions; but neither are they temporary groups set up for a particular purpose. Instead, according to the analytic (rather than empirical) definition given by Lave and Wenger, they are self-sustaining because of the recurring cycle of incoming members replacing 'old-timers'. Members have an interest in maintaining the practices of the community, and their actions are shaped by the shared repertoires, interpretive logics, ongoing debates and disagreements that infuse the community. Communities interpret artefacts (such as feedback) in their own ways. If we assume that 'tutor feedback' is relevant to students, and if we further assume that tutors and students inhabit different but perhaps overlapping communities of practice, then 'tutor feedback' may be valued and interpreted quite differently in each community.

Tutor feedback, once it passes into the student community, is no longer a tutor constructed artefact, but it becomes part of what Lave and Wenger (1991) term a learning curriculum. This means that the feedback becomes part of the group of learning resources (shared repertoire) that students are going to use (or choose to ignore) as part of their overall learning. Feedback, an institutional artefact, then enters the community through joint enterprise negotiations and a community's understanding of meaning will be established. This meaning may differ from that desired by the tutor. A community of practice therefore allows for tutor feedback to be manipulated, translated and hence perceived and understood by students in different ways over which the tutor may have little control. As Wenger (1998: 80) states, 'the enterprise [in this case feedback] is never fully determined by an outside mandate'. This translation of meaning is discussed further in the next section when the role of the 'self' and community practice are considered.

This chapter goes on to consider the 'self' in community social learning in three ways:

1   self-assessment;
2   thinking dispositions;
3   agency.

Community learning and self-assessment

It is helpful when thinking about the role of self-assessment in community learning to consider the notion of distributed cognition. Lave (1988) discusses distributed cognition from the perspective of social anthropology rather than as a psychological phenomenon. She considered cognition to be stretched, encompassing mind, body and activities. Stretched cognition is a complex social phenomenon in the sense that knowledge in the head and in the social world is organised in such a way as to be indivisible. Within a community, the learner is seen as a 'whole person' and not from the perspective of a cognitive learner who internalizes knowledge in the absence of, or separated from the world in which he or she is learning. Learning therefore occurs at the relational interface between the objective social world and the subjective student 'self'. In terms of the objective world, tutor feedback is just one 'function' in a broader system of relations of which the student is conscious. Thus within the learning curriculum, peer discussion regarding tutor feedback is important. This is because within a community, learning, thinking and knowing are relational among people in activities that allow for expression of practice, and discussing tutor feedback is part of the student practice. Such discussion is important because it leads to peer assessment and the associated peer feedback. Hence, in terms of tutor feedback, once engaged in these peer community discussions the student identifies 'bits' or discerns certain aspects of information that they need in order to make sense of the feedback. Discerning in this way encourages students to recognise variation in the feedback, and it is through this variation, or seeing the feedback in different ways, that students begin to learn.

Thus, at the relational interface, students appropriate aspects of the objective world and make sense of them and in order to carry out this sense-making task, the subjective self makes self-assessments. Self-assessment is defined by Boud (1995: 1) in the form of a series of questions:

> Whenever we learn we question ourselves. How am I doing? Is this enough? Is this right? How can I tell? Should I go further? In the act of questioning is the act of judging ourselves and making decisions about the next step.

As a situated activity, self-assessment is not an isolated act. It only has meaning when it acts as an integral part involved in the broader system of community relational activities. Self-assessment allows 'knowing' within the community to occur and emphasises the person in action. This leads to a change in how the subjective 'self' understands the objective world. Thus learning from tutor feedback is often defined by the community because meaning is sought through participation, for example, negotiations. Once meaning is achieved, the tutor feedback can be effectively used. How effective it is will depend on the level of negotiations and the quality of the resulting self-generated feedback.

Therefore high-achieving students with their strong ability to self-assess develop a sustainable assessment practice achieving very different understandings of feedback compared to non high-achieving students who tend to have poor self-assessment abilities, and thus rely on tutor (external) regulation. Feedback as a community joint resource forms part of student participation in situated negotiation and renegotiation.

> Once I had a problem [regarding feedback] with my dissertation supervisor. I thought I'd done things wrong . . . but I spoke to other people who were also his project students . . . and had the same problem . . . It wasn't a case that we were doing something wrong . . . it was more the feedback he was giving wasn't relevant to what *we* were trying to say.

This quote from a high-achieving student (Orsmond and Merry 2012: 9) conveys the nature of negotiation and the coming to a community 'we' perspective. Therefore, tutor feedback is used by individuals in such a way as to give form to the community's experience, with histories of interpretations creating shared points of reference.

Community learning and thinking dispositions

In making 'self' judgements students are influenced by what Perkins and Tishman (2001) call 'thinking dispositions'. They argue these dispositions are necessary to fully account for intelligent behaviour. They recognise patterns of thinking in everyday language and behaviour. Furthermore, they act as 'explanatory constructs that address the gap between ability and performance' so allowing some people to marshal their abilities (p. 237). Thinking dispositions can be categorised into three logically distinct and separate components – *sensitivity, inclination* and *ability*. Sensitivity concerns awareness of occasion, inclination concerns motivation or learning and ability concerns capability to follow through appropriately. As a consequence of these components being separate it is possible to be aware of a certain situation, but not be inclined to do something about it. That is to allow opportunities to pass by that another learner would be happy to invest in. Therefore, as part of a self-assessment process, it is necessary to consider the role of disposition. In terms of tutor feedback, students may not be sensitive or have the inclination or the ability to change. Either of these factors may make students appear to ignore or disregard the feedback.

In terms of the whole person and considering the interface between the objective world and the subjective self, the notion of thinking dispositions brings together both subjective psychological and sociological attributes in order to understand tutor feedback and subsequent peer discussions. In this context, thinking dispositions relate well with the notion of agency.

Community learning and agency

Agency has been defined as 'a sense of oneself as one who can go beyond the given meaning in any one discourse and forge something new' (Davies 2000: 67). Agency in terms of social learning can therefore be seen as part of the negotiating process, finding a meaning or determining a set of goals.

Regarding tutor feedback and learning, students developing a 'sense of oneself' can be seen in how judgements are made. The following is a series of previously unpublished responses made during an interview with the same student. This high-achieving student, when discussing how they 'understand' feedback, stated three separate processes that they used

> I tend to look at it more as a scientist . . . [from] that point of view . . . this is my way of assessing feedback.
>
> Some of them [tutors] actually put it [criteria] on a cover sheet on the front and their [standards] are circled.
>
> Looking back over previous grades and what comments they made about it, I kind of got in my mind what level I think my essays are generally at.

In this example, a student is finding understanding from feedback in three separate ways. First, as a scientist, so developing professional judgement; second, by using tutor-constructed marking criteria, so developing awareness of how others judge work; and, third, judgement is also made in terms of previous experience, a form of ipsative assessment (Hughes 2011) where a sense of intuition seems to be used. These processes may develop and be used in synchrony or in an a-synchronistic fashion. They will influence peer discussion and how sense is made of the objective tutor marking criteria. Furthermore, while marking criteria may be fairly static in structure, the subjective self is dynamic, developing understanding and utilising knowledge in different ways. Thus, once an understanding of criteria is grasped, its meaning begins to change. Hence, interpretation of marking criteria will change with time. This may be one explanation why students appear not to use criteria as tutors would want them to.

In order to 'forge something new', students can change their practice, for example by changing the way they talk, as indicated by this student quote (Orsmond et al. 2011):

> I like to talk to different types of groups [to find out what they know] and if they're [a specific group] not interested I'll try and change my personality . . . to fit.

A change in practice may also result in finding meaning when students approach tutors to discuss coursework. Students in their peer discussions do not regularly refer to aspects of marking criteria. However, when talking to tutors they will discuss marking criteria, particularly when discussing guidance and improvements that can be made. That is not to say students do not use marking criteria in peer discussions. It is just that student discussions use a language that does not explicitly refer to criteria. Contrastingly, when talking to tutors students' language makes, often, more explicit use of criteria terminology. A possible explanation for this is that students, when discussing criteria, are not 'owners of a common language, but shareholders in it' (Rommetveit 2003). Thus students may be reluctant to talk about criteria with peers (and possibly with tutors) as the social language they invoke involves what Bakhtin (quoted in Wertsch 1991) terms 'ventriloquation', that is, one voice speaking through another voice. Furthermore, such limited verbal expression of criteria does not mean that criteria are not being used. When thinking, students may well visualise their assignment in the context of criteria, but do not incorporate these particular thoughts into their peer discussions (Orsmond *et al.* 2011).

In terms of tutor feedback, the objective world consists of many information sources and the subjective self subsequently makes assessments of those sources. Tutor discussions may lead to new information being brought into the community and information can also be brought in from other 'communities' that students may be part of. This illustrates the notion of brokering defined as 'a common feature of the relation of a community of practice with the outside' (Wenger 1998). The subjective world meets the objective world at the interface in self-judgements that are influenced by thinking dispositions and 'self' learning histories that result from previous practice and experiences. Therefore students' engagement with tutor feedback involves social learning processes where internal factors, behaviour and environmental factors operate as 'interlocking determinants of each other' (Bandura 1978).

A learning curriculum (Lave and Wenger 1991) is thus constructed and, as a result of their practice in engaging with this, the student becomes a different person. The interface between objective world and subjective 'self' shifts and the student understands the world, their fellow participants and other communities differently. Learning has thus occurred.

Enriching communities of student practice: a way forward for students to learn effectively from tutor feedback

Encouraging students to learn from tutor feedback does not necessarily require a direct focus on the feedback provided. Rather it involves developing a student's ability at recognising 'self' in the learning process. There are a number of ways to do this. Peer learning with a focus on self- and peer-assessment with the associated feedback is a helpful way to engage students that may enrich community discussions. This is not the type of self- and peer-assessment practices that require students to mark work, or where student marking has to be compared with tutor marking. Rather, self- and peer-assessment activities can be arranged so that 'assessment' is seen in terms of making a judgement, or making sense of some aspect of learning. Peer feedback may not necessarily provide the same level of expertise that tutor feedback does, but peer learning activities do not have to occur in the absence of tutors.

Exemplars (see also Hendry, this volume) may be used as a way to develop peer dialogue and consequently peer feedback. Peer feedback and the development of a shared repertoire from the use of exemplars could be potentially more effective in promoting learning than tutor feedback. Handley and Williams (2011) have also discussed exemplars in terms of students' communities of practice. The use of exemplars may allow students to develop the ability to recognise how task specifications can be written. They are thus more likely to be able to write their own, something considered important by Perkins (2008). Students may, with the development of expertise, develop or create their own exemplars. One way of doing this could be through the development of 'patchwork texts' (Winter 2003). The patchwork is formed through the development of a variety of small self-contained sections of written work, which, when brought together into a patchwork have an overarching coherence. In terms of exemplars, the individual sections of the patch can be studied and students in peer discussion can evaluate changes in their provisional knowledge as the texts are brought together. In terms of evaluation and students recognising their own learning, the patchwork text approach is suitable for use within the GOALS process discussed below.

The GOALS process

While tutors cannot control student communities of practice and they cannot reproduce them in the classroom, they can influence them indirectly through developing and refining students' ability to self-assess. Enriching the quality of curriculum design allows this influence to take place by providing students with opportunities to recognise and develop their own self-assessment practice, which they can then translate into their community practice. Tutors need to provide scaffolding, particularly for non high-achieving students, to enable them to recognise the importance of self-assessment in their learning. One way of doing this is to provide course design with an infrastructure so that both tutors and students are able to focus on the role of 'self' in learning. A framework for achieving this is the GOALS process (Orsmond 2011), which is a model for developing self-assessment practice and uses as its source Boud's definition of self-assessment (Boud 1995).

The GOALS process is student-focused and considers learning from a student perspective initially in the *now*: G = what outcomes do *I* need to **G**rasp? These can be self-generated outcomes or tutor outcomes that are translated by the student so that they understand them. O = how can *I* **O**rientate to 'self', perhaps through asking questions such as 'What am I trying to achieve?' A = what **A**ctions do *I* need to take to achieve *my* outcomes? This could be seen in terms of 'Who do I need to speak to?' or 'How can I most effectively use the tutor provided exemplars?'

The GOALS process also considers learning for the *future*. L = what type of Learning evaluation do *I* need to make. Asking questions such as 'How have I done?', 'How am I different now compared to when I started?' or 'What has changed?' Finally S = what **S**trategies do *I* need to develop in order to successfully move on? Here students need to think about the experience of doing an assignment, perhaps in terms of how they can reduce 'error' in their approach.

Tutors can use the GOALS process when designing various programme structures such as curriculum design including pre- and post-assessment activities, assignment tasks and peer learning experiences. Through the GOALS process, tutors are able to direct students to their own learning and to allow students to be aware that they do have their own 'learning experiences'.

Therefore, if the curriculum is seen in broad terms, that is, as a dynamic and interactive process of learning, rather than just categories of description (Fraser and Bosanquet 2006), it is possible to see how a learning experience can be developed where student and tutor practice can be brought together, thus allowing students to learn because they recognise, for example, the tutor practice of being a biologist or a historian. Therefore students recognise what it means to 'be' a professional and learning is co-created as a result of both tutor and student recognising what is significant in their practice in terms of personal learning. Research-informed teaching (e.g. Jenkins *et al.* 2007) is a way in which 'learning through practice' environments can be created, and both personal and community research informed learning occurs. In this way, tutor feedback is integrated into the participation in practice and is not a 'bolt-on' accessory. An example of this integrated practice, investigative group practical work, has been shown to provide a vehicle whereby students receive extensive feedback on their ideas from other group members and this can develop students' awareness of their professional identity and the lifelong learning skills that their careers will require (MacKenzie and Ruxton 2007; Merry *et al.* 2010).

Conclusion

This chapter places the delivery and utilisation of feedback within the theoretical parameters of social learning models. It places the emphasis upon feedback being integrated into the practice of student communities and illustrates, within current teaching paradigms, how students' self-awareness of their individual community practice is a necessary condition for learning to occur from tutor feedback. Furthermore, consideration of student communities of practice provides opportunities for tutors to enrich the student learning that occurs outside the overt curriculum. Tutors are able, through suitably designed practice via the GOALS process, to enrich high-achieving students' feedback practice and develop non high-achieving students' self-assessment qualities, thus enhancing their learning abilities. Additionally, the implementation of research informed teaching practices can provide opportunities for situated research informed learning within the curriculum and then for that learning to pass out into the community.

References

Bandura, A. (1978) 'The self system in reciprocal determinism', *American Psychologist* 33(4): 344–58.

Boud, D. (1995) *Enhancing Learning through Self Assessment*, London: Kogan Page.

Davies, B. (2000) *A Body of Writing 1990–1999*, Walnut Creek: AltaMira Press.

Engeström, Y. (1987) *Learning by Expanding: an activity-theoretical approach to developmental research*, Helsinki: Orienta-Konsultit.

Fraser, S.P. and Bosanquet, A.M. (2006) 'The curriculum? That's just a unit outline, isn't it?' *Studies in Higher Education* 31(3): 269–84.

Handley, K. and Williams, L. (2011) 'From copying to learning: using exemplars to engage students with assessment criteria and feedback', *Assessment and Evaluation in Higher Education* 36(1): 95–108.

Hughes, G. (2011) 'Towards a personal best: a case for introducing ipsative assessment in higher education', *Studies in Higher Education* 36(3): 353–67.

Jenkins, A., Healey, M. and Zetter, R. (2007) *Linking Teaching and Research in Disciplines and Departments*, York: The Higher Education Academy.

Lave, J. (1988) *Cognition in Practice*, England: Cambridge University Press.

Lave, J. and Wenger, E. (1991) *Situated Learning: legitimate peripheral participation*, Cambridge: Cambridge University Press.

MacKenzie, J. and Ruxton, G.D. (2007) 'Effective experimental project work and its role in developing the academic identity of bioscience undergraduates', in C. Rust (ed.) *Improving Student Learning: improving student learning through teaching*, Oxford: Oxford Centre for Staff and Learning Development.

Merry, S., Skingsley, D.R. and Orsmond, P. (2010) 'Fostering lifelong learning within a social constructivist environment', in C. Rust (ed.) *Improving Student Learning for the Twenty-First Century Learner*, Oxford: Oxford Centre for Staff and Learning Development.

Orsmond, P. (2011) *Self- and Peer-Assessment: guidance on practice in the biosciences* (2nd edn), Leeds: The Higher Education Academy Centre for Biosciences. Available at: ftp://www.bioscience.heacademy.ac.uk/TeachingGuides/selfpeer/Self&PeerAssesment(2ed).pdf (accessed 1 October 2012).

Orsmond, P. and Merry, S. (2012) 'The importance of self-assessment in students' use of tutors' feedback: a qualitative study of high and non-high achieving biology undergraduates', *Assessment and Evaluation in Higher Education*, 1–12, iFirst Article DOI: 10.1080/02602938.2012.697868.

Orsmond, P., Merry, S. and Callaghan, A.A. (2011) 'Communities of practice and ways to learning: charting the progress of biology undergraduates', *Studies in Higher Education*, 1–17, iFirst Article DOI: 10.1080/03075079.2011.606364.

Perkins, D.N. (2008) 'Beyond understanding', in R. Land, J.H.F. Meyer and J. Smith (eds) *Threshold Concepts within the Disciplines*, Rotterdam: Sense Publishers (pp. 3–19).

Perkins, D.N. and Tishman, S. (2001) 'Dispositional aspects of intelligence', in J. M. Collis and S. Messicks (eds) *Intelligence and Personality: bridging the gap in theory and measurement*, Mahwah, NJ: L. Erlbaum (pp. 233–58).

Rommetveit, R. (2003) 'On the role of "a psychology of the second person" in studies of meaning, language and mind', *Mind, Culture and Activity* 10(3): 205–18.

Vygotsky, L.S. (1978) *Mind in Society: the development of higher mental processes*, Cambridge: Harvard University Press.

Wenger, E. (1998) *Communities of Practice: learning, meaning and identity*, Cambridge: Harvard University Press.

Wertsch, J.V. (1991) *Voices of the Mind: a sociocultural approach to mediated action*, London: Harvard University Press.

Winter, R. (2003) 'Contextualizing the patchwork text: addressing problems of coursework assessment in higher education', *Innovations in Education and Teaching International*, 40(2): 112–22.

Chapter 12

Integrating feedback with classroom teaching

Using exemplars to scaffold learning

Graham Hendry

Introduction

> I was like 'oh my God this is . . .', I would not have thought to do it that way, there is no way I would have done [it] that way, I would have definitely done it the first way, checking all the legislation and showing what I know. Just like [secondary] school you know you just want to show how much you know.
>
> (Hendry *et al.* 2011b)

This is a quote from a student in a first year undergraduate Law programme at a large metropolitan Australian university. He is talking about his experience of seeing an *exemplar* of a good assignment – a legal letter of advice to a client – before he had handed in his own letter assignment for grading. An exemplar is a typical example of work of a particular level of quality; for example, a distinction exemplar is a typical example of work at a distinction grade level.

The point of this quote is that this student would have needlessly performed poorly had he not seen an example of what his teacher was expecting him to produce. Had he gone ahead with his plan of 'checking all the legislation and showing what I know' his teacher may have found it necessary to give detailed feedback about how he could have improved his assignment. In the worst case, they may have simply awarded a fail grade.

This chapter is about seeing task-level feedback (Shute 2008) in a different light. I define feedback as any information a teacher (or peer) can provide that helps a student to understand how they could have completed the task in a better way to produce work at a higher level of quality. I suggest that in higher education teachers have for too long been exhorted to *load up* on assignment or assessment task feedback. By 'load up' I mean that teachers wait until students have completed a task to provide a sufficiently useful amount of information to help students learn how to do the task better, or at the very least correct their errors. Put another way, loading-up means storing up feedback until the end of the task. What is needed is a re-orientation in which the feedback that teachers are expected to give is integrated with their direct instruction *before* assessment tasks, so students know more clearly what they need to produce in their assessment tasks and depend less on being told what they did well, or could have done better, after the event.

I prefer the term 'scaffolding' for guidance provided to students before their assessment tasks, based on Vygotsky's (1978) social constructivist principle that guidance from a knowledgeable other helps learners reach the top limit of their *zone of proximal development* (Handley and Williams 2011). In its broadest sense, scaffolding is 'intentional assistance provided to "another" for learning ends' (Pifarré 2007: 392). So from a Vygotskian perspective, teachers need to provide scaffolding to students both before an assessment task, to help them achieve their best, and after the task, to help them see how they could develop further.

All of this is not to say that conventional after-task feedback is not important; it is, particularly when woven into a cycle of interactive teaching that involves the teacher presenting material, students applying their understanding of the material, and discussing and receiving feedback on the quality of their application (Petty 2009). We know from meta-analyses of educational research that feedback has one of the highest effects on student achievement (Hattie and Timperley 2007). Petty (2009) asserts that the effect is equivalent to a leap of two grades. We also know from the literature that feedback in higher education is rated by students as one of the most important factors in their learning, yet is often perceived as consistently unsatisfactory.

The remainder of this chapter is about ways in which teachers can effectively scaffold learning about assessment task expectations both before students attempt tasks and afterwards. I describe previous research and more recent work that my colleagues and I have conducted in Law and Education on students' perceptions and the effects of teachers using assignment exemplars in subject teaching. I also describe work by colleagues at the University of Sydney focused on providing large student cohorts with automated timely and personalized after-task feedback (Bridgeman and Rutledge 2010). I conclude with implications for university teachers' subject teaching and feedback practice, and how change in feedback practices might be incorporated across an institution.

Do students know what is expected of them in assessment tasks?

For after-task feedback to be effective in the first place learners must have some idea of what is expected of them (Sadler 1989) or they must know 'where am I going' (what are the goals?) (Hattie and Timperley 2007). The answer to the question, 'Do university students know what is expected of them in assessment tasks?' appears to be a clear 'No' from the results of our most recent research on helping students understand the expected standards for an essay (Hendry and Anderson 2012).

We asked third and fourth year students enrolled in a teacher education programme for secondary mathematics teachers to individually mark essay exemplars from the previous year (written on a different topic) using the teacher's marking guide or rubric. The grades students awarded were varied, to say the least. A majority of students (68 per cent) gave a credit essay a credit, but less than half the students (40 per cent) gave the distinction essay a distinction; one student failed the distinction essay, and four students gave it only a pass, while two students gave a credit essay a high distinction (Hendry and Anderson 2012). Even after small group discussion in class, students differed in their views about what was a good essay and why. Only after an explanation from the teacher about what her expectations were, and why the distinction essay was graded distinction, did most students think that they were clearer about what was expected in the task. In our most recent study involving pre-service secondary mathematics teachers, at least one student might have still needed more convincing: 'I'm somewhat surprised about the overall grade on paper A. I think I'm going to read it again.' (Essay A was the distinction or best essay.)

For most students, the marking class led them to reflect on their understanding of what the teacher expected in an essay and how they might improve their own essay writing. The teacher scaffolded students' learning for the task by asking students to look at examples of work of different quality and grade them (using the marking guide that would be used for their own work), and then explaining in class how the exemplars were actually graded. In other words, she clarified students' performance for them before they attempted the task, and did not load up or rely solely on her future feedback to help students correct their understanding and improve their approach. Most students found the exercise a highly valuable one:

> I think it's great preparation, it enables me to think about what my essay will be like and highlights some issues that I can keep in mind from the beginning instead of realising later on.

> This is fantastic. I would have been confused without the examples.

How does scaffolding with exemplars affect quality and quantity of feedback?

Can scaffolding with exemplars help teachers to lighten the after-task feedback load, both for themselves and students? A key point from Sadler (1989) is that if a person knows more about how they are expected to perform in a task then they should also be able to interpret more clearly the feedback that they receive on how they have performed. Their cognitive load (Kirschner *et al.* 2006) for interpreting the feedback should be reduced. They may also experience a stronger feeling of certainty about what the feedback will be about (Shute 2008). So teachers may need to spend less time and effort on explaining the feedback.

However, after-task feedback still needs to focus on learners' needs for improving, with specific or concrete suggestions about how they might go about changing their performance on similar tasks in the future (Hounsell *et al.* 2008; Nicol and Macfarlane-Dick 2006; Shute 2008).

In research that involved undergraduate Law students in marking exemplars using a marking guide, and participating in student- and teacher-led discussion of the exemplars in class (Hendry *et al.* 2011b), most students (72 per cent), after receiving their letter assignment back, were satisfied with a series of ticks on the marking guide combined with a *limited number of personalized, concrete suggestions* for improving the way they write legal letters of advice.

It may be that students who often adopt a surface approach in the end still choose to minimize their effort in completing the task, but if they are clearer about what is expected, then they will also know what feedback to expect (and so not be as dissatisfied). Other students may attempt the task knowing what a good assignment should look like, but still not produce a high standard of work in the time available. So a teacher's feedback might focus on what these students could have done to achieve the next higher level of quality, particularly by *making more time* for themselves. Students who complete the task to a high standard may be satisfied with feedback that simply lets them know they are 'well on track'.

Effects of scaffolding with exemplars on students' levels of self-monitoring, achievement and confidence

Finding an optimal level of after-task feedback that is manageable for teachers in the context of scaffolding students' learning for assessment tasks will depend on the task, how what students learn in doing the task helps them prepare for the next task, and the size of the class or cohort. If teachers can be confident that students have enhanced understanding of the expected task standards, then perhaps they can give brief feedback that is specific and individually targeted to help a student make a maximum developmental gain in some aspect of their work. Carless *et al.* (2011) also argue that helping students to become more self-regulated in their learning can transfer some of the onus from teachers to students, and make giving feedback more manageable.

While I would argue that the onus is always on teachers to 'make student learning possible' (Ramsden 2003) and so scaffolding for assessment tasks is a moral imperative, I agree that in higher education we need 'to place less emphasis on conventional feedback practices and develop further those in which student autonomy and self-monitoring capacities become paramount' (Carless *et al.* 2011). Carless *et al.* suggest that 'dialogic cycles applied to exemplars' may be key strategies in helping students develop self-monitoring capacities. Indeed in recent research (Hendry and Anderson 2012) students report reflecting on the quality of their own future work, and thinking about it in a more critical way or from a 'teacher's perspective', as a result of engaging in marking and student- and teacher-led discussion of exemplars. A student commented about the usefulness of the experience, as follows: 'I really liked it. It encouraged me to reflect on thinking critically on what our own response should be like.'

Students' enhanced reflection and self-monitoring of the quality of their work should lead them to produce higher quality work. From the results of research – that began with the work of Berry O'Donovan, Margaret Price and Chris Rust at Oxford Brookes University – the positive effects of marking classes on students' achievement are clear and consistent.

To help undergraduate business students understand criteria and standards for an assignment, Rust *et al.* (2003) provided students with a marking guide, an exemplar of a borderline and an exemplar of an 'A' grade assignment, and asked students to individually mark the assignments. In an optional 90-minute workshop held one week later, students discussed their grades with their peers, and staff explained how the assignments had actually been graded. Students who participated in the optional workshop subsequently achieved significantly better results in their assessments compared with those who did not attend the workshop (O'Donovan *et al.* 2004; Rust *et al.* 2003).

More recently these results have been replicated in undergraduate Law (Hendry *et al.* 2011a) and Sport Science (Payne and Brown 2010) programs. Hendry *et al.* (2011a) found that Law students who participated in marking and discussing exemplars in class, and received a balanced explanation from the teacher about why the exemplars were graded the way they were, performed significantly better on their assignment than students in classes who only marked and discussed the exemplars (with no teacher explanation) or received a teacher explanation that focused mainly on errors that past students had made in the exemplars.

Payne and Brown (2010) found that students in a Biomechanics course who used a marking guide to mark examples of the previous year's final written examination scripts and discussed their marks in class, and engaged in teacher-led discussion in class, achieved higher grades in their final examination than students who did not receive the marking guide and were not given the opportunity to participate in a marking class. Students in the marking class reported using the marking guide and past papers to guide their exam revision, and reported feeling more confident about sitting the final examination (Payne and Brown 2010). Students in our most recent research (Hendry and Anderson 2012) have also reported feeling more confident: 'There was more confidence working on this assessment than other assessments because . . . the expectations were clear (p. 8).' These results indicate that teacher explanation of grading decisions is not only important for helping students to understand the quality of work expected, but is also important for motivating students.

Giving students confidence in their ability to improve is also a feature of good after-task feedback that respects students' efforts, and 'encourages positive motivational beliefs and self-esteem' (Nicol and MacFarlane-Dick 2006). Feedback that is formative or provides students with suggestions about how to achieve a learning goal enhances learners' perceived self-efficacy (Chan and Lam 2010).

Self-efficacy influences goal setting, motivation, and the effort a person expends on a task, even in the face of difficulties or obstacles; higher self-efficacy is associated with increased effort and persistence (Bandura 1997). Scaffolding that focuses mainly on peer errors, like after-task feedback that is poor because it is overly critical (Carless 2006; Weaver 2006), can reduce students' self-efficacy for completing assessment tasks.

Enhancing students' self-efficacy is never more important than in very large classes where students' experience of learning is often impersonal (Bridgeman and Rutledge 2010). Faced with a first year cohort of up to 3,500 students and declining student satisfaction with feedback in first and second year undergraduate Chemistry, Bridgeman and Rutledge developed innovative open-source software to process quiz 'marks files to [rapidly] produce individual reports and emails for every student in a class' (2010: 62). The after-task feedback email addresses a student by their first name and is personalized according to their subject, degree programme and own results; it is concrete because it provides explanations for answers and links to relevant resources for students to use in improving their performance: 'when a student has chosen a distractor within the multiple choice set, the software can explain why their answer is incorrect: what error they made or what extra step was needed' (Bridgeman and Rutledge 2010: 63). The student response has been overwhelming, with their satisfaction with feedback increasing from a low of 36 per cent in 2007 to over 80 per cent and in some subjects to 100 per cent in 2009 after the initiative was implemented. As one student commented: 'I'm surprised how personal our feedback is. The fact that it's 260 students or something, I would have expected impersonal feedback but it really is personal allowing us to know where we went wrong' (Bridgeman and Rutledge 2010: 65). Another student responded: 'I took the quiz, got the bus home and my email was there waiting for me. How did you do this?' (Bridgeman and Rutledge 2010: 65).

Where to go from here?

Research on teachers' scaffolding of students' learning for their assessment tasks shows clearly that students develop greater understanding of what constitutes quality work; experience enhanced confidence or self-efficacy to attempt tasks; and achieve at higher levels, than if they had not received the scaffolding. These results are consistent with predictions of Vygotsky's (1978) theory and the social constructivist approach about the way we learn. Instead of prevailing upon teachers to load up on their feedback to improve students' learning after a task is completed, we should be supporting teachers to integrate their scaffolding for learning for assessment tasks into their everyday classroom or course teaching.

Key sources of institutional support for teachers include providing leadership for the renewal of institutional assessment policy, and committing resources for policy implementation (Duck et al. 2011). In a recent review of assessment policy at a large Australian University, Duck *et al.* 2011 concluded that 'major cultural change is needed' and that 'the process of developing policy . . . should include active participation by students and all those responsible for teaching' (Duck *et al.* 2011: 2). Support for teachers to integrate their scaffolding for learning for assessment tasks can also come from encouraging staff engagement in discussion forums, in which they can identify challenges to the implementation of new policy, and evaluate evidence and examples of successful practical strategies.

A potentially successful practical strategy to help establish scaffolding for learning for assessment tasks is for teachers to identify assessment task exemplars and clarify for themselves, and with their colleagues (e.g. in markers' meetings), why the exemplars typify the grades awarded to them. This process may even lead to modifying assessment task standards and rewriting marking guides (Anderson 2011). Permission must be sought from former students to use their de-identified work, and exemplars must be formatted in the same way to reduce cognitive load on students when they are marking (Anderson 2011). Our recent research (Hendry and Anderson 2012) shows that senior students find it acceptable to read and mark up to three relatively short, or two longer, exemplar essays. Assessment tasks need to be set on different topics to the exemplars from the previous year, so as not to tempt students into plagiarism. Setting different assignment topics each year is in any case best practice for supporting students' development of academic honesty (James *et al.* 2002).

Teachers then need to allocate time in class to discuss and explain the standards of work expected. Taking time to allow students to reword and negotiate criteria and standards with teachers may take the whole enterprise to another 'community of practice' level (O'Donovan *et al.* 2008). This means allocating less time for teacher instruction that delivers discipline or subject content to students, which staff often see as challenging, particularly in professional courses that receive external accreditation. Staff feel they have a professional responsibility to cover or present a certain quantity of content. However, I would argue that time 'lost' by the teacher scaffolding students' learning for an assessment task is made up by students themselves during their completion of the task because they can spend more time on learning content rather than working out the task, which is what learning-oriented assessment (Carless *et al.* 2006) is all about. As one student commented in our study in Education (Hendry and Anderson 2012): 'It helps you do the task better, rather than you spending the time, figuring out how to do it, if you have a bit more [of an] example then you can actually achieve more with that task.'

Conclusion

Staging assessment tasks, so that one task provides students with an opportunity to learn something that they can then use in the next task, and scaffolding the learning for these tasks through a dialogue around the standards of work expected, should mean that teachers need to provide brief, targeted after-task feedback only. Students' dependency on after-task feedback can be reduced. Instead of loading up, teachers can lighten their after-task feedback load and practice giving feedback in the best ways: in a timely fashion to be used by students before the next task; affirming that students are in some respect on the right developmental path (helping them to maintain their self-efficacy); and suggesting at least one concrete way that they might improve their work, and so facilitating their success in the next task, in relation to the expected standards.

References

Anderson, J. (2011) 'Do I have to write an essay? I'm going to be a Maths teacher', *Synergy* 31: 6–8. Available at: www.itl.usyd.edu.au/synergy/31/ (accessed 5 September 2011).

Bandura, A. (1997) *Self-efficacy: the exercise of control*, New York: W.H. Freeman & Co Ltd.

Bridgeman, A. and Rutledge, P. (2010) 'Getting personal: feedback for the masses', *Synergy* 30: 61–8. Available at: www.itl.usyd.edu.au/synergy/30/ (accessed 5 September 2011).

Carless, D. (2006) 'Differing perceptions in the feedback process', *Studies in Higher Education* 31(2): 219–33.

Carless, D., Joughin, G. and Liu, N.F. (2006) *How Assessment Supports Learning: learning-oriented assessment in action*, Hong Kong: Hong Kong University Press.

Carless, D., Salter, D., Yang, M. and Lam, J. (2011) 'Developing sustainable feedback practices', *Studies in Higher Education* 36(4): 395–407.

Chan, J.C.Y. and Lam, S. (2010) 'Effects of different evaluative feedback on students' self-efficacy in learning', *Instructional Science* 38(1): 37–58.

Duck, J., Hamilton, S. and Robb, C. (2011) *Assessment Policy and Impact on Practice: sharpening the policy review in Australian universities*, Strawberry Hills, NSW: Australian Learning and Teaching Council. Available at: www.olt.gov.au/system/files/resources/PP8-874%20UQ%20Duck%20Final%20Report%202011%20FINAL%20DRAFT.pdf (accessed 5 September 2011).

Handley, K. and Williams, L. (2011) 'From copying to learning: using exemplars to engage students with assessment criteria and feedback', *Assessment and Evaluation in Higher Education* 36(1): 95–108.

Hattie, J. and Timperley, H. (2007) 'The power of feedback', *Review of Educational Research* 77(1): 81–112.

Hendry, G.D. and Anderson, J. (2012) 'Helping students understand the standards of work expected in an essay: using exemplars in mathematics pre-service education classes', *Assessment and Evaluation in Higher Education* DOI: 10.1080/02602938.2012.703998.

Hendry, G.D., Armstrong, S. and Bromberger, N. (2011a) 'Implementing standards-based assessment effectively: incorporating discussion of exemplars into classroom teaching', *Assessment and Evaluation in Higher Education* 37(2): 149–61.

Hendry, G.D., Bromberger, N. and Armstrong, S. (2011b) 'Constructive guidance and feedback for learning: the usefulness of exemplars, marking sheets and different types of feedback in a first year law subject', *Assessment and Evaluation in Higher Education* 36(1): 1–11.

Hounsell, D., McCune, V., Hounsell, J. and Litjens, J. (2008) 'The quality of guidance and feedback to students', *Higher Education Research and Development* 27(1): 55–67.

James, R., McInnis, C. and Devlin, M. (2002) 'Assessing learning in Australian Universities', Melbourne: University of Melbourne, Centre for the Study of Higher Education. Available at: www.cshe.unimelb.edu.au/assessinglearning (accessed 5 September 2011).

Kirschner, P.A., Sweller, J. and Clark, R.E. (2006) 'Why minimal guidance during instruction does not work: an analysis of the failure of constructivist, discovery, problem-based, experiential, and inquiry-based teaching', *Educational Psychologist* 41(2): 75–86.

Nicol, D.J. and Macfarlane-Dick, D. (2006) 'Formative assessment and self-regulated learning: a model and seven principles of good feedback practice', *Studies in Higher Education* 31(2): 199–218.

O'Donovan, B., Price, M. and Rust, C. (2004) 'Know what I mean? Enhancing student understanding of assessment standards and criteria', *Teaching in Higher Education* 9(3): 325–35.

O'Donovan, B., Price, M. and Rust, C. (2008) 'Developing student understanding of assessment standards: a nested hierarchy of approaches', *Teaching in Higher Education* 13(2): 205–17.

Payne, E. and Brown, G. (2010) 'Communication and practice with examination criteria: does this influence performance in examinations?' *Assessment and Evaluation in Higher Education* 36(6): 619–26.

Petty, G. (2009) *Evidence-Based Teaching: a practical approach*, Cheltenham: Nelson Thornes.

Pifarré, M. (2007) 'Scaffolding through the network: analyzing the promotion of improved online scaffolds among university students', *Studies in Higher Education* 32(3): 389–408.

Ramsden, P. (2003) *Learning to Teach in Higher Education*, London: RoutledgeFalmer.

Rust, C., Price, M. and O'Donovan, B. (2003) 'Improving students' learning by developing their understanding of assessment criteria and processes', *Assessment and Evaluation in Higher Education* 28(2): 147–64.

Sadler, D.R. (1989) 'Formative assessment and the design of instructional systems', *Instructional Science*, 18: 119–44.

Shute, V. (2008) 'Focus on formative feedback', *Review of Educational Research* 78(1): 153–89.

Vygotsky, L.S. (1978) *Mind in Society: the development of higher psychological processes*, Cambridge, MA: Harvard University Press.

Weaver, M.R. (2006) 'Do students value feedback? Student perceptions of tutors' written responses', *Assessment and Evaluation in Higher Education* 31(3): 379–94.

Part III

Fostering institutional change

Overview

Margaret Price

So far in this book there has been a focus on why there is a need to rethink our assumptions and beliefs about the nature of feedback and to reshape our conceptions of feedback and how it works. Ideas and evidence of how this can work in practice have been put forward and discussed. However, what has not yet been considered is how we bring about large-scale transformation. So Part III is concerned with outlining and critically examining frameworks and models that have been used to try to achieve large-scale change in feedback processes and practices in order to better support student learning.

Each chapter draws on the experience of an institution in attempting major change. The change approach in Rust *et al.*'s chapter uses an assessment 'compact', based on comprehensive research, aimed at (re)framing the understanding of assessment and changes to practice. Senior management recognised the need for something beyond rule and policy changes and used expertise in assessment within the institution to drive the change. By contrast, it is partnership with students that is foregrounded in the campaign-based approach that is the focus of Holden and Glover's chapter. The campaign was aimed at fostering a more positive view of feedback across the institution and aimed to achieve this by engaging students and staff in dialogue at every level of the university.

Russell *et al.* consider an externally funded initiative to facilitate change and the use of technologically enhanced assessment and feedback practices in two of its academic schools. The project used appreciative enquiry and a guiding thematic framework to shape the direction of changes. It developed a range of tools that are described and evaluated in the chapter.

Finally, Draper and Nicol draw on their reflections of the REAP project (also externally funded with a focus on technology enhanced assessment and feedback) and the work of Twigg in the USA to identify seven key decisions that are needed to shape an educational change project. They illustrate the presentation of these decisions and the problems to be overcome with experiences of REAP and its effects. This chapter raises key points about the nature and outcomes of any planned educational change process and therefore provides a fitting end to the section.

These change initiatives were designed by and for particular institutions but it is interesting to note that while their contexts are different there are several similarities in their approaches that can be discerned. Many of these similarities seem to point to some key success factors.

First of those is that the initiative must have a clear and explicated theoretical underpinning. Such an underpinning is translated into principles, tenets, themes, etc. to more easily communicate the ideas to all stakeholders. In addition, providing evidence of practical benefit is powerful and it seems to be important to set up processes to collect such evidence right from the early stages of the initiative to provide further evidence to persuade others beyond early adopters to change.

Linked to this is the importance of building and providing a bank of resources such as case studies (including evaluations), diagnostic or analytical tools, information sheets, etc. that can spread understanding, inspire or reassure.

Such resources also have great importance in relation to another key factor, namely that the change initiative, while driven by a common theoretical perspective, must allow freedom in its interpretation and application for different contexts, for example relating to different disciplines and epistemologies or different organisational structures in departments or programmes.

Change can be initiated at many different points in the organisational structure or by targeting particular stakeholders. However, all the initiatives reported here chose to focus on programme or module teams. Working with teams allowed joint exploration of the ideas and innovative ways in which to put them into practice.

It seems rather obvious to say that initiatives should have a clear purpose. However, for those reported here it involved more than just stating a purpose; it was also about trying to engender a collective envisioning of the change to be achieved. Changes that require reconceptualisation can be very difficult to envisage, which is why factors already mentioned such as a bank of resources and team discussion are so important.

One other factor in all the examples is that each had some dedicated funding, either external or internal. Such funding is very important not only for providing some time for 'extra' work or collecting and processing evaluation data but also for signalling the importance of the initiative.

Finally, the issue of time is also important. First in relation to the launch of the initiative, each of these initiatives was timely – the institutions were ready for change. Second, it was acknowledged that all the initiatives required effort over a long time period. However, sustaining such interest in a project is difficult and requires commitment from senior management and champions. Identifying phases of the project and/or using a variety of activities did help to keep the initiatives near the top of stakeholders' agendas and even after 'completion' each one is still having a ripple effect. Nevertheless it is clear that such major change needs far longer to achieve its goals than most decision makers anticipate and it pays to maintain the focus on change long after the initiative began to ensure early gains are not lost.

Chapter 13

An assessment compact
Changing the way an institution thinks about assessment and feedback

Chris Rust, Margaret Price, Karen Handley, Berry O'Donovan and Jill Millar

Introduction

In September 2009, Oxford Brookes University introduced an Assessment Compact – defined as a non-legally enforceable agreement – between the university and its students (see Figure 13.1). The aim of the Compact is to bring about significant change in both assessment practices, and attitudes to assessment and feedback among staff and students, rather than just consolidate current practice. It is both values- and evidence-based, and seeks to reconceptualise thinking about assessment and feedback in the institution whereby assessment and feedback are seen as a relational and integrated learning process involving on-going dialogue within an active learning community of staff and students.

This chapter explores the approach to institutional change and, in doing so, aims to help you, the reader, consider (a) whether the introduction of such a compact might be appropriate in your institution, and (b) if so, how you might improve the chances of successful introduction by judicious consideration of the Brookes' experience. It will offer this experience as a case study, and consider which factors enabled the development of the Compact and identify issues arising in the translation of the Compact into practice. In particular, difficulties in understanding the ideas within the Compact and the capacity to envision radical change are discussed. There will also be consideration of the degree to which this strategy has succeeded so far in changing thinking about and practice of assessment in the institution.

Institution ready for change

A number of factors combined to make the institution ready for significant change. By the autumn of 2008, the Assessment Standards Knowledge exchange (ASKe), a Higher Education Funding Council of England funded Centre for Excellence in Teaching and Learning, had existed at Brookes for three years actively promoting changes to assessment practices and funding research projects into assessment across the university. Concern, interest and awareness of assessment issues had grown as a result. Despite this, as with the sector at large, the

UK National Student Survey (NSS) scores for assessment and feedback for the university were not good. In addition, on the basis of those scores, a new student union vice president (academic affairs) (SUVP) had been elected on a platform of 'doing something about assessment' and the university also had a new deputy vice-chancellor (DVC). The final positive factor was that a mass course redesign was about to happen as part of a rationalisation of all the undergraduate courses offered at Brookes, which offered an opportunity for changes in assessment strategy and practice to be made as part of this process.

The process of creating the Compact

Origins

The original idea for a Compact came out of a discussion at the university's Academic Enhancement and Standards Committee (AESC), which was considering the NSS scores. Some initial suggestions by committee members included rule changes, such as introducing a maximum length of time for assessment to be returned and feedback given, or a requirement to use standardised feedback templates, etc. These were similar to actions taken by many other institutions. But fortunately the newly appointed DVC wanted to draw in university based expertise in this area in ASKe and therefore the committee decision was to commission one of ASKe's Directors to lead the project of developing the Compact.

Two other important decisions followed. It was agreed that the ASKe team would write a first draft of the Compact, informed by explicit principles and research-based evidence. A cross-university working group was then formed comprising sufficiently senior representatives from each academic school (deputy heads where possible) who had interest in learning and teaching issues, plus representatives from the student union including the SUVP.

Ideas in the Compact

ASKe drew on its extensive knowledge of research and current thinking about assessment practice from around the world. While having no illusions about the difficulties involved in bringing about significant cultural and institutional change, there was a determination to produce a document that got to the heart of the assessment and feedback issues, rather than just tinkering with existing practices, or imposing simplistic standardised 'rules'. It needed to propose a new and holistic approach to assessment and feedback that reflected new understandings and practices for a modern Higher Education sector, and focussed on principles, not rules. It was recognised that the ideas contained in the Compact were complex and many staff and students had not previously been asked to think deeply about the assessment process. Engagement with, and commitment to, the Compact would inevitably mean some major changes to assessment attitudes and practices. The Compact had to have academic integrity and require the application of relevant principles but also recognise the need for contextual interpretation (e.g. for different disciplines, courses and so on).

The Compact was very much influenced by both the *Assessment Standards Manifesto* and the *Feedback Agenda for Change*, which had each been the result of earlier ASKe initiatives. These initiatives, one on assessment standards (2007), one on feedback (2009), followed the same model, bringing together a group of national and international experts in the field for two days of discussion and debate. The outcomes, in the form of the Manifesto and the Agenda for Change, both call for necessary changes in assessment and feedback policy and practice. The Agenda for Change is discussed in Chapter 4 of this book.

It is not our intention in this chapter to go into detail about the theoretical literature and research evidence and underlying debates that influenced the Compact's content. Much of this is significantly covered in Chapter 4, and for full detail of the Manifesto and the background arguments behind it, see Price *et al.* (2008).

In summary, the Compact is informed by the following key principles:

- To be effective, assessment must be recognised as a joint responsibility between staff and students (Rust *et al.* 2005).
- Assessment and pedagogic literacy among staff and students are prerequisites for increased effectiveness of assessment and feedback (Price *et al.* 2010).
- Students need to actively work with assessment standards in order to gain a full understanding of them (Rust *et al.* 2003).
- Understanding and emphasising the relational and dialogic nature of feedback and its processes is crucial for effective student engagement and learning (Price *et al.* 2010).
- Interactions within a learning community (Astin 1997; O'Donovan *et al.* 2008) are of primary importance in enhancing the student learning experience.

The wording of the Compact

As a first step, to appeal to busy staff and students and increase the likelihood of it being read, it was decided that the document should not exceed one page of A4. However, while being succinct it also needed to capture and communicate the complex ideas at its heart, without ambiguity. With this in mind very special attention was paid to the choice of words and the precise meaning of phrases and sentences. The consequence of this is that, in achieving the required brevity, it is not always clearly understood by staff and students, especially on first reading. It contains some language that has particular technical meaning and requires very careful reading. This in turn has led to a number of problems, with some staff dismissing some of the chosen terminology as overly complex jargon, and some reading other parts somewhat superficially, believing what is said to be

Assessment* Compact

**OXFORD
BROOKES
UNIVERSITY**

[* Assessment encompasses all judgements made about the work of a student and/or their skills, abilities and progress, and the associated provision of feedback.]

1. There are five fundamental tenets behind this compact, namely that:

1.1   Effective assessment is central to learning.

1.2   To be effective the relational nature of the assessment and feedback process needs to be emphasised, particularly in terms of the need for active dialogue between students and staff.

1.3   To be effective, assessment must be recognised as a joint responsibility between staff and students.

1.4   The ability to assess the work of both self and others is an essential skill for all graduates.

1.5   For the above tenets to be met in full, students and staff need to be 'assessment literate' and actively participate in disciplinary communities of assessment practice.

2. The University will therefore ensure that:

2.1   Assessment is central to the curriculum, and there should be no distinct boundary between assessment, teaching and learning. All academic staff will therefore be encouraged to regard assessment as a fundamental and integral part of programme design, and one that is intended to shape and develop learning, as much as to judge and measure it.

2.2   Assessment is designed at programme level, to integrate module assessment and ensure that assessment shapes learning in a coherent and holistic fashion, consistent with the aims and learning outcomes of the programme so that identified knowledge, skills and qualities can be developed and recognised, and validly assessed, whilst recognising progressive levels of attainment and different modes of study.

2.3   The relationship between learning outcomes and assessment tasks is made explicit. In addition, clear assessment criteria should be provided whenever possible, and always when the assessment contributes to marks, grades, or decisions about progression. Assessment judgements must focus on the achievement of the learning outcomes against the assessment criteria, and this achievement authenticated as the student's own.

2.4   Every effort is taken to ensure that there is no bias in the type of assessment task, or method chosen, or the criteria applied that would unfairly disadvantage any student.

2.5   Students are given supportive, constructive and timely feedback as an essential part of their learning. Such feedback will enable students to build on their positive achievements and have a clear sense of what they need to do to improve, with subsequent opportunities provided to act on the feedback and to put the advice given into practice.

2.6 Programmes include activities (e.g. marking exercises, self- and peer-assessment, etc.) specifically designed to involve students in assessment, to encourage dialogue between students and their tutors, and students and their peers, and to develop their abilities to make their own informed judgements (assessment literacy).

2.7 Programmes produce assessment schedules of summative assessment, and make every effort to avoid the concentration of assessment deadlines.

2.8 Academic staff are provided with staff development in assessment literacy, and awareness of new ideas and techniques.

2.9 Disciplinary communities of assessment practice are developed through, for example, regular peer discussion and student involvement.

2.10 Institutional values and policies consistently support this compact, and adequate resources are provided.

3. Students will be expected to take responsibility for their own learning through:

3.1 Actively engaging with assessment tasks, including carefully reading the guidance provided, spending sufficient time on the task, ensuring their work is authentic and their own (whether individual or groupwork), and by handing work in on time.

3.2 Actively engaging in activities designed to develop assessment literacy, including taking the initiative when appropriate (e.g. asking for clarification or advice).

3.3 Actively engaging with, and acting on, feedback provided.

3.4 Actively engaging in the development of assessment policy at course and pro-gramme level through the established processes and student representative system.

Figure 13.1 The Oxford Brookes University Assessment Compact.

simpler than the ideas the words are actually trying to convey. These problems are discussed further below.

Whole university involvement

A draft of the Compact was presented to and discussed by the working group. Given the robust interrogation to be expected from academics when confronted with proposed changes it was pleasantly surprising how few adverse comments were raised, with most representatives being very supportive. However, it should be acknowledged that these were academic staff with particular roles that reflected some interest in teaching and learning and, in that sense, were probably not truly representative of Brookes' academics as a whole. The SU VP was very supportive and had a particularly good understanding of the ideas behind the Compact, which had been developed by working with ASKe and the DVC over a long period of time since her election.

After several meetings, and some minor redrafting and rewording, the final version had a relatively trouble-free ride through the university's committee structures to become policy.

Factors and issues regarding creating the Compact

The ease of formal agreement of the Compact was undoubtedly largely due to the championing of it by the DVC, along with the SUVP, and the fact that so many senior staff had buy-in through their involvement in the working group, as well as responsibility for improving assessment and feedback ratings in the NSS. The SUVP had even sent a copy to the National Union of Students and had had the response from the national executive that they saw it as 'exemplary practice'. However, another reason for its easy passage may also have been that not everyone understood all the ramifications of the commitments made in the Compact.

The wording of the Compact was an issue raised by the working group and has proved to be an on-going issue. Words like 'relational' and 'dialogic' were seen to be especially difficult by staff, let alone students, and there have been repeated suggestions that the wording should be simplified. However, we have consistently resisted calls to simplify the wording on the grounds that this would inevitably change the meaning. The ideas *are* complex, and we believe that part of the argument for dialogue is that it will only be through dialogue that understanding of the concepts will be achieved. The Compact cannot, and should not, be seen as something that can just be handed out as a self-explanatory document.

Another major issue has been the understanding and appreciation of the scale of the issues that the Compact is trying to address and differing abilities to envision the fundamentally new approach and reconceptualisation that it advocates. There was ready agreement to the Compact by many, both managers and academic teaching staff, because there was a belief that, to a large extent, 'we are doing it all already'. However, there was, and is, little evidence in practice to corroborate that belief.

Translating the Compact into practice

It is fully recognised that successfully getting a policy accepted through the committee structure is not the same as getting a policy implemented. As has already been mentioned, it was fortunate to be able to link introduction of the Compact with a university-wide initiative to redesign all programmes. A staff development programme was launched to take place over the academic year 2009–2010, which ended up continuing into the following academic year. The programme focused on development for whole programme teams (including student reps) coming together to consider how the theory-based principles and commitments of the Compact could be applied in the assessment and feedback processes in their new programmes. These were known as Assessment Design Intensives (ADIs) and were based on a successful formula of 'Course Design Intensives' (see https://wiki.brookes.ac.uk/display/CDIs/Home) pioneered by the Oxford Centre for Staff and Learning Development (OCSLD). They were jointly run by ASKe and the OCSLD and offered to each academic school. It was through these ADIs that it was hoped that 'grass-roots' buy-in to the

Compact could be achieved. Take-up for the ADIs was mixed, but by the end of the year some staff from all schools had taken part and well over 200 academic staff had attended some form of support training. Following the staff development interventions it was up to the programme teams to fully translate the Compact's tenets and obligations of the university into the plans for the new programmes.

Factors and issues in translating the Compact into practice

- The backing of the senior management, as exemplified by the DVC sending instructions to all Schools that they should participate in ADIs.
- Many staff really welcomed seeing in the Compact the educational values they would like to follow but could not always achieve.
- Initiative fatigue – staff had been asked to engage with several major initiatives in the recent past and not all were enthusiastic to engage with yet another one.
- There was great difficulty in holding ADIs in semester time when students could attend, because of lack of staff availability to attend. Consequently most were held outside semesters, with limited or no student involvement.
- Concerns about the complexity of the wording used in the Compact (as mentioned above) were raised frequently in the ADIs by staff. Their comments were often framed around concern for the students and many were worried that the Compact must be discussed with students to develop their understanding of it, which would take time. In addition, some staff felt that their own understanding of the Compact was not strong enough to discuss it with students.
- We have also recently discovered that the concern about the complexity of the language of the Compact has led to some staff writing their own 'simpler' handouts in support of, and/or as additional guidance to the Compact. While some of these clearly try to capture aspects of the Compact, they do not encompass all the meanings within it.
- In line with those approving the Compact, the ability to envision the change being proposed both in scale and nature was limited and consequently the initial changes planned were minor. Some staff even concluded their practice was already aligned with the Compact, so did not require change, even though they could not illustrate the claim with examples.

The challenges to understanding the Compact

There are possibly three main reasons why, for at least some staff, there have been problems of understanding.

First, as has been said already, there is the issue of terminology. For some staff, terms like 'communities of practice' and 'relational' are seen as jargon and therefore dismissed as such rather than stimulating engagement and deeper consideration.

Second, partially because of the enforced brevity in order to keep the Compact to one page, and especially if read quickly and superficially, it is possible to see much of what is written in the Compact as obvious and something that, of course, everyone does. For example, a word like dialogue, taken at face value, can be assumed to simply mean 'talking about' assessment – and most staff can claim to do that at some point or other. And who would question that 'assessment is central to learning', or that it should be seen as a 'joint responsibility between staff and students'? However, when examined in more detail these simple and largely uncontested statements raise questions such as:

- How, and in what ways, do we give students responsibility within our assessment practices? How might we and should we?
- In practical terms, how do we recognise the centrality of assessment in our course design?
- To what extent do we consider the effect of our assessment choices on student learning behaviours?

And so on.

Third, the Compact (Figure 13.1) includes a tenet that almost certainly requires most staff to reconceptualise much of their approach to assessment. Once one accepts that 'the ability to assess the work of both self and others is an essential skill for all graduates' (tenet 1.4) one needs to see that skill as a learning outcome in its own right. Self- and peer-assessment cease to be simply choices amongst a range of possible assessment processes. This, combined with the importance of student responsibility and the need for true dialogue between staff and students within the development of a 'community of assessment practice', is arguably a huge conceptual shift for the majority of academic staff and also for students.

Therefore, both the complex wording and the apparently deceptively simple parts of the Compact need to be examined and discussed at length by staff and students if the full meaning is to be understood and enable them to envision new practice and bring about significant change. ADIs were a start in this process as they challenged staff to look at the ideas and implications of the Compact. It is critical that staff and students are supported to achieve the assessment literacy referred to in the tenets of the Compact.

Evaluation

In recognition that what is being attempted through the Compact is significant culture change and a shift in conceptualisation of assessment and feedback, a long-term approach to evaluation was planned and is still in process at the time of writing.

A two-year multi-faceted evaluation study was started in 2010–2011 to research the implementation of the Compact and whether it is having an impact. The evaluation process comprises:

- an annual questionnaire gathering data on awareness, understanding and impact on practice.
- a focused study of the Compact related to changes in a number of specific modules.
- examination of annual programme reviews.
- student focus groups exploring assessment issues and understanding of the Compact.

While the university will continue to monitor future NSS scores regarding assessment and feedback they do not form part of the formal evaluation of the Compact because we have always maintained that sound assessment practice may not necessarily lead to increases in student satisfaction. In fact, without a developed assessment literacy, students may express a preference for practices with which they are familiar but which the Compact is seeking to change.

Alongside this evaluation, there is also a qualitative study being undertaken by ASKe, investigating the concept of assessment literacy and how, if at all, students develop it. This study uses audio diaries, where students provide commentary on their assessment experience, and also semi-structured interviews as data collection methods. While not directly focused on the Compact, it is possible that this study may also supply data that can be used in the evaluation as well as to further efforts to bring about change through the implementation of the Compact.

The impact so far

Awareness

In autumn 2010 the survey of all students and staff revealed that the majority of teaching staff respondents had heard of the Compact (78 per cent), with nearly a third stating that awareness of it has changed their assessment practice; disappointingly, student awareness of the Compact was very low with just over 18 per cent of student respondents stating they 'had heard of it'.

It seems that the staff development programme had had the effect of at least raising awareness but results suggested that many academics were not engaging in the necessary dialogue with students about the Compact nor was it being sufficiently promoted through other avenues such as the Student Union.

Following the first evaluation report for the university AESC a target of 85 per cent awareness among students was set for the 2011 survey with the onus largely on Faculties to achieve this target and improve student understanding of the Compact. In addition, recommendations were accepted to interrogate assessment strategies in relation to the Compact, as part of course validation processes, and for programmes to report, in annual review, progress made towards alignment with it.

The extent of initiatives in Faculties is unclear but unfortunately the next survey carried out in autumn 2011 which was directed only at students revealed that the awareness rate remained low at 23 per cent. Subsequent to this, ASKe mounted a publicity campaign directed at students that will be continued into the autumn semester. To assist in the publicity campaign, ASKe produced a leaflet (in its '123 leaflet' series – see www.brookes.ac.uk/aske/resources/index.html) focused on the Compact, designed to convey ideas within the Compact and to prompt dialogue between staff and students. This leaflet has been widely distributed in the university.

Practice

As already stated, the initial survey indicated that about a third of staff were changing practice as a result of the Compact. The annual review documents focusing on 2009/2010 provided limited information on changing practice but annual reviews focused on 2010/2011 were required to specifically address changes made in response to the Compact. Although change has not been consistent throughout all departments in the university, the reviews have revealed many initiatives and new practices within programmes and modules, such as time devoted to enhancing student understanding of assessment standards and increased use of peer review. Regarding the focused study of specific modules, in most cases, the data collected shows positive signs that the Compact related changes have had positive effects as measured in different ways, including student performance, student attitude, and staff perception. A resource of case studies, exemplars and innovative ideas about how to implement the messages of the Compact is now being developed to support further change.

Student understanding

Student focus group data is very limited because the cascade method used to set up and run the groups did not work well. The first focus groups run by ASKe consisted of student representatives who were then themselves trained to set up and run focus groups within their own constituencies. Very few focus groups actually took place. However, the data that was collected revealed that within exploratory discussion students understood and supported the ideas and ambition of the Compact. Student diary data from the qualitative study has not yet been fully analysed but initial impressions suggest that students' understanding of assessment purpose, process and outcome is extremely variable, ranging from a focus on learning to a focus solely on marks. Most of the diarists respond positively to new assessment initiatives they have encountered, especially opportunities to engage in discussions about assessment with staff and their peers.

Reflections

Aiming to achieve reconceptualisation around difficult ideas is ambitious, so inevitably some initiatives within the change process have worked while others have been less successful.

What worked?

- The use of a strong theoretical and practical evidence base for the proposals for change. This provided a strong and persuasive rationale for the Compact.
- Provision of a single, succinct, values based framework to which everyone can reference their practice.
- Adherence to unambiguous, if technical, language has helped to prevent oversimplification or changes to meaning.
- High stakeholder involvement and commitment especially from senior management and the SU.
- Commitment to the need for fundamental reconceptualisation of assessment and assessment processes, rather than looking for 'quick fixes'.
- Commitment to embedding as a long-term process, including monitoring and evaluation.
- Persuading a critical mass of staff and, although staff are not yet talking enough to students about the Compact, they are changing practice in the classroom.

What have we learnt, and what could we have done better?

Envisioning a changed assessment landscape is very difficult, especially for those who are fairly unfamiliar with the complexity of assessment and the research in the area. The introduction of the Compact instigated a steep learning curve for many staff. A staged process to raise awareness before attempting to reshape practice might have been preferable. The opportunity to piggy back on the programme redesign may have led to the initiative seeking to achieve too much too fast. In order to bring about significant changes in staff attitudes to assessment and the pedagogic culture staff first need to be able to engage in a considerable amount of discussion. But the opportunity and time for such discussion has in fact been very limited. And to bring about the necessary structural change needs considerable commitment and buy-in from staff.

The failure, due to the need to hold workshops outside semester time, to involve students in the ADIs meant that dialogue with students in the planning and development of practice was insufficient. If there had been greater opportunity for such dialogue it may have served to illustrate the need for such dialogue in the classroom and build staff confidence to engage in that dialogue. This could be the focus of future course team development.

The process of developing and adopting the Compact within the university was relatively smooth but the extent of real buy-in by stakeholders has to be questioned. Perhaps, rather than just involving those with a particular interest in learning, teaching and assessment, there should also have been a broader consultation so that the barriers to embedding the ideas could have been more clearly understood at an early stage.

Ongoing issues

This chapter has made it clear that throughout the process there has been a tension between precision of language and communication. As noted above, an insistence on retaining the wording of the carefully crafted Compact is seen as important in providing a reference point throughout the university. So has the eventual production of a '123 leaflet' compromised the Compact? It is too early to say but the '123 leaflet' does not seek to replace the Compact; it is intended to be read alongside it, i.e. inviting students (and staff) to look at the Compact. It is hoped that it will boost engagement rather than become a substitute.

Until the Compact's ideas are part of the broad culture of the organisation, the tensions arising from the current wide range of different views of assessment (e.g. purpose, relationship to learning, role of peers, etc.) will be a constant challenge to envisioning and fully achieving the desired changes. The Compact calls for staff and students to become assessment literate but, until that is more fully achieved, it is likely that staff seeking to change will face conflicting messages. For example, while the SU may be promoting the Compact, and the ideas behind it, a large majority of the student body are still requesting practices such as more traditional, teacher-written feedback (in preference to involvement in self- and peer-assessment – activities that they may even initially be resistant to); and anonymous marking – practices that are counter to those promoted by the Compact. Staff have a major role to play in supporting the development of students' assessment literacy but they need to feel confident in their own understandings of assessment theory in order to do this.

Measuring the impact of the Compact is a challenge in line with capturing evidence of cultural change. It is essential that the evaluation is multifaceted. The revelation, in a survey, that students are not aware of the Compact may not particularly matter if other data reveals that the assessment practices they encounter are aligned with the Compact, enhance their learning and their assessment literacy. Clearly there is still much work to do, and within the evaluation reports for AESC it has been noted that '[t]he real impact of the Compact, where its messages have become unrecognisably interwoven with practice, can only be measured long-term via a variety of measures and only indirectly evidenced by such indicators as changed practice at the modular and programme level' (Benfield *et al.* 2011: 1).

Conclusions and messages for others

It is still too early to judge whether a device such as a Compact can bring about institutional change in its approaches to assessment or if this initiative will, in the long run, prove successful – but the initial signs are at least tentatively positive.

Many aspects of the Compact's introduction and adoption have gone well but if we were starting again we would definitely consider taking longer, with a staged process to raise awareness and achieve 'grassroots' buy-in, thereby essentially educating both staff and students to understand the terminology and underlying concepts, so that they could then, more confidently, reshape practice.

We would therefore provisionally recommend adopting a similar process of constructing a compact for your own HEI and, although wording and presentation might vary, we hope that the content of your compact would turn out significantly similar to ours, certainly avoiding more simplistic, piecemeal approaches; but the process of its creation is a vital contribution to the institutional 'owning' of it. In terms of implementation the organization of a focused but long-term campaign that does not have to compete with many other initiatives for attention would seem to be ideal if the necessary reconceptualisation is to be fully achieved.

References

Astin, A. (1997) *What Matters in College? Four critical years revisited*, San Francisco: Jossey Bass.

Benfield, G.D., Price, M. and den Outer, B. (2011) *Assessment Compact Survey: early messages report*, OCSLD/ASKe, Oxford Brookes University, May 2011.

O'Donovan, B., Price, M. and Rust, C. (2008) 'Developing student understanding of assessment standards: a nested hierarchy of approaches', *Teaching in Higher Education* 13(2): 205–17.

Price, M., Carroll, J., O'Donovan, B. and Rust, C. (2010) 'If I was going there I wouldn't start from here: a critical commentary on current assessment practices', *Assessment and Evaluation in Higher Education* 36(4): 479–92.

Price, M., O'Donovan, B., Rust, C. and Carroll, J (2008) 'Assessment standards: a manifesto for change', *Brookes eJournal of Learning and Teaching* 2(3). Available at: http://bejlt.brookes.ac.uk/article/assessment_standards_a_manifesto_for_change (accessed 28 August 2012).

Rust, C., O'Donovan, B and Price, M. (2005) 'A social constructivist assessment process model: how the research literature shows us this could be best practice', *Assessment and Evaluation in Higher Education* 30(3): 233–41.

Rust, C., Price, M and O'Donovan, B. (2003) 'Improving students' learning by developing their understanding of assessment criteria and processes', *Assessment and Evaluation in Higher Education* 28(2): 147–64.

Chapter 14

Fostering institutional change in feedback practice through partnership

Graham Holden and Chris Glover

Introduction

This chapter reviews the development and implementation of a collaborative project (the Feedback for Learning Campaign) between students and staff that aimed to influence student perceptions of assessment feedback. In doing so it sought to raise awareness of the role of feedback in enhancing student learning, thereby encouraging dialogue at all levels of a higher education institution. Ultimately it was hoped that the campaign would improve the experience of assessment feedback for all students, and as a result improve the institution's scores against assessment and feedback in the National Student Survey (NSS). The chapter looks at the background, impetus and context of the campaign, describes its strategy and the lessons learnt.

Background to the campaign

The importance of feedback in the learning process is well documented and has already been set out in the introduction to this book along with evidence of on-going dissatisfaction on the part of students with its quality and usefulness. However, the picture presented is not a gloomy as it looks and it is important to acknowledge that student dissatisfaction with feedback is not universal. There is significant variability within and across the sector, its disciplines and courses (Williams and Kane 2008). Clearly in some instances the quality of feedback, as perceived by students, is high and the issue therefore appears to be consistency across an institution and the identification and dissemination of the many instances of good and excellent practice in the provision of feedback. The challenge of how to improve student perceptions, and to maximise the impact of good practice formed the basis for the Feedback for Learning Campaign described in this chapter.

The view from across the sector: how are universities responding to these issues?

In the UK the National Student Survey (NSS) has played an important role in raising the profile of feedback in higher education and many institutions have developed interventions, with various degrees of success, to improve feedback processes. The response from students, coordinated by the National Union of Students (2008a), has been to develop and disseminate principles for 'good' feedback in the form of a Charter (2008b), aimed at influencing institutional policy and individual academic practice.

Prior to the initial conceptualisation and subsequent development of the Feedback for Learning Campaign, an analysis of the content of websites, content of external conference programmes and staff development activities at other UK higher education institutions was undertaken. This analysis was one aspect of the information that formed the basis of a staff development event held to reflect on the University's current position with regards to assessment, feedback and the NSS. The outcomes of this analysis indicated a tendency for institutions to address the issues surrounding feedback by improving feedback processes, seeking to improve the feedback practice of academic staff and by engaging students in the feedback process. The following provides a summary of the actions that have been adopted across the UK higher education sector to enhance the experience of students of feedback on their assessed work.

Modifications to the feedback process

For example:

- setting targets for the return of assessed work;
- making the schedule of feedback on assignments clearer to students and timetabling of assignments more evenly through the academic year;
- introducing standardised feedback systems, such as standardised forms, hand-in and return procedures;
- reviewing quality processes to ensure feedback is given promptly and not delayed by external moderation.

Changing feedback practice

For example:

- developing and disseminating principles of good feedback practice;
- auditing and encouraging the spread of effective practice;
- staff development events focused on providing feedback in alternative forms such as audio feedback, and encouraging feedback practices that indicate how future improvement might be achieved (feed forward).

Engaging students with the feedback process

For example:

- activities that involve students in the feedback processes, such as peer feedback;
- student involvement in staff development activities, bringing an authentic voice into discussions around developments in feedback practice.

The basis for the Feedback for Learning Campaign

The Feedback for Learning Campaign was based on educational research that had been undertaken at the University from 2005.

Early beginnings: the Formative Assessment in Science and Technology (FAST) project

The FAST project (FAST 2005) was based at the Open University and Sheffield Hallam University and was funded by the Fund for the Development of Teaching and Learning. It aimed to examine how students' formative assessment experiences affected their learning, initially within the physical and biological sciences. A particular focus for the project was to look at how feedback to students could be made more effective and to maximise the learning students gain from assessment activities.

It was an outcome of the work of the FAST project which was to prove pivotal in informing the actions taken as part of the *Feedback for Learning Campaign*. A key finding from the FAST project was that students, in spite of receiving a variety of types of oral feedback, were claiming it didn't exist and were calling it something else, even though the reality was that students received as much, if not more, oral feedback as they did written. This outcome suggested that one way of enhancing student engagement with feedback is to raise awareness of the range of feedback available to them, and to focus on how they can use this feedback to contribute to the development of their learning. Furthermore this should also enable better informed responses by students to the assessment and feedback questions in the NSS.

FAST forward: three years on what are our students telling us?

In 2008 a detailed analysis was undertaken of free text comments received from students within the NSS and how these differed over the three years since the outcomes of the FAST project (FAST 2005). This analysis revealed that the key issues identified by students in the FAST project had not changed and remained those of consistency, clarity and usefulness. These issues could be seen explicitly in student responses and the analysis indicated that concerns over inconsistency focused on the handing in and return of assessed work; the availability and quality of assessment criteria; the amount, quantity and quality of feedback; and inconsistency of feedback practice between tutors.

In addition, although the 'evidence' is anecdotal, there were also indications that more staff were using electronic forms of feedback than by the end of the FAST project. Equally, students were using electronic means of communicating with tutors and each other more than they did by the end of the FAST project in 2005. Perhaps more importantly, the analysis indicated that students considered this feedback to be more useful than previously and perceived, for example, an e-mail communication from a tutor as being feedback, and that they are 'expected' to do something with it. Raising awareness of the importance of electronic feedback, and the different forms it takes, was to become a key feature of the Feedback for Learning Campaign.

The institutional context: The Assessment for Learning Initiative (TALI)

Building on the work of the FAST project, TALI was established at Sheffield Hallam University in 2006, as an internally funded university-wide quality enhancement project. TALI aimed to identify and implement the deliberate steps needed to enhance the student and staff experience of assessment and feedback, and to embed assessment for learning as the key underpinning principle for academic practice and that the University's regulations, processes and systems reflect and support this. A key priority was to address the issues that were identified by the FAST project and to develop an institutional-wide approach to addressing them.

TALI set out to engage large numbers of staff across the institution in this agenda using a wide range of formal and informal activities and through:

- research-informed change with a strong focus on the student experience of assessment;
- the development of resources and case studies sharing good practice supported by the appointment of teaching fellows as local authentic voices (Holden et al. 2008);
- innovative use of technology to improve the efficiency and effectiveness of assessment and feedback practice (Parkin et al. 2011).

The Feedback for Learning Campaign: fostering change through partnership

The Feedback for Learning Campaign arose from the work of FAST and then TALI and was a collaborative project between the university, and the student union. The campaign's objective was to improve the experience of assessment feedback for *all* students, and as a result to improve the institution's scores against assessment and feedback in the NSS.

From the outset TALI engaged students in dialogue about their experiences of feedback through surveys, focus groups, case studies and culminated in a university-wide conference run jointly with students. These activities placed the student voice at the heart of changes to assessment policy and practice. The outcome of these activities was an excellent working relationship with the Students Union, with whom there was regular dialogue on how to enhance the student experience for all students at the university. The work of FAST suggested the benefits of engaging students in dialogue about different forms, and the value, of feedback, and it was therefore a natural next step to work collaboratively to tackle the issue of feedback. The result was a Feedback for Learning Campaign led by the Students Union but working in close collaboration with the assessment initiative.

The campaign set out to enhance both student and staff engagement by engaging them in a university-wide dialogue at every level of the university. By engaging students and staff in a dialogue on the purpose of feedback, its role in improving learning and the range of types of feedback available, the campaign aimed to influence student perceptions of feedback, and in particular to:

- raise awareness of the role of feedback in enhancing learning and assessment performance;
- develop awareness of different types of feedback that students routinely receive during their studies;
- encourage students to share their positive experiences of using feedback for learning;
- encourage students to 'feel good' about using their given feedback, to foster positive, better informed responses to the assessment and feedback questions in the NSS;
- promote student engagement through involvement in a university-wide campaign.

An institutional approach to encouraging dialogue

From the outset the campaign was faced with the challenge of how best to encourage a university-wide dialogue on feedback. Inspiration was drawn from an unusual area for educational development – marketing. Marketing campaigns are an established part of everyday life and are an effective tool to increase awareness for a particular product or service, or to increase consumer awareness of a business or organisation. By designing a campaign using a memorable slogan combined with eye-catching images based around collectable cartoon characters, the Feedback for Learning Campaign adopted a very different approach to those normally employed on campus when it comes to teaching and learning.

As detailed in Table 14.1, the Feedback for Learning Campaign was made up of two phases and was timed to start at the beginning of the teaching year with activities running throughout the year to support student responses to the NSS in 2009. It culminated in a university-wide conference towards the end of the academic year to disseminate the outcomes from the campaign.

Phase one of the campaign was designed to catch attention with blanket coverage of both of the university's campuses through posters and screensavers on PCs, all emblazoned with the slogan 'How do use yours?' (Figure 14.1). After a gap of two weeks this was followed by 16 roadshows where students were invited to complete prize draw cards (Figure 14.2) about their experience of feedback. Students were asked to identify five types of feedback and to give an example of how they had used feedback to help improve their learning. The stalls were staffed by individuals (student representatives and staff) who wore branded t-shirts emblazoned with the slogan 'How do you use yours?' on the front and 'Feedback the key to your success' on the back. Branded bags and bookmarks (Figure 14.3) were also handed out. The bookmarks were designed to be collectable and attractive to students.

The roadshows created a real buzz on campus and one of their key features was the dialogue about feedback that occurred between those involved. In total, during the roadshows hundreds of conversations took place, staff–student, and student–student, and over 1,500 competition entries were received. Data from the cards was analysed and the text comments from students used to inform phase two of the campaign.

A key feature of the campaign was the role of the student union student representatives who ran the stalls and were encouraged to begin the dialogue with fellow students and staff. This dialogue was continued into formal committees and into student–staff consultative committees held during the academic year as part of the university's quality review processes.

Phase two of the campaign ('Feedback – the key to your success') again featured blanket coverage of the campuses through a range of media. This time, however, the posters featured students' free text comments drawn from the prize draw in phase one of the campaign. This phase of the campaign was complemented by a range of staff development activities (workshops, seminars, etc. on feedback practice), culminating in a university-wide student-led staff development conference that featured significant input from students.

Throughout the campaign items were placed on the agenda of key university meetings both at university and faculty level to reflect the key messages from the campaign and to further promote the importance of dialogue on feedback with students.

A joined up approach

The Feedback for Learning Campaign was supported by a range of complementary activities aimed at enhancing the experience of feedback for staff and

Table 14.1 Outline design of the Feedback for Learning Campaign

Week	27 Oct	03 Nov	10 Nov	17 Nov	24 Nov	01 Dec	08 Dec	15 Dec	22 Dec	29 Dec	05 Jan	12 Jan	19 Jan	26 Jan	02 Feb	09 Feb	Beyond
Teaching	5	6	7	8	9	10	11	12						1	2	3	
Phase	How do you use yours?					Feedback – the key to your success											Campaign evaluation
Activity	Launch of campaign with blanket coverage of campuses using posters, etc.		Roadshow with stalls and prizes		Maintain interest with repeated messages	Launch phase two to encourage deeper engagement; Celebration event to hand out prizes	Maintain interest with repeated messages										
Methods and resources	Posters (size A2, 1 design; 250 copies; + e-copy for online distribution); Roadshow (stands; t-shirts, posters. . .); Competition (entry postcard – 1,000 copies) to win a laptop or USB stick (200); Handouts – bookmarks (4 designs), bags					Fold-out feedback guide handout to all students; Posters with student comments from phase one; Follow-up publicity (students union publications, university newsletters, VLE, staff intranet, etc.); Student representatives follow through with dialogue in staff–student committees; Capture and disseminate student stories about their experience of feedback											Completion of NSS Survey

Communications: newsletter (university, faculty), student portal, staff intranet, university committees, etc.

Staff development activities culminating in university-wide conference

Course approval – focus on feedback linked to requirement to respond to principles embedded in new assessment and feedback policy

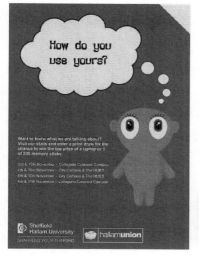

Figure 14.1 'How do you use yours?' campaign poster.

Figure 14.2 Prize draw cards.

Figure 14.3 Bookmarks handed out to students.

students across the university. These activities followed the change model adopted by TALI (described below) with the intention of bringing about institutional change in the student and staff experience of feedback. The outcome was an integrated and systematic approach to encouraging change in feedback practice across the institution.

This change model recognises the advantages in promoting institutional change through key personnel at ground level (Newton 2003). The approach adopted by TALI was to adapt this approach, to recognise the complex nature of assessment and to understand how change happens in organisations, particularly with regard to the notion of emergent change and the need for connectivity across the institution (Seel 2000). The result was a joined up approach to changing assessment and feedback practice (adapted from Macdonald and Joughin 2009), which comprised five principal levels of the organisation (module, course, faculty, institutional and external) with the introduction of the student voice, a key feature of the campaign, as an additional level in the model.

The Feedback for Learning Campaign was complemented by different related activities at each level of the organisation, reflecting the widespread responsibility for changing feedback practice within the university.

- **Student level:** *the student experience* of assessment and feedback.
  Feedback for Learning Campaign, as detailed above, with students union, supported through student representatives encouraging dialogue between students on their positive experiences of feedback.

- **Module level:** *Where assessment happens.*
  For example, staff supported to develop and adopt new innovative approaches to feedback for example using audio feedback through staff development sessions co-ordinated by faculty teaching fellows.

- **Course/programme level:** *Supporting good practice.*
  For example, course approval/validation quality process adapted to provide a focus on feedback. This included change to formal requirement for module/course descriptor to meet the requirements of a new assessment and feedback policy that identified key principles to be adhered to.

- **Faculty level:** *the faculty context.*
  For example, staff development activities were held at subject/faculty level, co-ordinated by faculty teaching fellows.

- **Institutional level:** *the institutional context for good practice.*
  University-wide assessment conference following the feedback campaign provided a focus for sharing good practice in feedback.

- **Wider level:** *the external context.*
  External speakers were invited to share their experience of assessment and feedback with colleagues across the university through a wide range of development activities.

The approach adopted was therefore to recognise the complex nature of the problem and to identify deliberate actions at each organisational level of the change model, as outlined above, with a strong focus on developmental activity and on changes to key institutional processes and policies. In this way the change model provided a clear framework within which the complex nature of assessment and feedback could be understood, thus enabling the formulation of a quality enhancement strategy to enhance the student and staff experience of feedback. The Feedback for Learning Campaign contributed to this change model by capturing the student voice, acting as vehicle for dialogue on the student experience of feedback, informing the development of policy and providing a bridge between the different activities within the framework.

What impact did the campaign have?

The analysis of responses received from students during phase one of the feedback campaign indicated a strong move towards electronic forms of feedback. More significantly, the analysis also indicated that students considered this type of feedback to be more useful than previously (i.e. at the time of the FAST project). Only a small proportion of the responses (3 per cent) received were negative, and these generally reflected that students had not received any returned work at that point in the academic year. The remainder of the comments either implied, or stated directly the usefulness of the feedback received articulating the contribution that feedback had made to their learning:

'Helped me understand what was expected of me within the essay and what the tutor was looking for.'

'I read the comments on my essay and used them to improve my next draft.'

'Used it to reflect on and improve my learning style and assignments.'

However, despite the significant level of activity, undertaken as part of the campaign, at institutional, faculty and course level these comments were in stark contrast to the free text comments received from the NSS that followed the campaign. These comments overwhelmingly focused on the deficiencies of the feedback that students have received, reflecting many familiar issues, such as consistency, legibility, timeliness and usefulness, suggesting little improvement from the analysis done as part of the FAST project. A deeper analysis of the NSS scores clearly indicated that student dissatisfaction with feedback was not universal and, despite significant improvements in NSS scores in some subject areas, there remained significant variability within and across the university, its disciplines, courses and even modules.

Concluding remarks

The pressing challenge, then, after all the concerted effort detailed in this chapter, is to identify the lessons learnt from this approach and to consider how best to respond to the issue of consistency particularly between subject disciplines. This situation is not unique, and is reflected in responses from students across the sector, which show that student dissatisfaction with feedback remains a significant issue.

So what can we draw from the model of partnership working described in this chapter?

First, the feedback campaign mirrored the dialogic nature of a feedback process and showed the benefits of working in partnership with students, which resulted in high levels of student and staff engagement, creating a real sense of momentum across the institution.

Second, placing partnership working within a structured change model was a key feature of the approach adopted. It did lead to the development of a coherent strategy to take developments forward across the different levels of the university to enhance the student learning experience in a coherent manner. It also consolidated the strong partnership between the university and students union in working to enhance the student experience. In addition, working in this way meant that dialogue on feedback was held at all levels of the institution, from formal university committees to informal discussions between tutors and students. However, working with sabbatical officers in the students union can make continuity challenging, as the nature of the roles they play mean that the incumbents change on an annual basis. This means that this model of partnership working has potentially a built-in weakness – the need to establish new working relationships annually. Further, newly elected officers often wish to follow their own priorities rather than those of their predecessors and so a campaign such as the one described in this chapter is difficult to sustain.

Finally, it is important to recognise the variability between subject areas and the associated student experiences. By its nature, the messages and materials coming out of the Feedback for Learning Campaign were generic and, with no formal requirement to engage, participation of students and staff in different subject areas was not uniform. This meant that different subject areas responded in different ways and in different timescales to changes in practice, resulting in inconsistency in levels of student satisfaction, at least in the short term.

Achieving institutional change therefore requires time to embed, as effective change in the student experience of feedback across all subject disciplines cannot be introduced and implemented in the short term; it requires concerted action over an extended period of time. Further this action needs to be undertaken at the course/module level where actions have a direct impact on the student experience. This is a cautionary lesson for all those responsible for instigating and delivering institutional change programmes.

Acknowledgements

Special thanks to Sheffield Hallam University (Creative Services) for allowing the use of the illustrations in this chapter plus other marketing materials.

References

FAST (2005) *Formative Assessment in Science and Technology*. Available at: www.open. ac.uk/science/fdtl/ (accessed 12 February 2012).

Holden, G., Wilson, R., Bradley, S. and Ackroyd, L. (2008) *Authentic Voices – Teaching Fellow, Educational Developer and Administrator – Working in Partnership*, 13th Annual SEDA Conference, Birmingham. Available at: http://seda.ac.uk/confs/birm08/ abstracts/22_HoldenWilsonBradleyAckroyd.pdf (accessed 12 February 2012).

Macdonald, R. and Joughin, G. (2009) 'Changing assessment in higher education: a model in support of institution wide improvement', in G. Joughin (ed.) *Assessment, Learning and Judgement in Higher Education*, New York: Springer.

National Student Survey (NSS), Bristol: Higher Education Funding Council for England. Available at: www.hefce.ac.uk/learning/nss/ (accessed 12 February 2012).

National Union of Students (2008a) *Feedback Amnesty*. Available at: www.nus.org.uk/ en/campaigns/higher-education/Assessment-feedback-/ (accessed 12 February 2012).

National Union of Students (2008b) *Feedback Charter*. Available at: www.nusconnect. org.uk/asset/news/6010/FeedbackCharter-toview.pdf (accessed 12 February 2012).

Newton, J. (2003) 'Implementing an institution-wide learning and teaching strategy: lessons in managing change', *Studies in Higher Education* 28(4): 427–41.

Parkin, H., Hepplestone, S., Holden, G., Irwin, B. and Thorpe, L. (2011) 'A role for technology in enhancing students' engagement with feedback', *Assessment and Evaluation in Higher Education*. Available at: www.tandfonline.com.lcproxy.shu.ac. uk/doi/abs/10.1080/02602938.2011.592934 (accessed 12 February 2012).

Seel, R. (2000) 'Culture and complexity: new insights on organisational change, culture and complexity', *Organisation and People* 7(2): 2–9.

Williams, J. and Kane, D. (2008) *Exploring the National Student Survey*, The Higher Education Academy. Available at: www.heacademy.ac.uk/assets/documents/nss/ NSS_assessment_and_feedback_issues.pdf (accessed 12 February 2012).

Chapter 15

Making learning-oriented assessment the experience of all our students

Supporting institutional change

Mark Russell, Dominic Bygate and Helen Barefoot

Introduction

Assessment and feedback have consistently been the lowest rated aspects of the student learning experience within the UK annual National Student Survey (NSS) and like many universities, the University of Hertfordshire recognised the importance of improving the assessment experience and prioritised this as an action for the Institution.

Previous studies within the Institution (Gillett and Hammond 2009) had identified a number of challenges prominent in certain parts of the University:

- students receiving feedback too long after the assessment experience;
- students being given insufficient opportunities to demonstrate how they have learned in response to feedback;
- teachers not using information about their students' understandings to inform their teaching as effectively as they might;
- an over-reliance on summative assessments rather than formative, learning-orientated assessments.

This chapter provides a reflection on a strategic, externally funded project designed to respond to the assessment and feedback challenges. It also presents a set of assessment for learning themes that were developed throughout the project and are now being used institutionally to effect sustained improvements in assessment and feedback. Aspects of the project, including the assessment for learning themes, have featured in a series of national workshops presented by the Joint Information Systems Committee (JISC).

The University of Hertfordshire context

The University of Hertfordshire (UH) primarily offers campus-based education to around 28,000 students. Currently (2011) the disciplinary areas are located in 14 academic schools.

The University has a positive predisposition to the use of technology to support its learning, teaching and assessment endeavours. The institutionally designed virtual learning environment is used to engage students on all modules and the widespread use of technologies in teaching indicates that staff at the University are receptive to the value of technology enhanced learning. Evidence of the embedded practice supported the bid to establish a Blended Learning Unit (BLU) (2005–2010) as part of HEFCE's funding for Centres for Excellence in Teaching and Learning (CETL). The BLU's remit was to support cross-university innovation as well as to reduce barriers for large scale uptake of technology enhanced learning. Through the work of the Blended Learning Unit, its successor, the Learning and Teaching Institute (LTI) and the support of institutional policies and processes, technology enhanced learning is well embedded throughout the whole University.

As part of the University's enhancement agenda the use of technology to support assessment and feedback was recognised as an area of focus. The University has, for example, run a number of workshops related to assessment and feedback and offered Small Scale Innovation funding for teaching and assessment related developments. Although there have been many interesting projects, the widespread dissemination and further uptake has often been limited. For example, staff in the School of Computer Science developed a Personalised Formative E-Assessment Tool, for students on multimedia modules in levels 5 and 6. The project was clearly beneficial for staff and students on these modules but the tool has not been used beyond the School because it was not designed within the Institution's virtual learning environment.

To stimulate strategic activities, larger scale funding was offered to teams/academic schools to support projects responding to the prevailing priorities of the Institution. Despite the intention of the activities funded under the Prevailing Priority Initiative, the projects still tended to be limited in terms of their scope and wider uptake.

The ESCAPE project

In 2008 the JISC released a funding call to seek projects that 'wished to transform how they deliver and support learning across a curriculum area through the effective use of technology, in response to a particular challenge faced by the discipline(s), department(s) or institution(s)'. The JISC is a UK government-funded body aiming to 'inspire UK colleges and universities in the innovative use of digital technologies, helping to maintain the UK's position as a global leader in education' (JISC 2011).

Drawing together the expertise and experience of the BLU along with the growing Institutional enthusiasm to improve assessment and feedback practice, the JISC call presented an opportunity for the BLU to work with academic schools within the University to help revisit their current practice and create more learning-oriented assessment. Our response to the JISC call, the Effecting Sustainable Change in Assessment Practice and Experience (ESCAPE) project, was funded.

The ESCAPE project was one of 15 projects funded over a two-year period, within the JISC Curriculum Delivery programme. The overall aim of the programme was to explore how technology can support and engage learners more effectively within different disciplines (JISC 2011).

The centrally managed ESCAPE project worked with two academic schools, the School of Life Sciences and the Business School, and had a particular focus on assessment and feedback. The Schools were chosen to be part of the project for a number of reasons. Both Schools had previously run Prevailing Priority projects associated with assessment and had conducted ten Small Scale Innovation projects over the previous four years, indicating a commitment to enhancement activity. They shared general challenges associated with assessment and feedback as evidenced in NSS scores and student performance data.

Between them the Schools used a broad spectrum of assessment and feedback methods yet also shared a number of specific concerns. These included:

- an over-emphasis on assessment *of* learning;
- disengagement in study activity outside of class;
- difficulties providing timely feedback;
- poor student use of feedback;
- diverse and large student cohorts;
- reduction in teacher–student contact;
- poor attendance/engagement at lectures.

To support the Schools the ESCAPE project focused on three broad areas of activity:

- working with staff to develop their understanding of the interrelationship of assessment, feedback and student learning;
- helping staff to identify educationally effective assessment that aligns with the disciplinary context;
- supporting staff to identify how technology might support their assessment activity and enable resource efficiencies.

Recognising that projects have different phases of activity, six complementary and sequenced work packages were identified to support the aims. Dissemination within the sector ran throughout the whole project (Figure 15.1).

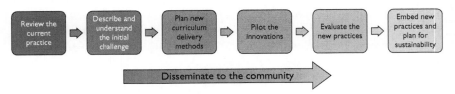

Figure 15.1 ESCAPE project work packages.

Ways of working

Seeking to bring about sustainable and pedagogically sound change dictated a need to draw on principles of good assessment and feedback practice and change management principles. Working with the Schools the project team was particularly keen to unearth areas of assessment and feedback that were working and led to good student learning. Indeed the project team avoided any overt suggestions that the Schools were failing in their current assessment and feedback practice. Hence, many of the conversations between the project team and the Schools were framed with the appreciative inquiry approach (Annis-Hammond 1998). Rather than fixate on challenges and issues, appreciative inquiry starts with the notion that organisations and individuals are already engaged in good work. Appreciative inquiry seeks to 'surface and spread' the good work.

A variety of interactions took place between the partner schools and the project team. The initial interactions helped the project team share their aspirations of the project, describe the ways of working and start to understand the local context. Importantly, the initial interactions sought to identify modules and teams with whom the project would work.

Nine modules were identified as being of particular interest. The modules were chosen for a number of reasons, including: core programme modules with large student numbers; modules with an emphasis on end of process assessment; modules with a reliance on singular modes of assessment; modules where staff felt the assessment was not as influential on learning as it may have been; modules with large numbers of teaching staff; and modules led by teachers that had strategic influence in the school.

The interactions with the module teaching teams began with one-to-one discussions using appreciative inquiry techniques to review current practice. These semi-structured interviews explored the modules and the current assessment and feedback methods.

Following the initial interviews, all teams participated in a two-day, off-site, event. The project team drew on their experiences of change management activity, which had been a key component of the work of the BLU. Based on the Higher Education Academy's national Change Academy[1] work, the BLU developed a local version, the Change Academy for Blended Learning Enhancement (CABLE). A two-day event was described as a key component within CABLE (Anderson and Bullen 2009) and was hence included within the ESCAPE project. Having identified specific challenges, the teams shared their current experiences, their pedagogical values and beliefs and were presented with research informed principles of good assessment and feedback practice. The event comprised a designed mix of presentations, small and large group discussions and active planning. The intended outcome of the event was for module teams to begin the process of assessment redesign in light of their understanding of good assessment and feedback.

While the ESCAPE project had a focus on technology enhanced assessment and feedback the project did not have any fixed ideas on the technologies to be used. The teams developed their technology enhanced assessment solutions based on their contexts. Emerging examples of the re-engineered module assessment that came from the two-day event included:

- use of blogs and student-generated videos (short rationale: to develop improved student reflection and to establish student to student and student to teacher dialogue);
- extended use of electronic voting systems (short rationale: to check student understanding in class, provide more student-centred teaching sessions and improve lecture attendance and engagement with lecture material);
- use of group areas and wikis within virtual learning environments (short rationale: to establish opportunities for collaboration and co-creation);
- use of a web-based reflective questionnaire at the end of a peer assessment process (short rationale: to stimulate student self-reflection and enhance understanding of the benefits of peer feedback);
- use of weekly online assessed tutorial sheets (short rationale: to stimulate regular student engagement with subject matter and provide rapid feedback to students and teachers on performance).

As the module staff began the implementation of their redesigned assessment and feedback activities, the project team maintained on-going dialogue with the module leaders and supported the evaluation process. The module teams identified evaluation measures relevant for their modules. For example:

- formal and informal feedback from students regarding how the assessment and feedback benefited their learning;
- increased engagement in, and out of, classes;
- gains as measured in enhanced assessment performance.

The project team were also interested in considering the work burden of staff to ensure that the assessment redesigns were not only educationally effective but were also resource efficient.

Towards the end of the project the module teams reconvened to share their experiences, articulate their reasons for the redesign, identify the outcomes of their redesign and importantly to hear of plans to sustain and grow their successes through their schools. Case studies were prepared and shared within institutional workshops and specifically within the Schools (Figure 15.2).

ESCAPE assessment for learning themes

Why were the ESCAPE themes developed?

Throughout the whole process, the project team did not offer quick fixes nor present ready-made hints and tips. It was essential that the modules teams

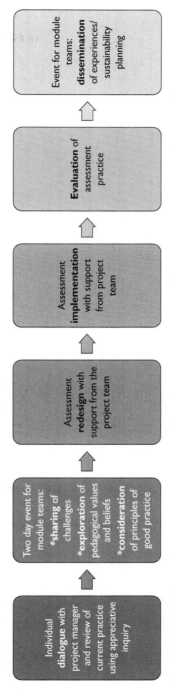

Individual **dialogue** with project manager and review of current practice using appreciative inquiry

Two day event for module teams:
*   **sharing** of challenges
*   **exploration** of pedagogical values and beliefs
*   **consideration** of principles of good practice

Assessment **redesign** with support from the project team

Assessment **implementation** with support from project team

Evaluation of assessment practice

Event for module teams: **dissemination** of experiences/ sustainability planning

Figure 15.2 ESCAPE project process.

articulated their own challenges and then identified solutions relevant for them. Imposing ideas and solutions onto module teams could have i) caused hostility and resulted in a lack of engagement, and/or ii) stifled the development of their own understanding of good assessment and feedback practice. All interactions were therefore framed around a number of existing sets of principles of good assessment and feedback practice (Gibbs and Simpson 2004; Nicol and Macfarlane-Dick 2006; Weston Manor Group 2007). As the project progressed it became evident that presenting multiple research findings led to some initial confusion for staff. Although the project team were very familiar with the large body of work associated with assessment and feedback, for many staff, the pedagogic literature was new to them and was something they hadn't previously engaged with. Not wanting to overwhelm staff with multiple models and lists of principles/conditions for ways of working, it was identified that a shortened summary of the key messages from the literature would have been more beneficial for busy academics.

The ESCAPE themes

Mirroring the work of Chickering and Gamson (1987), the project team developed a set of assessment for learning themes that were limited in number, had face-validity and were relevant across all disciplines. The themes were shaped by input from staff in the BLU and the LTI and were tested with staff attending institutional wide workshops on assessment and feedback. The ESCAPE themes became a central area of activity for the ESCAPE project.

Good assessment for learning:

- engages students with the assessment criteria;
- supports personalised learning;
- stimulates dialogues;
- ensures feedback leads to improvement;
- focuses on student development;
- considers staff and student effort.

The ESCAPE themes intend to help staff develop pedagogic values, rather than offering specific solutions. Working on conceptions of good assessment and feedback rather than solutions is likely to yield more sustaining and growing changes in assessment and feedback practice. They are designed to provide an overarching framework for ways of working, and not being subject-specific enable staff from any discipline to apply the themes to their specific assessment and feedback contexts.

As with Chickering and Gamson's (1987) seven principles for good practice in undergraduate education, the themes have underpinning questions to help unpack some of the detail. Specifically, and it is here that the link is made to existing work, the starting questions are extracted from the principles of Gibbs and Simpson (2004), Nicol and Macfarlane-Dick (2006), National Union of Students (2012) and the 'Assessment standards' manifesto (Weston Manor Group 2007).

Using the ESCAPE theme 'ensures feedback leads to improvement' as an example, Figure 15.3 shows the link between the ESCAPE themes and the existing research-informed principles. The link is made via the five questions.

Outputs and resources

Outputs and impact on practice

Each module involved in the project evaluated the assessment redesign in ways appropriate to the change. To share the benefits of the project and disseminate findings, the project team collated ESCAPE examples, one of which is provided below.

Overview of one of the module assessment redesigns

Module: Principles and Practices of Sports Science on the BSc Sports Studies programme.

Previous module assessment: comprised four long, paper based, written assignments plus a final written examination.

Good practice in assessment-for-learning:

3 Ensures feedback leads to improvement

Feedback is an essential aspect of assessment activity. Feedback will be more effective if it is prompt and makes sense to the students. Moreover, good feedback provides a commentary on the student's submissions, offers advice on how the work could be developed and provides opportunities for students to demonstrably engage with the feedback.

Q3.1 I ensure that my feedback is produced quickly enough to be of use to students.

Q3.2 I provide feedback that is detailed and frequent.

Q3.3 I ensure that feedback makes sense to students.

Q3.4 I ensure that my students have the opportunity to act on the feedback.

Q3.5 I deliver high-quality feedback information related to assessment criteria that helps learners self-correct.

Figure 15.3 Linking the ESCAPE themes to existing assessment and feedback principles.

Module challenge: Student engagement was low – students did not always realise that they needed a grasp of the principles of science within their sports studies degree. The assessment workload, for teachers and students, was arduous. There were difficulties in providing feedback that students could use to support their ongoing studies.

Assessment redesign: The first step in revitalising the module was to make better use of the University's virtual learning environment, StudyNet. The students were divided into groups of up to five and a group page on StudyNet for each was created. Each group was tasked with producing a scientific report through the use of a wiki.

Redesign benefits: The students received early, and ongoing, evaluations of their contributions to the report as well as their contributions to the group effort (all of this was traceable through the wiki). The module lead was able to monitor the students' work throughout the process and provided short, timely interjections supporting and critiquing their thinking. The tutor feedback was demonstrably used in future edits and iterations.

Module leader reflection: 'Assessment redesign has been a win–win experience for all of us. The whole process is paperless: the reports are written, submitted, marked, moderated and returned with feedback online, which is both efficient and effective. Students are more engaged and supportive of one another, and I am left wondering why we ever thought marking 250 essays four times over was an appropriate way to assess this module' (James Johnstone, module leader).

School benefits

As well as specific improvements on modules, the Schools have shown improvements on institutional measures such as student performance and NSS scores. Specifically, since the project started in November 2008, both Schools have shown improvements in the assessment and feedback sections within the NSS.

Importantly, to show the benefits of working with staff and their conceptions of good assessment and feedback, we have seen:

- embedding of redesigned assessment within the ESCAPE modules;
- a growth in assessment redesign within modules not initially targeted by the ESCAPE project;
- an increase in dialogue, across the Institution, about assessment, feedback and learning (through monthly assessment and feedback workshops; a learning and teaching conference themed around good assessment and feedback practice and enhancement awards associated specifically with improving assessment).

Resources

In addition to the production of case studies directly from the project modules, the team were keen to provide additional resources enabling staff who hadn't been directly involved in ESCAPE to support enhancement of their own assessment and feedback practice.

Case studies demonstrating application of ESCAPE themes

Using examples of existing assessment and feedback, the ESCAPE themes have been overlaid to show teachers that their existing practice is, in some ways, aligned with good assessment and feedback practice, whilst also highlighting areas that might need enhancing (Figure 15.4).

Through the analysis of current assessment activities in light of the ESCAPE themes, it became evident that existing descriptions of assessment and practice showed limited engagement with elements of the theme 'ensures feedback leads to improvement'. Although the assessment descriptions highlighted the provision of 'prompt feedback' there was very little written about the students' use of feedback. In such situations, it was arguably the design of the assessments that needed reviewing; there was little or no demonstrable opportunity for students to use their feedback and improve their future work. Providing feedback without designing the intent for its use may be a contributory factor in the number of marked assessments that remain uncollected.

The growing resource bank of case studies proved useful for teachers both within the project and others beyond. The examples are used in workshops both

A themed assessment case study from the *Effecting Sustainable Change in Assessment Practice and Experience (ESCAPE)* **project**

2 The first assignment: formative feedback to aid academic writing

Tags: formative, large group, level 1, personal tutor, skill, academic writing, referencing, plagiarism, biosciences

Level   1

Number of students 150

Discipline   **Biosciences**

Brief overview of assessment activity

A formative essay is set within the first two weeks of term and submitted online in week four. The students write a 1,500 word essay about a named infectious disease including a discussion of the symptoms, its diagnosis, treatment and social/economic importance. The essay is marked by personal tutors (each member of staff mark approximately eight essays). The aims of the assignment are to: engage students with subject matter early within their programme; provide an opportunity for students to receive feedback on academic writing ;and discuss how to use, and reference, resources appropriately,

> Author
> **Comment:** Focuses on student development (Focus on learning not marks)

> Author
> **Comment:** Ensures feedback leads to improvement (feedback makes sense to students)

Description of how the assessment supports student learning

The assignment ensures early engagement with subject material, encouraging students to explore the LRC for relevant books and to look at online resources. The assignment provides students with a

Figure 15.4 Part case study overlaid with the ESCAPE themes.

within and beyond the Institution, as well being available online. The case studies are 'tagged' such that teaching staff can see which of the case studies relate to which of the ESCAPE themes.

Additional resources

As the project progressed, a number of additional resources were developed based on the findings. The resources are tools that teaching staff can use with colleagues and/or with students to develop their own assessment and feedback practice beyond the support of the project team. These additional resources are being used to frame continuing discussions regarding assessment/curriculum design.

Assessment patterns

Exploration of current assessment practices confirmed a suspicion of over-reliance on high stakes summative assessment, particularly within level 6. End of module assessments, by definition, do not encourage student use of feedback as there are no further scheduled opportunities for the feedback to be acted upon. To help staff consider alternative assessment schedules and to encourage appropriate student study behaviours, a number of assessment patterns were developed to demonstrate that other types of regular assessment activities could be incorporated within the curriculum. The intention of the assessment patterns was not to over-prescribe solutions but rather to highlight that different assessment patterns exist and that with each different pattern different consequences are likely to arise. The assessment patterns are used within workshops for staff on enhancing their assessment and feedback, as well as forming part of the resources available within the Assessment for Learning strand of the University's Curriculum Design Toolkit. They are also useful teaching aids on the Post Graduate Certificate in Learning and Teaching in Higher Education and in Programme validation guidance.

In creating the assessment patterns the project team set out to create accessible visual representations rather than lengthy text descriptions. Three example assessment patterns are shown in Figure 15.5.

To help provide a focus the assessment patterns have been grouped into three broad areas. These are:

- providing opportunities to make more use of feedback;
- moving away from high stakes/end of process assessment;
- taking a programme view of assessment.

White circles indicate low stakes assessment, grey circles indicate medium stakes assessment, black circles indicate high stakes assessment.

As with the majority of the ESCAPE work, the assessment patterns were presented to stimulate thinking. The patterns were not overly value laden but rather offered alternative ways of working. The examples presented in Figure

P1

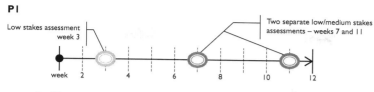

Possible consequences:
- engages students early with the curriculum;
- student workload reasonably well spread out;
- not reliant on high-stakes assessment activity;
- opportunities exist for the provision of feedback after each assessment;
- the three assessment tasks are seeen as being too discrete, i.e. there is no obvious link between the assessments;
- little explicit need for students to collect, read, seek to understand or act on any feedback.

P2

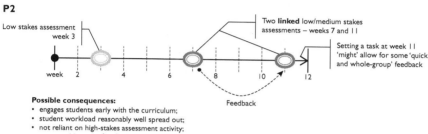
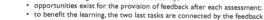

Possible consequences:
- engages students early with the curriculum;
- student workload reasonably well spread out;
- not reliant on high-stakes assessment activity;
- opportunities exist for the provision of feedback after each assessment;
- to benefit the learning, the two last tasks are connected by the feedback

P3

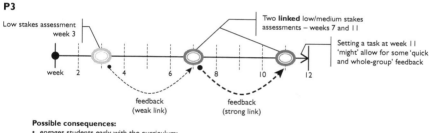

Possible consequences:
- engages students early with the curriculum;
- student workload reasonably well spread out;
- not reliant on high-stakes assessment activity;
- opportunities exist for the provision of feedback after each assessment;
- task two 'suggests' feedback from one is important – weak feedback link;
- task three is directly related to the feedback students receive in task two – strong feedback link;
- because of the linking of feedback (both weak and strong) students are more likely to *pick up, read,* seek *to understand* and subsequently *use their feedback.*

Figure 15.5 Examples of assessment patterns – making more of feedback.

15.5 comes from the set relating to 'making more of feedback' and shows how the assessment tasks could be designed such that the feedback from one task is used and feeds into the upcoming task (P2). The notion of a weak and a strong link (P3) suggests that the first feedback (weak link) may be of a more general nature (e.g. structure/referencing) whereas the second feedback (strong link) is content focused and specifically linked to the next task.

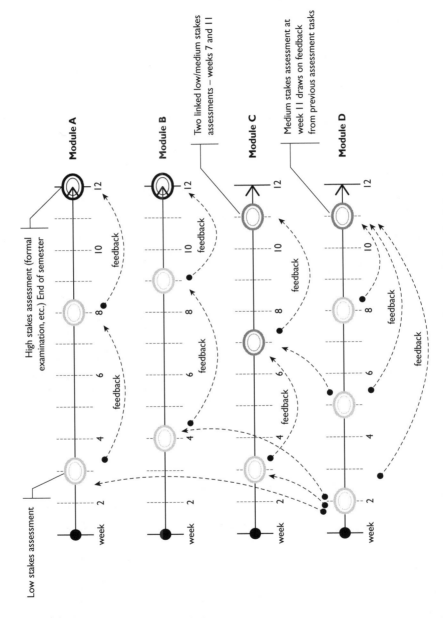

Figure 15.6 Examples of assessment patterns – a programme view of assessment (one level shown).

Assessment patterns reflecting programme assessment schedules were also produced (Figure 15.6). Mapping the assessment patterns of all modules within a programme enables staff to identify bunching of assessment and to then redesign assessment schedules to improve student study behaviours. The programme assessment patterns also demonstrate how feedback on module assignments can support assessments in parallel modules within the programme.

Student facing resources

The significant intent of the ESCAPE project was to work with teachers and their conceptions of good assessment and feedback practice. Recognising that assessment is undertaken by students and that students have a role to play in terms of helping themselves led to the development of a set of student facing resources.

The student facing resources were created towards the end of the project and again are part of the project's legacy. Using the ESCAPE themes as a common thread, the resources include a set of questions to describe the sorts of activities students might undertake to help create a better personal assessment experience. A set of six postcards have been produced – one for each theme. An example postcard on the theme 'ensures feedback leads to improvement' is shown in Figure 15.7 on page 186.

Given the issues regarding students lack of engagement with feedback, an additional resource was developed – a feedback hierarchy. The hierarchy draws on the framework offered by Maslow's Hierarchy of Needs (Maslow 1943). In the ESCAPE feedback hierarchy the implication is that students are not able to use the feedback (top level of the hierarchy) until a series of other steps have been met. Two versions of the hierarchy have been produced, one that is focused on the students (Figure 15.8, p. 187) and one that is teacher focused (Figure 15.9, p. 188).

Legacy and institutional change

The legacy

The ESCAPE themes and associated resources feature in numerous conversations and activities relating to assessment and feedback across the University.

As part of the University's staff development programme monthly workshops support staff in considering their assessment and feedback practice. The ESCAPE resources focus the discussions and enable staff to develop their assessment such that feedback creates more positive consequences for learning. It is apparent that staff from outside the targeted Schools have benefited from the ESCAPE resources and have used them to shape their own assessment design.

4. Focuses on student development

4.1 When constructing my assessment submission I focus my effort on learning (i.e. linking concepts together) rather than just presenting information.

4.2 When I receive feedback on my assessment I look carefully at the comments, advice and encouragement and do not just concentrate on my mark/grade.

4.3 I take the time to review my own assessment (self assessment) before and after I submit my work.

4.4 I make sure I identify the positive aspects of my own work as well as areas for improvement.

4.5 I ensure any misconceptions I have about my learning are voiced.

How about YOU?
The ways I use assessment to support my learning include…

ESCAPE Project Funded by the JISC

http://tinyurl.com/escape-project

University of Hertfordshire

"Assessment feedback allows me to IDENTIFY the POSITIVE ASPECTS of my work as well as areas for IMPROVEMENT."

Figure 15.7 An example of a student-facing postcard.

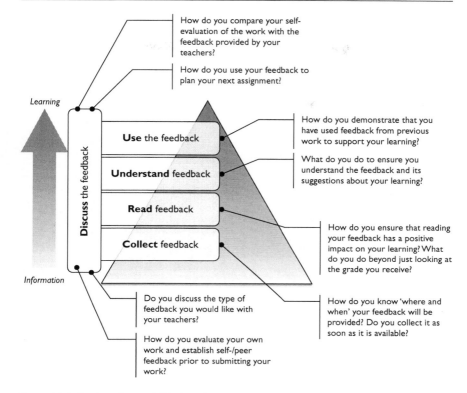

Figure 15.8 Student-focused ESCAPE feedback hierarchy.

The ESCAPE themes are being piloted in a new programme review process. It is encouraging that a quality enhancement activity is now being more embedded in a quality assurance process.

As well as making effective use of project outputs within the University of Hertfordshire the findings have been widely disseminated through the JISC Design Studio. The resources have also been used as components of a JISC national workshop series in relation to Effective Assessment in a Digital Age.

Embedding the ESCAPE findings, ways of working and resources in institutional process ensured the sustainability of the project. The commitment to enhancing assessment and feedback has led to year on year increases on institutional NSS score for the assessment and feedback and the focus on this work continues to improve the assessment experiences for students and staff alike.

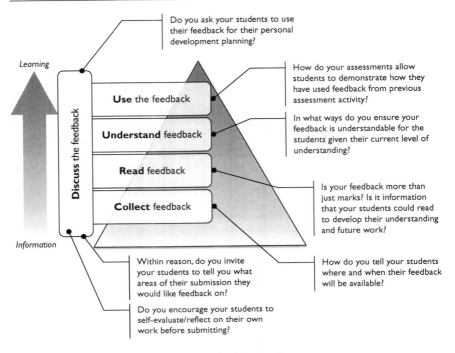

Figure 15.9 Teacher-focused ESCAPE feedback hierarchy.

Institutional change

The ESCAPE project met a recognised need within the Institution and was timely in that there was an institutional readiness for change. From our experiences, stimulating institutional change relied on a number of factors:

- identification of a specific challenge;
- institutional support for change;
- benefit of external funding;
- the importance of a research informed approach;
- the value of flexibility – creativity and innovation within the project – responsive to needs of participants;
- production of accessible resources (development of evidence based themes for persuasion, as tools of analysis, for framing development and resources, for sustainable change);
- usefulness and applicability of resources;
- engagement with, and adoption of, technology enhanced learning.

The ESCAPE project ultimately met its aim of effecting sustainable change in assessment practices, which has led to improved experiences for students and for staff.

Notes

1 The Change Academy was organised through a partnership between the Higher Education Academy and the Leadership Foundation for Higher Education and brought together cross-institutional teams to think creatively and develop a major change initiative. Projects tended to last for a year and provided opportunities for planning and developing strategies for lasting change through ongoing support and a four-day team residential event.

References

Anderson, I. and Bullen, P. (2009) 'The change academy and institutional transformation', in T. Mayes, D. Morrison, H. Mellar, P. Bullen and M. Oliver (eds) *Transforming Higher Education Through Technology Enhanced Learning*, York: Higher Education Academy (pp. 149–63).

Annis-Hammond, S. (1998) *The Thin Book of Appreciative Inquiry*, Bend, OR: Thin Book Publishing Company.

Chickering, A. and Gamson, Z. (1987) 'Seven principles for good practice in undergraduate education', *American Association of Higher Education Bulletin*, 39: 3–7.

Gibbs, G. and Simpson, C. (2004) 'Conditions under which assessment supports students' learning', *Learning and Teaching in Higher Education* 1(8): 3–31.

Gillett, A.J. and Hammond, A.C. (2009) 'Mapping the maze of assessment: an investigation into practice', *Active Learning in Higher Education*, 10: 120–37.

JISC (2011) Available at: <http://www.jisc.ac.uk/> (accessed 30 November 2011).

Maslow, A.H. (1943) 'A theory of human motivation', *Psychological Review*, 50(4): 370–96.

National Union of Students (2012) *Feedback: what you can expect.* Available at: www.nus.org.uk/en/advice/course-reps/feedback/feedback-what-you-can-expect-/ (accessed 14 May 2012).

Nicol, D. and Macfarlane-Dick, D. (2006) 'Formative assessment and self-regulated learning: a model and seven principles of good feedback practice', *Studies in Higher Education* 31(2): 199–218.

Weston Manor Group (2007) *Assessment standards: a manifesto for change.* Available at: www.business.brookes.ac.uk/learningandteaching/aske/Manifesto%20final (accessed 20 October 2008).

Chapter 16

Achieving transformational or sustainable educational change

Steve Draper and David Nicol

Introduction

Researchers and practitioners often feel that the demonstrated merits of their work should be sufficient to drive adoption by others. However, in practice, in education, new research findings or even best practices spread slowly, if at all. Achieving significant adoption usually requires a project specifically addressed to this: a change project. Even when change is explicitly called for and funded, only some projects can truly be characterised as change projects. Many others claim this while retaining a structure which only leads to research outcomes. Research and change projects have different goals and therefore must be constructed quite differently. The aim of a research project is to establish new knowledge, whereas the aim of a change project is to persuade people to change their practice based on existing knowledge. We discuss seven major decisions that shape a true change project.

One decision concerns the level at which the intervention to promote change is applied. While some suppose that in education, transformational change requires interventions at the institutional policy level, this chapter argues that achieving educational change across a whole institution is not always done by directly intervening at that level. Many of the most far-reaching change initiatives have been driven from other levels. Six levels are considered, with examples of success or failure at each: the individual learner, the individual teacher, the course, the institution, the discipline, and the sector.

The main activity in a change project is persuasion: almost all the project has to do is to persuade a range of people that the project is worth doing; that is the main deliverable. Success depends on the prior assembly of resources on which to base the persuasion and then the implementation of the changes envisioned. The main barrier to these is generally disciplinary differences which, as elaborated later on, make it difficult for academics to appreciate that educational innovations in other disciplines are relevant to their own.

Background

This chapter derives from our attempts to generalise from the institution-wide change at the University of Strathclyde achieved by the REAP project (Re-engineering assessment practices in HE) (Nicol 2011). It started with the redesign of assessment and feedback practices in nine departments across five faculties, and with student numbers ranging from 190 to 560. Of the 10 redesigned modules, six showed measurable gains in student test results, and all showed high student satisfaction and positive staff attitudes about the teaching benefits to the department. Some redesigns showed reduced teacher workload, and none increased it, after allowing for the cost-to-change. Indicators of wide-spread organisational change were the take-up of the project ideas in other departments beyond those funded by REAP, the incorporation of the REAP principles of assessment and feedback into a new university-wide project, the continuing reference to the ideas and principles in reporting documentation, and a 'feedback as dialogue' initiative designed and developed through the student union.

This chapter is a companion piece to Draper and Nicol (2006), and Nicol and Draper (2009). The latter analysis gives more details of REAP, is structured around Lindquist's (1974) barriers to institutional change, and offers seven principles for constructing a project to achieve such change. Readers are referred to it for example cases of course designs, REAP's list of 11 design principles, and further discussion of rhetorical resources. This chapter develops that theme in a different way, asking what the key decisions are in shaping any such project.

Seven big decisions in shaping an educational change project

In this section we identify seven of the biggest decisions taken, whether explicitly or not, in shaping an educational project intended to change practice significantly. (And we invite the reader to consider, for any project that seems to have omitted some of them, whether it might have been more successful if it had addressed them.) They will be illustrated mainly in relation to the REAP project summarised above, and Twigg's Programme in Course Redesign (PCR).

The PCR, conceived and directed by Carol Twigg (2003) and funded by $8.8m from the Pew charitable foundation, ran 1999–2002 and gave $6m to 30 course teams in HE across the USA to introduce redesigned courses. They spanned many disciplines (including English, Maths, Chemistry, Psychology), and institutions of many kinds from community colleges to private four-year universities. All 30 showed significant cost reductions, and 25 showed significant measured improvements in the learning outcomes.

It achieved its strategic purpose of demonstrating, contrary to what almost everyone in HE, particularly researchers, had assumed: that it is possible to reduce costs and raise learning quality simultaneously in HE. This fundamentally breaks the assumption of an inevitable trade-off between cost and time: in particular, that raising quality requires increasing costs. The PCR also, we believe, showed that in educational designs you achieve only what you aim for. Many projects have taken (and achieved) the use of new technology as the goal but it seems that unless you have the explicit and consistently pursued goals of reducing costs and raising learning quality, then you do not get them in course redesigns. Potential benefits are not normally, let alone automatically, realised.

A. Selecting the project research type, and its consequences for cost and quality control

The most basic, and the first, decision for an educational project is where you intend it to lie on a generalised pure-applied spectrum running from pure research through development to 'rollout' (i.e. spreading a new practice). Shayer (1992) characterised a version of this as a developmental sequence of educational project types: studying the primary effect (establishing that with the new method a gain is possible at all), replicating it without the original researcher, and finally demonstrating that teachers who were not volunteers can get the same effect.

Projects at different points on the spectrum have different characteristics and purposes that must be clearly acknowledged and not conflated. This chapter is concerned only with achieving widespread change, i.e. essentially with rollout projects, which differ from other educational projects. For example, an experiment to test the value of introducing a novel teaching method or technology, while perhaps being mindful of costs, should not have this as the driving criterion, but should be concerned with studying the primary effect. In contrast, rollout is generally only worthwhile or even permissible if costs and quality are favourable. Almost certainly, then, any large-scale change needs at least to contain and preferably to reduce costs; and similarly at least to maintain or preferably to raise learning outcomes. However, Twigg's PCR showed that these requirements will not be met unless they are explicitly required and designed for in every case, a lesson the REAP project followed. Consequently, the decision to aim for widespread change immediately entails making cost and learning quality explicit and high-priority requirements, with pervasive consequences for the project. It is this which makes the selection of the project type the first and most important decision. Failure to recognise and act on this will usually doom a project, like so many others, to being (despite any intentions to the contrary) not a rollout project but at most a demonstrator with no sustained change achieved.

B. Select the level at which to apply the primary lever for change

Even if the project purpose is to change a whole institution, that does not necessarily mean that the institutional level is the one to which to apply the lever, only that it is the level on which final success or failure is to be judged. As an analogy: to bring down a dam (the intended ultimate, but perhaps indirect, effect), is it most effective (as a primary direct action) to blow it all up, or to drill a small hole in it somewhere, or to knock a small gap in the lip and let erosion enlarge it? In many ways the second biggest decision about method which a transformational project takes is what primary change (direct intervention, as opposed to indirect but intended effect) it will attempt, and the major part of this decision is selecting which level to act upon. Six levels are discussed here.

The level of the individual teacher

Very many people (funders, pupils, parents) clamour for training of teachers (i.e. in HE, academics) as an important way to improve learning quality and quantity. Introducing more teacher training is in fact a common indirect institutional intervention. Evidence from learner ratings of teachers tends to support this (Gibbs 2010). However, the evidence based on learning outcomes suggests *no* effect from the quality of the teacher's training (Chingos and Peterson 2011) in the school sector, still less in HE. This seems to imply no effect of training on learning outcomes (although there may be an effect of practice initially). In the field of feedback, there are many sets of published advice for teachers on how to give better feedback, but we know of no studies showing whether this translates into better learning outcomes for students. The first job (research) would be to demonstrate that such interventions affect learning outcomes at all. It would then remain to be proven that this could be a successful level for rollout.

This section mentioned conflicting primary evidence about effects at this level, and an absence of primary evidence about feedback changes applied at this level. If primary evidence emerges, then a rollout project could be planned at this level.

The level of the individual learner

Interventions at the level of the learner but independently of normal classes may certainly be powerful: for example, prior selection for IQ or academic achievement is the biggest single factor predicting dropout rates. After entry, training students in study skills is another example of this kind of intervention. In the field of feedback, requiring students to specify what feedback questions they want answered (elective feedback, see Draper 2011) is a promising method. If strong primary evidence for this effect (not just student approbation but learning outcome improvements) emerges, then a rollout project would be worthwhile at this level.

The course level

Many research projects, including interventions detailed in some chapters of this book, have demonstrated that the course design level can be effective in changing learning outcomes significantly and repeatedly. Twigg's PCR and REAP selected course (re)design as the main lever of change, and thereby demonstrated that this level can be the basis for successful rollout.

The institutional level

However, the above levels are far from the only possibilities on the face of it. For example, we could imagine a university introducing a policy that required that all course proposals, including renewal of approval for courses, produce both direct evidence from test outcomes and student feedback, and evidence from the published educational literature to justify each course's learning and teaching design. This would transform learning and teaching into an evidence-based activity from the current folk medicine/'traditional practice' basis. The field of medicine illustrates both how slow this shift is in coming, but also its benefits. Another example would be the University of Surrey's Professional Year Programme, an institutional policy from its founding, which now sees 80 per cent of students across all degree programmes include a sandwich year (between their second and fourth years) of professional training placement outside the university.

There has been a recent flurry in the UK of institutions imposing a policy about uniform deadlines for the return to students of feedback (e.g. two weeks). However, this seems to be aimed at improving NSS ratings, rather than learning outcomes. It is also unrelated to both the two relevant times for receiving formative feedback. The first is immediately upon completion of the work, when the student's mind is filled with the whole exercise, and which can be achieved, for example, by online testing software, or by an assessment being marked on the spot in the same session by displaying the right answers and having students mark the work. Two weeks is four orders of magnitude slower than this. The second relevant time is when the student is attempting the next similar piece of work, which might be three months later for a termly essay, and earlier delivery is irrelevant to the feedback being applied by the learner.

It seems that this level could be successfully used for rollout, although in many cases it has not been.

The disciplinary level

Still more interesting because it seems so indirect, yet has some of the best evidence of success in improving learning, is the strategy embodied in Hestenes' work. Hestenes invested considerable person-years of work in developing the Force Concept Inventory (FCI) (Hestenes et al. 1992), a test for physics students that shows what qualitative understanding they have of some basic (HE year 1) topics. He did not primarily develop and promote any new ways of teaching, no new learning activities, no special teacher training. Nevertheless the FCI led to some of the biggest published educational improvements in HE (e.g.

Crouch and Mazur (2001) who report a near-tripling of the amount learned on a course).

We might view this, after the fact, as a remarkable transformational strategy: the FCI has such tremendous 'face validity' that academics teaching relevant courses simply cannot bear it when they see the poor results their own students manage on the test. The FCI worked by delivering a simple tool by which each academic can measure the effectiveness of their own teaching, both before and after any change of method. Subsequently they have then either devised new methods, or sought to adopt others' methods that have shown success at this. Hake (1998), in his noteworthy paper drawing on 62 courses with 6,542 students, reports the success following on from this due to the spreading adoption within HE physics teaching of new methods. This is the educational equivalent of a medical project which, rather than developing a single new treatment, simply collects and publishes reliable cause-of-death statistics, or five-year survival rates for different cancer treatments, thereby establishing a measure plus benchmarks that all researchers and practitioners can use.

The CLA (Collegiate Learning Assessment; Klein *et al.* 2007) is another interesting example of a measure already in existence, offering a test for graduate attributes such as problem solving. A suggestion for other disciplines might be to devise and publish measurement instruments based on 'threshold concepts' (known problem barriers for learners) for that discipline. The spread of Problem Based Learning (PBL) in medical schools amounts to a different kind of example of disciplinary level transformational change. Note that in the UK this was initiated only after heavy pressure from the disciplinary licensing body (the General Medical Council).

Rollout has certainly been demonstrated at this level, and might perhaps be applied to feedback. Disciplinary level standards of feedback to students certainly exist (and so could be the object of change projects): for example, in teacher training, requirements for reflection by trainees on their practice, or for observation of their practice by supervisors or mentors.

Sector level

Twigg's longer term strategy is to bring about sector-level change using a course-level primary intervention, and for the PCR and successor projects to spread the ideas now convincingly demonstrated. (She therefore selected a wide range of disciplines and of types of institution so as to demonstrate the sector-wide implications of her project.) Sector-level primary interventions can and do occur in terms of government policy and funding changes, but have more often concerned broad curriculum specifications (i.e. which subjects get funded) than learning and teaching methods. It could be argued that the assessment and feedback subscale of the NSS is a sector-level intervention that has brought widespread change, in that feedback return deadlines have been introduced in many HEIs, although as noted above their educational effectiveness may be disputed. Rollout of rather different content (e.g. curricula) has certainly occurred at this level, and it seems a possibility for feedback projects.

Summary

Thus there are in fact a range of quite different strategic approaches for bringing about educational change. REAP demonstrated an institutional-level *effect*, but using a course-level primary *intervention*. PCR demonstrated a sector-wide effect, again using a course-level primary intervention. Hestenes precipitated a discipline-level effect, from a discipline-level primary intervention. Requiring (more) teacher training in a HE institution (e.g. a university) attempts an institution-level effect from an individual teacher-level intervention.

C. The recognised problem area

The next crucial choice for a project is that of the 'issue': the widely recognisable educational problem to be tackled. In the context of this book, it is 'feedback', an issue widely seen as poorly handled in HE. This is important in getting immediate recognition from others of the relevance and importance of the project. Funding is often tied to initiatives defined by such pre-recognised issues. We could say this is the level of the apparent problem, of 'symptoms': like the 'black death' as opposed to identifying the plague bacillus.

REAP's choice was 'assessment and feedback' for this decision; while Twigg's choice was cost-benefit ratios with new learning technology. Any tour of recent funding initiatives throws up many alternative candidates, e.g. student retention, flexible learning, graduate attributes, etc.

D. The educational aspiration

Popular perceptions of problems, however, correspond to symptoms, and may not turn out to correspond to underlying causes (diagnoses). An important feature of a good project will be a less obvious idea about educational good that can serve as the source for innovative suggestions about new learning designs. In Twigg it was 'active learning'; in REAP it was 'self-regulation', i.e. the idea that the real aim of feedback should not be correcting the current product (e.g. an essay) but making the learner increasingly able to detect and remedy their own errors in the discipline. Without an aspiration of this kind, a project could have a collection of traditional remedies to draw upon, but would be less likely to achieve significant learning gains beyond the norm of current practice.

E. Design principles

Even given a target symptom and a putative diagnosis, there is still a large gap before arriving at a plan of action that is practical in a specific context, and can be communicated to the people who must carry it out. REAP's approach to this was to have a set of 11 'design principles' prepared in advance of the project. These are short (6–14 words long) action-oriented heuristics, designed to start the process of bridging between abstract theory and practical action (e.g. 'Provide opportunities to act on feedback'). From the viewpoint of communication, they need to be ready in two forms: the short principles themselves, and slightly longer descriptions that clarify their meaning and head off any misinterpretations that the slogan form may allow, and to have justifications prepared in terms of published evidenced – see below.

Design principles play the role of families of remedies or treatments (cf. pain-killers, anti-inflammatories, antibiotics), as opposed to specific remedies (cf. aspirin, penicillin) which are analogous to specific learning designs from the library discussed in the next subsection. Design principles are also comparable to Alexander et al.'s (1977) 'patterns' in the field of architecture, in that they do not specify a whole design or solution, but express a functional element that is common across many different good designs. The clauses of the Agenda for Change (see Chapter 4), which encapsulate the ideas on which this book is based, would provide a design framework.

F. A library of learning designs to suggest

In both REAP and PCR a crucial part of the project was discussions of course designs between project members and course teams. For this, another resource was vital: having key project members know about a large set of possible designs, mainly from the literature. Thus if a client says, 'The principle of "Encourage teacher-student and peer dialogue around learning" sounds good, but how could that be done?', then the advisor might suggest feedback vivas (where students must discuss feedback with staff in interviews), or EVS-mediated class tests. (For descriptions, see Draper 2011.)

Experience both within REAP, and in REAP-based talks to other audiences, shows how important such a 'quiverful' of designs is to the dialogue that is triggered, and to the inspiration they give to audiences. The nearest this resource came to a written form in designing the REAP project may be the literature review (Nicol and Macfarlane-Dick 2006); but it could also be embodied in a repository of 'interesting' designs like the one generated during the REAP conference (Nicol 2011). In REAP, at least, this library was not a resource finalised in advance so much as one constantly expanded and updated during the project.

G. The role of evidence

Published evidence in the literature from past work is also important to per-suading some people. This is an overlapping set with the previous one of learning designs, but by no means identical since learning designs are often published as 'how-to' accounts, with little or no substantial evidence of their effect on learning outcomes. Having evidence to hand can be important in persuading clients.

Another major decision is whether to invest resources in collecting and publishing evidence of the effect of the project on learning outcomes. It is a decision, not a detail that can be left for the project to decide later, because it takes resources: hiring people to collect and process data, extracting commitments from clients to support this. (PCR and REAP both found that it was advisable not to pay clients anything until the evaluation data was supplied.) However it is also an important decision because evidence has a large effect on persuasion, both within the project (convincing course teams) as well as externally, and for persistence i.e. sustainability (why should newcomers to a course team maintain the change in future?).

Barriers to direct action

Two barriers to the easy spread of research findings to widespread uptake in education are now discussed, which in part explain why rollout requires major additional work in order to succeed.

Disciplinary differences

Although this section of the book is about institutional change management, as if a university were the natural unit of organisation, in reality HE is fundamentally cross-organised by discipline. Even at the level of first year students, a literature student learns and is taught in fundamentally different ways from, say, a chemistry student. The lives of the academic staff are much more bound to their discipline than to the HEI. Their next job is either in another HEI, or depends upon publications in journals controlled not by the HEI but by their discipline. More fundamentally, their ways of learning themselves and of teaching others, both good and bad, come from their discipline and not from any general theory or practice of education. It is because of this that the institutional level is not the only possible way to initiate transformational change: it has been done at the disciplinary level (among others).

It also means that even when an educationalist finds a concept about learning and teaching that applies across disciplines, academics will not recognise its meaning in their own discipline. At the simplest level, if we give a talk, we have to illustrate each method or idea with both an example from an essay based-discipline and one from a calculation-based discipline, or else the other half of the audience will shake their heads politely and say the idea is not relevant to them. If we simply talk in our own, to us natural, disciplinary language of education, then no-one at all other than educationalists will understand us. This matters to a change project when (like REAP) it needs to enlist staff across disciplines as fundamental participants. In that case, the problem of translating ideas across disciplines is fundamental to both the design and execution of the project. Thus a rollout project usually has to support the work of translating educational ideas between disciplines, and/or via the educational literature.

Constructivism applies to rollout projects

As discussed in Nicol and Draper (2009), in REAP we repeatedly experienced that at the end of presentations, people would approach us to discuss ideas they had had about applying the ideas in their own contexts, and that these ideas would go beyond what we could have suggested ourselves. This means that to communicate across disciplinary divides, we need not simple precision but a suggestive lack of exactness that draws the recipient into the process of making practical sense of the ideas. Thus something more than just 'translation' is involved. We find we must apply constructivism not just to basic teaching of students, and not only to feedback (i.e. get away from prescriptions about feedback as if this were something teachers must do to passive students), but also and most radically to our interaction with colleagues in rollout projects. This cannot be 'staff training' or instruction. Simple assertions are not what bring about the desired effect. It is about trying to combine general educational ideas with knowledge of the course specific context: the discipline, the particular set of students, the existing learning and teaching practices there. Thus, again, the work of transfer or translation, i.e. re-construction of an idea in a new context, is substantial, and is a major part of the work of a rollout project.

Many rollout projects consist of persuasion

Some strategies for large-scale change avoid a focus on communication difficulties. Hestenes, by addressing the discipline level, did not need to work on cross-discipline translation. Furthermore, by providing a validated test instrument, he did not even rely on convincing colleagues either by theory or by his own evidence: he manoeuvred them into themselves collecting the data that would convince them from their own classes. (Advanced constructivism is the facilitation of the 'autonomous' learning you wish to come about!)

However, projects such as PCR and REAP which address the course level must get large numbers of people to change their ideas and behaviour in response to the project. This is also true of many other rather differently structured projects, e.g. redesigning a university course database. That would involve enlisting those in central university units (registry, room bookings, etc.). All such projects must get large numbers of people to change their ideas and behaviour in response to the project. Consequently they are necessarily mainly about persuasion and communication, as opposed to producing some object or piece of software or new knowledge.

In the light of this we can review the seven project design decisions, and see that most of them are each associated with a resource for persuasion and communication. The relationships of decision steps and resources, and some aspects of the resources that need to be managed in a project, are illustrated in Table 16.1. The parenthesised row numbers refer to rows in the table; for example '(row 5)' refers to whether the resource is updated during the project. The following bullet points are steps in the argument about the relationships amongst project design decisions, persuasion, and rhetorical resources.

- All seven are decisions that need to be taken (shows as ✔ in row 1 of the table) and together largely shape the project.
- Inducing people to collaborate with and in the project is a task of persuasion. The decisions define the nature of the project, and people are persuaded to the degree these features of the project coincide with their existing interests, and/or are convincing to them.
- While one source of persuasion is evidence and reasoning, short memorable phrases expressing powerful ideas can be important as well (e.g. 'self-regulation', 'feedforward', 'time on task'). Like symbols and proper names in general, they may attract attention and convey some meaning before the recipient properly understands them; they are helpful in manipulating the idea as a chunk in thinking and planning; and they may be recalled after recipients have forgotten the detail of the explanation that originally convinced them. They are therefore 'rhetorical' devices in that they are important to persuasion in a way beyond naked evidence or logic, but not in the sense of being insincere. This is in line with Putnam's (1975) argument that ordinary people (including ordinary professors of philosophy) do not in fact themselves know exactly what they mean by the most ordinary words such as 'water' or 'gold', but ground their meaning in what other experts mean by the terms. Inventing or selecting such phrases can be important work in achieving persuasion that persists.
- A persuasive resource may thus be classified (row 2) into whether it is a **memorable phrase**, or an **explanation** ('making plain in detail') such as a case study or evidence. In the case of design principles, both are needed: both a summary slogan, and a longer, clarifying description. In other cases, the idea may be generally well understood and neither slogans nor evidence required. (A wish for this chapter is that it will make phrases such as 'rollout project' more recognisable; cf. table row 2, first two columns.)
- When a resource is explicitly assembled for the project, then a feature of it is its degree of novelty: whether invented, or taken as-is from the literature, or an intermediate case where a term is taken but a particular definition of it is developed for the project. In the case of evidence, both existing evidence and new evidence of the project's own successes are important. In brief: whether the resource is **adopted**, **adapted**, or freshly **created** (row 3).
- When a resource is explicitly assembled for the project, then at least a nucleus of it may need to be ready in advance (row 4).

Table 16.1 An example of the relationship of design decisions to resources for persuasion in the course-level REAP project (this kind of table would aid planning this kind of rollout project)

Aspects of persuasive resource creation	Project design decisions / steps						
	Rollout project type	Level of the intervention	Problem area	Educational aspiration	Design principles	Learning design library	Evidence
	A	B	C	D	E	F	G
1 Decision?	✓	✓	✓	✓	✓	✓	✓
2 Memorable phrases and/or explanations	(?)	(?)	M- phrase	M-phrase	M-phrase; and explanations	Explanations	Explanations
3 Created, adapted, or adopted	Adopted (cost, quality)	Adopted	Adopted	Adapted	Created	Adopted; some adapted or created	Adopted; created
4 At least a nucleus ready in advance			✓	✓	✓	✓	✓
5 Update during project					(✓)	✓	✓

- A resource may alternatively or additionally be updated during the project (✔ in table row 5 where it has been).

Thus the project design decisions mostly serve directly to promote the persuasion that is the heart of rollout projects like PCR and REAP. In those cases, communication with course teams across many disciplines is the biggest target, but other stakeholders are also important, e.g. HEI management, funding bodies, students. As sketched in Nicol and Draper (2009), the same resources can be used in different sequences and mixes for each audience. (Cf. Latour (1988) for a view of Pasteur's 'scientific' success in terms of progressively persuading ever more and bigger interest groups within French society to promote his programme.)

Assemble communicative resources before the project

The communicative resources required to change minds need to be largely assembled before the project begins. This is the reverse order to that in pure research projects, where evidence is a final product, along with catchphrases that improve post-project dissemination of new ideas that have been created during the project. Here, however, the persuasion needs to be the focus of not only action but preparation in a project like this, just as the experimental design and required equipment are in an experimental project.

This has implications for funding decisions. Judging project proposals by which has signed up the best clients means awarding money for nothing after the real work has been done, like increasing your advertising budget only after your sales have increased, not in order to bring them about. Conversely, funding a proposal that has not already assembled its rhetorical resources means that no persuasion will be done until after the end of the project. Creating the resources can be a project in itself, and has somehow to be funded separately. The need for communicative resources to be assembled largely in advance is another way in which rollout projects are quite different from research projects.

Conclusion

The most important message of this chapter is that rollout projects are quite different from research projects. Failing to understand the need for them, and their different nature, is a major reason for the common failure to achieve widespread and sustained educational change, which has seldom been effectively addressed and managed. Seven major decisions that feed into rollout projects are identified. The second message is the possibility, when planning to precipitate transformational change in education, of selecting a level for the intervention that may not be the institution at all. Alternatives are reviewed. Third, given that the main business of a rollout project is persuasion, the notion of rhetorical resource was discussed, and linked (in the table) to the decision stages.

References

Alexander, C., Ishikawa, S. and Silverstein, M. (1977) *A Pattern Language: Towns, Buildings, Construction*, New York: Oxford University Press.

Chingos, M.M. and Peterson, P.E. (2011) 'It's easier to pick a good teacher than to train one: familiar and new results on the correlates of teacher effectiveness', *Economics of Education Review*, 30(3): 449–65

Crouch, C.H. and Mazur, E. (2001) 'Peer instruction: ten years of experience and results', *American Journal of Physics*, 69: 970–77.

Draper, S.W. (2011) 'Assessment and feedback in HE'. Available at: www.psy. gla.ac.uk/~steve/rap/ (accessed 12 December 2012).

Draper, S. and Nicol, D. (2006) 'Transformation in e-learning', paper presented at ALT-C Edinburgh, 5-9 September. Available at: www.reap.ac.uk/public/Papers/transf1. pdf (accessed 12 December 2012).

Gibbs,G. (2010) *Dimensions of Quality*, London: Higher Education Academy.

Hake, R.R. (1998) 'Interactive-engagement versus traditional methods: a six-thousand-student survey of mechanics test data for introductory physics courses', *American Journal of Physics*, 66(1): 64–74. Available at: www.physics.indiana.edu/~sdi/ajpv3i. pdf (accessed 12 December 2012).

Hestenes, D., Wells, M. and Swackhamer, G. (1992) 'Force concept inventory', *The Physics Teacher*, 30: 141–51.

Klein, S., Benjamin, R., Shavelson, R. and Bolus, R. (2007) 'The collegiate learning assessment: facts and fantasies', *Educational Review*, 31(5): 415–39.

Latour, B. (1988) *The Pasteurisation of France*, London: Harvard University Press.

Lindquist, J. (1974) 'Political linkage: the academic–innovation process', *Journal of Higher Education*, XLV(5): 323–43.

Nicol, D. (2011) 'Re-engineering assessment practices in HE'. Available at: www.reap.ac.uk (accessed 12 December 2012).

Nicol, D.J. and Draper, S.W. (2009) 'A blueprint for transformational organisational change in higher education: REAP as a case study'. Available at: www.psy.gla.ac.uk/ ~steve/rap/docs/NicolDraperTransf4.pdf (accessed 12 December 2012). (A shorter version appeared in T. Mayes, D. Morrison, H. Mellar, P. Bullen and M. Oliver (eds) (2009) *Transforming Higher Education through Technology-Enhanced Learning*, Higher Education Academy, pp. 191–207.)

Nicol, D.J. and Macfarlane-Dick, D. (2006) 'Formative assessment and self-regulated learning: a model and seven principles of good practice', *Studies in Higher Education*, 31(2): 199–218.

Putnam, H. (1975) 'The meaning of meaning' in *Mind, Language and Reality*, Cambridge: Cambridge University Press.

Shayer, M. (1992) 'Problems and issues in intervention studies', in A. Demetriou, M. Shayer and A. Efklides (eds) *Neo-Piagetian Theories of Cognitive Development: implications and applications for education*, London: Routledge, pp. 107–21.

Twigg, C.A. (2003) 'Improving learning and reducing costs: new models for online learning', *Educause Review*, 38(5): 28–38. Available at: www.educause.edu/ir/library/ pdf/erm0352.pdf (accessed 12 December 2012).

Conclusion and reflections

Stephen Merry, Margaret Price, David Carless and Maddalena Taras

The chapters in this book explore feedback in higher education from the perspectives of different stakeholders including students, tutors and institutions. Previous considerations of feedback by researchers, managers and practitioners have often seen it as a one-off product consequent to assessment. A feedback product of this kind has been invested with the status of a magic bullet which, if optimised, will, by itself, target and change students' understandings and learning.

However, as we made clear in the introduction there are many other factors that make the effectiveness of feedback complex and far from automatic. The authors of this book have proposed that feedback be reconceptualised as a process rather than a product and within this section emergent themes from their work are highlighted using representative quotes and views expressed in the preceding chapters.

Feedback must involve ongoing dialogue with students in order for it to become meaningful and to allow them to fully integrate it into their learning. In the absence of dialogue attempts to optimise feedback provision through such initiatives as the imposition of time limits and standardised templates are likely to meet with limited success. The effort put into reengineering only the feedback product is likely to be problematic and wasted as has been illustrated within this book:

> Results from the NSS [UK National Student Survey] have led to some institutions specifying time-limits within which feedback should be provided.
>
> (Yorke)

but

> there are often concerns raised about the administrative burden of turning around large quantities of individualised feedback so quickly.
>
> (Bols and Wicklow)

and

explanatory comments designed to be copied and pasted and so not tailored to the individual . . . may, in fact, have been a waste of time to write because they are simply not understood.

(Bloxham)

The last quotation also suggests that anonymous marking procedures might further compound these difficulties. While anonymous marking has a place in ensuring fairness in summative assessment if feedback is also blind to the identity of the student it cannot be personalised or contextualised or form the basis of a dialogue.

The heart of the feedback conundrum is illustrated by the following:

Research into human learning shows there is only so much a person typically learns purely from being told.

(Sadler)

Transmission modes of feedback are thus often limited in their impact on students.

This book has begun to explore the effect of reconceptualisation of feedback as a dialogic process in terms of its theoretical meanings, practical implementation and policy implications. Within the chapters of the book a range of perspectives have been taken concerning the scope and purposes of feedback. Feedback has been given multiple meanings arising from its different contexts. For example, the use of exemplars may generate feedback that has a *'task level'* focus (Hendry) and this may be subtly different to Orsmond *et al.* where feedback relates to the overall learning practice and personal development of individuals within communities. It *is* recognised that such distinctions may be artificial (for example feedback is provided which is often a mixture of task improvement comments concerning work itself together with suggestions as to how future assignments might be tackled) and there can be blurring of the boundaries as to what is seen as feedback and what is seen as part of teaching. The editors of this book have not sought to constrain, limit or judge the merits of these interpretations since they reflect variation on the use of the term *feedback* within the broader academic community. The reconceptualisation we propose is sufficiently broad to encompass these multiple understandings and purposes and reflect the idea that feedback, teaching and learning are inevitably entwined.

The subtly differing perspectives of stakeholders within and outside the feedback process are illustrated by their evaluation of feedback which varies from measuring input through to looking at the impact on learning. If each stakeholder wishes to improve student learning, then students must truly be at the centre of assessment and feedback processes, which can only be achieved through dialogic negotiations. Formative assessment will be carried out by the learner who can demonstrate how considered understanding of feedback through dialogic processes impacts on future learning. It is not sensible to begin with the expectations of the feedback provider and endeavour to force a square peg into a round hole. Feedback and assessment must be mediated and take place through dialogic processes with learners who seek shared understandings.

It is a dialogic feedback process that provides a basis for a shared understanding within a specific context. It is only through dialogue that feedback can become more interpretable and hence effective and efficient. This book, therefore, represents a clarion call for a fundamental change in the way that feedback is perceived; a reconceptualisation of feedback as a process rather than a product and as dialogue, not monologue.

> Feedback as a delivered message is a commonly held conception among stakeholders in higher education. However, we fail to see the potential value of feedback if we conceptualise it (implicitly or otherwise) as a product that is the culmination of an earlier assessment process . . . What is overlooked is what mediates the exchange: the interactions between sender and receiver; and the network of social relations that shape the interpretation processes and make possible the development of shared understanding.
>
> (Price et al.)

Dialogue, which may be with either peers or tutors, serves to enrich previous feedback and also provides further feedback in an ongoing process. For example, Carless exemplifies how oral presentations can be used as a site for peer feedback. The process of peer interaction around what constitutes a quality oral presentation heightens students' awareness of their own strengths, weaknesses and how to improve. Students' judgement capabilities are developed by participating in peer dialogue around quality, but it is mainly through repeated practice of self-assessment that students develop their ability to self-monitor their own work. Taras highlights that self-assessment processes are not monolithic or fixed and she explores five different possible alternatives in use in higher education.

An alternative use of dialogue is that proposed by Hendry, who sees peer and tutor dialogue concerning exemplars as a means of scaffolding students' approaches to assessment tasks. He argues that time spent on such scaffolding activities prior to assessment tasks is a valuable investment that may streamline post-assessment feedback. The student understanding that these processes generate means that extensive explanations can be reduced to succinct messages. Furthermore, Bloxham, when considering the use of exemplars to make assessment standards more explicit, regards dialogue as the key element to achieving better understanding of assessment and feedback.

Dialogue can also be seen as central to the sustainability of feedback. Carless regards feedback as sustainable when it supports students in making judgements about their work so that they can continue to improve independently without being over-reliant on teacher guidance. A dialogic approach to feedback emphasises students' role in making sense of feedback and these sense-making judgements develop students' self-assessment capabilities, enabling them to make better sense of subsequent feedback. Without such self-assessment capabilities, students may not be able to use feedback effectively. McArthur and Huxham argue for feedback as dialogue that should be embedded throughout the learning process, not merely as an aspect of formal module assessment.

While it is argued that changes to the feedback product may have limited impact and dialogue is required, an important point is that the introduction of dialogic processes regarding feedback does not make the feedback product redundant. The product can still be stimulus for dialogue and, if necessary, an institutional resource for quality assurance procedures alongside evidence of the dialogic processes. The point is that the feedback product becomes an integral part of learning. Dialogue functions to enrich and develop this feedback product rather than to be a replacement for it. This means that what this book advocates is not simply a critique of current feedback practices; the authors do not want to discard the positive aspects of what we have and totally replace it with something else. Rather, the book is an expression of frustration that current feedback practices do not go far enough because they are often limited by current paradigms of feedback as 'one-way telling' (Sadler). The challenge to established educational practices, however, is the implication that existing curriculum designs may not facilitate such dialogue and institutional quality assurance processes may not encourage or permit the dialogic component of assessment procedures. In this context Draper and Nicol review the potential for institutional change from interventions at levels ranging from individual tutors to whole institutions and subject disciplines. They argue that each form of intervention has its merits, but the effective widespread implementation of new educational practice needs to be carefully planned as a distinct 'roll-out' project. Such projects should be separate and distinct from research projects designed to appraise the situation either before or after the roll-out.

In sum, to evaluate more fully the implications of reconceptualising feedback the chapters within this book have considered and explored the potential of, and possible mechanisms for the introduction of more dialogic feedback processes within higher education. The question that arises is that if this reconceptualistion is to be more widely and more easily adopted in practice, what exactly needs to be done? Our considerations of teaching, course, programme and institutional effects suggest that no one single approach is likely to be fully effective in isolation.

Price et al., concerning the Feedback Agenda for Change, point to the need for stakeholders to recognise the position of feedback within an integrated system of educational practice and management. National bodies can provide the broad framework within which change can be facilitated. However, within such a framework institutions need to pay more attention to effects of feedback rather than the inputs into the process. They should seek to dispel myths and misconceptions concerning feedback among staff and students, and to engage students through development of their assessment literacy, relationships of trust and their greater involvement in assessment and feedback processes.

> For feedback to be re-engineered on a wide scale, it needs to engage with or even confront the belief systems and existing practices of staff.
>
> (Carless)

Although embarking on such change will be a long-term commitment, the rewards are great in terms of learning benefits and in defining new educational relationships in higher education. What is indicated is that the powerful potential of feedback to enhance learning is underutilised because it often excludes students as central instigators of their own learning and, furthermore, that the current dissatisfaction felt by feedback stakeholders will not be effectively subdued by providing more of the same type of feedback as in the past.

The proposed reconceptualisation of feedback moves away from the idea of feedback as instruction imposed on students and recognises that students navigate their own learning through a relational process with their work and a dialogic process with their teachers and peers. This book moves thinking in this direction, but it also recognises areas that need greater exploration.

First, what is the nature of this dialogue, how is it best facilitated particularly with large class sizes and, if students are reticent to participate, what encouragement can they be given? In various chapters of this book some vehicles to stimulate dialogue are considered including student presentations, exemplars and discipline-specific research, but it is noticeable that they are considered in the context of face to face teaching with relatively high staff input. The dialogue generated in such situations is likely to be rich and wide-ranging. It will be formative feedback in the sense that it will encompass not only feedback on the task outcome, but also concern personal development strategies applicable to future tasks. Recipients of feedback can also ask for clarification if they are unsure of what they have heard. Massification of higher education, however, makes such teaching scenarios less common and more problematic to engineer, hence research is required as to what aspects of the dialogue are particularly conducive to learning and how these aspects, or the rich dialogue in general, can be generated in less staff intensive situations. Can electronic discussion be as rich as personal discussion, and can rich discussion only be facilitated by highly trained and experienced staff?

Second, in what ways can tutors be supported to develop strategies that generate productive dialogic feedback? Motivated individual tutors will, as in the past, introduce dialogic feedback practices into their teaching, but making such practices mainstream requires intervention from management teams. Draper and Nicol suggest that the most successful interventions to date have been discipline-specific interventions involving professional bodies. Changes to the UK medical curriculum, which have involved the General Medical Council, are an example of this. They suggest that the particularly strong allegiance of academics to their discipline makes such approaches particularly effective. Alternatively, institutional- and programme-level interventions could be considered. It is recognised that no single approach is likely to be effective in all cases, but the characteristics which make interventions effective and sustainable are yet to be fully elucidated and acted upon.

We do not recommend that tutors wait for discipline or institutional change to overtake them. Tutors should be proactive in reconceptualising their own feedback practices, seeking to provide greater opportunities for students to give and receive feedback so that students have more opportunities to develop the sophisticated approaches to feedback used by practising professionals. Exemplars, brief presentations, whole class feedback or other discussion documents may serve as foci for such initiatives. Additionally, tutors should discuss their own feedback practices with their students to clarify their intentions as to the purpose of their feedback and to seek a common understanding with their students as to how the particular instances of feedback that they provide can be implemented to support overall learning development and to better prepare for subsequent work. Lastly, tutors should encourage a greater awareness in students concerning the value of self-assessment, because it is an integral component of the effective implementation of feedback. Possible strategies might include asking students to collect their feedback together for discussion of overall trends, encouraging students to set a 'what is required and why' agenda with the tutor when they undertake an assignment or asking students to write reflections on received feedback.

If this book promotes interest in these and other related areas, it has served its purpose.

Index

Abercrombie, M.L.J. 57–8
ability 126
accessibility of feedback 21, 23–5
achievement 136–8
active learning 85, 196
adapted/adopted resources 200, 201
agency 124, 127–8
Agenda for Change 4, 34, 41–53, 80,
    149, 197, 207–8; Clause 1 41, 42–6;
    Clause 2 41, 46–7; Clause 3 41,
    48–50; Clauses 4 and 5 42, 50–1
Alverno College 34
anonymous marking 205
appreciative inquiry 175
assessment: diagnostic 33; and feedback
    34; formative *see* formative
    assessment; learning-oriented 145,
    172–89; patterns in the ESCAPE
    project 182–5; student involvement
    in the scholarship of 77, 80–91
assessment compact 145, 147–59
Assessment Design Intensives (ADIs)
    152–3, 154, 157
assessment for learning (AfL): student-
    produced guides 77, 80–91; themes
    in the ESCAPE project 176–9
Assessment for Learning Initiative *see*
    TALI
assessment literacy 47, 49, 155, 158
Assessment Standards Knowledge
    exchange (ASKe) 41, 147, 148, 155,
    156
Assessment Standards Manifesto 149
assessment tasks: complex *see* complex
    tasks; exemplars *see* exemplars; nature
    of and feedforward 111; oral
    presentations 115, 119–20, 206;

students' knowledge of what is
    expected of them 134–5
Australasian Survey of Student
    Engagement (AUSSE) 12
Australia 3, 6–18; Course Experience
    Questionnaire 6–7, 8–9, 11–12, 16;
    political history 7–9; surveys of the
    first-year experience 12
award-winning teacher, case study of
    115–20

belief systems of teachers 121
Black, P. 31, 32–3
Blended Learning Unit (BLU) 173
Bloxham, S. 66
bookmarks 165, 167
boot grit feedback 77, 93–4, 95, 98–100
Boud, D. 114, 125
Brewer, W. 45
Bridgeman, A. 138
brokering 128
Brooks, V. 65
Brown, E. 104
Brown, G. 137
business school 174
business studies teacher, case study of
    115–20

Cann, A.J. 38
Carless, D. 108, 114–15, 136
case studies: application of ESCAPE
    themes 181–2; business studies
    teacher 115–20
Change Academy 175, 188
Change Academy for Blended Learning
    Enhancement (CABLE) 175
Chickering, A. 178

Chinn, C. 45
clarification of understanding 13, 15
clarity 97, 162–3
class participation 116–19; assessment of 118
cognitivism 43–4
Cole, M. 134
Collegiate Learning Assessment (CLA) 195
Commonwealth Tertiary Education Commission (CTEC) 7–8
communication 199–202; assembling communicative resources 202
communication trust 121
communities of practice 78, 123–30; enriching 128–30; situated learning in 123–8
community of learning 20
competence, and complex learning tasks 56–62
competence trust 121
complex tasks 47; development of peer feedback knowledge and skills 54–63
compulsory sector (CS) 30, 31–3, 33–4, 35
connoisseurship 114
consistency 50–1, 162–3
constructive alignment 86
constructive feedback 21, 26–7
constructivism 199; social 43–4, 67–8, 134, 138
contact hours 27
content: balance with process 118; students' relationship with 46
content comments 78, 104–11
contingency management 57
control 97
Course Experience Questionnaire (CEQ) (Australia) 6–7, 8–9, 11–12, 16
course handbooks 97–8
course-level change 168, 193–4, 208
course structures 49
created resources 200, 201
criteria 60, 62; community learning and 127–8; and standards 64–5
customers/consumers, students as 19–20

decisions, in educational change projects 191–8, 200–2

deep learning 84–5
definitions of feedback 4, 30–3, 107
departmental approach to feedback provision 110–11
design principles 196–7, 201
detailed comments 13, 15
diagnostic assessment 33
dialogue and dialogic feedback 56, 77, 79, 92–102, 113, 205–7, 208; Agenda for Change and 41, 42, 43–5; assessment compact 152, 154, 157; dialogue with experts 68, 70–1; end of course and 100; feedback as dialogue 94–6; institutional approach to encouraging 164–5; interactive dialogic whole-class teaching 116–19; practical moments for feedback as dialogue 93, 97–100; student guides to AfL 86, 88; sustainable feedback see sustainable feedback; TALK 27–8
differentiation by teachers 66–7
discipline-level interventions for change 168, 194–5, 198–9, 208
disciplines 15–16, 170; differences between 198–9; and online feedback 25; and usefulness of feedback 27; and verbal feedback 23
distance-learning students 103–7
distributed cognition 125
divergent assessment tasks see complex tasks
drafts 71, 71–2
Dreyfus, H.L. 58
Dreyfus, S.E. 58
dualist epistemology 44
Duck, J. 139
Dunbar-Goddet, H. 70, 71

e-assessment 25–6, 173
Edinburgh University 97–8
educational aspiration 196, 201
educational change projects 145, 190–203, 207; barriers to direct action 198–9; persuasion and 190, 199–202; seven big decisions 191–8, 200–2
Effecting Sustainable Change in Assessment Practice and Experience (ESCAPE) project 172–89
electronic feedback 163, 169

email feedback, personalized 138
empowerment 35
epistemological development 44
evidence 50–1, 197–8, 201
exams 24
exemplars 47, 82, 129, 205; standards
    frameworks 68, 69–70, 71; using to
    scaffold learning 78, 133–41, 206
expectations: feedback as dialogue 97–8;
    students' expectations of feedback 3,
    19–29; students' knowledge of what
    is expected in assessment tasks 134–5
expertise, development of 56, 58
experts, dialogue with 68, 70–1
explanation: persuasion and educational
    change projects 200, 201; in written
    feedback comments 105–7, 109–10

face-to-face dialogue 44, 45–6
face-to-face feedback 28
facilitation of learning 121
faculty context 168
Fanthorpe, U.A., 'Reports' 92, 94, 96,
    100
feedback: definitions of 4, 30–3, 107;
    and feedforward 107–8; and
    formative assessment 33–4; and
    guidance 64; as knowledge of results
    55–6; learners and 34–5; redefining
    in student guides on AfL 87–8
Feedback Charter 161
Feedback for Learning campaign 160–71
feedback hierarchy 185, 187, 188
'Feedback – the key to your success'
    campaign 165, 166
feedback moments 93, 97–100
feedback spiral 93
feedforward comments 107–8, 110–11
fees, undergraduate 19–20
Fernández-Toro, M. 106–7
FInALS 20
first lecture 98
first-year experience surveys: Australia
    12; UK 14–15
Force Concept Inventors (FCI) 194–5
format for feedback, choice in 24–5
formative assessment 4, 22, 23; feedback
    and 33–4
Formative Assessment in Science and
    Technology (FAST) project 162–3,
    164

formative feedback 22, 23, 31
free-text comments of students 16
Freire, P. 92, 94
Fund for the Development of Teaching
    and Learning (FDTL) project 47
funding decisions 202
future work, comments helpful for
    104–7

Gadamer, H. 43
Game, A. 99
Gamson, Z. 178
gap 31, 32, 107; future and retrospective
    gaps 107–8
gap-bridging comments 107–8, 109–10
General Medical Council 208
generic skills development see skills
    development
Gibbs, G. 70, 71
Glover, C. 104
goals 92–3
GOALS process 129–30
'good teaching' scale (GTS) 11
grade/mark, importance of 23–4
Grainger, P. 66
Great Feedback Amnesty 20, 26–7, 161
guidance: feedback and 64; principles for
    effective 68–73
guides to assessment for learning (AfL)
    77, 80–91

Hake, R.R. 195
Handley, K. 70, 71
Hendry, G.D. 133
Hertfordshire, University of 172–89
Hestenes, D. 194, 199
Higher Education Funding Council for
    England (HEFCE) 9
holistic standards 65–6, 68, 69
holistic view, need for 48–50
Hounsell, D. 114
'How do you use yours?' campaign 165,
    166, 167
HSBC/NUS Student Experience Survey
    3, 19–29

inclination 126
individual level: interventions for change
    168, 193; recommendations for
    written feedback comments 109–10

information 31; knowledge and 95
institutional change: initiatives 145–6;
    success factors 146; TALI model 167,
    168–9; *see also under individual change
    initiatives*
institutional level: assessment policy
    138–9; interventions for change 168,
    194, 208; sustainable feedback 121
integrated peer/tutor feedback model of
    self-assessment 36, 37
interactive dialogic whole-class teaching
    116–19
investigative group practical work 130

James, R. 12
Jarratt Report 9
joined-up approach to change 165–9
Joint Information Systems Committee
    (JISC) 172, 173; Curriculum
    Delivery programme 174; Design
    Studio 187; Effective Assessment in a
    Digital Age workshop series 187
judgements: developing evaluative
    capacity in students 59, 60–1;
    professional *see* professional
    judgement
justification of judgements 60–1

knowledge: and information 95;
    'knowing to' 57–9; learners'
    knowledge base and benefiting from
    feedback 56, 58
knowledge of results, feedback as 55

lack of understanding of feedback
    comments 103, 105–7
language distance-learning students
    106–7
large classes/lectures 99–100, 138
Lave, J. 123, 124, 125
league tables 6–7
learners *see* students/learners
learning: active 85, 196; for complex
    outcomes 54–6; deep and surface
    84–5; need to redefine in student
    guides to AfL 84–5; situated 123–8;
    social 78, 123–32; teachers as learners
    98–9
learning contract design (LCD) 36, 38
learning curriculum 124, 128

learning design library 197, 201
learning environment 85–7; safe learning
    space 99
learning-oriented assessment 145,
    172–89
learning pyramid 27
legibility of feedback 21, 25–6
levels of intervention for educational
    change 168, 190, 192–6, 201, 208–9
life sciences school 174–80
Linke Report 8, 9
Longden, B. 14

Macfarlane-Dick, D. 88–9
Maclellan, E. 112
management 50–1
mark/grade, importance of 23–4
marketing 164
marking classes 137
marking guides 111, 137
medical curriculum 208
memorable phrases 200, 201
Metcalfe, A. 99
modifications to the feedback process
    161
module level 168; ESCAPE project
    175–8, 179–80
moments for feedback as dialogue 93,
    97–100
Moore, M.G. 46
motivational comments 104–11

National Student Survey (NSS) (UK)
    35, 42, 48, 161, 172; Oxford
    Brookes University 148, 155;
    politicisation of feedback 6–7, 10,
    13–14, 15–16; sector-level
    intervention 195; Sheffield Hallam
    University 169
National Union of Students (NUS)
    (UK) 50, 152; *Feedback Amnesty* 20,
    26–7, 161; feedback and assessment
    campaign toolkit 20; *Feedback Charter*
    161; NUS/HSBC Student
    Experience Survey 3, 19–29
negotiation 125–6
Nicol, D. 42, 92–3, 108
Northedge, A. 70
Northumbria University 22; student
    engagement with the scholarship of
    AfL 82–90

online feedback 25–6, 173
opportunities to make more use of
    feedback 182–3
oral presentations 115, 119–20, 206
organisational culture 49–50
organisational level *see* institutional level
Orr, S. 66
Orsmond, P. 45, 124
Osney Grange Group Agenda for
    Change *see* Agenda for Change
Oxford Brookes University Assessment
    Compact 145, 147–59

partnership with students 145, 160–71
patchwork texts 129
Payne, E. 137
pedagogic literacy 47, 49
peer assessment 31, 81–2, 115;
    assessment compact 154
peer feedback 4, 115, 119–20, 129;
    development of knowledge and skills
    in relation to complex tasks 54–63;
    integrated with tutor feedback and
    self-assessment 36, 37; social learning
    128–9
peer interactions 86, 88, 99
peer review 28, 72; Agenda for Change
    41, 46–7
performance indicators 8, 9
Perkins, D.N. 126
Perry, W. 44
personalised email feedback software 138
personalised formative e-assessment tool
    173
persuasion 190, 199–202
physics 194–5
planned educational change *see*
    educational change projects
'pleased/encouraged by' comments 103,
    105–7
Polanyi, M. 57
policy: evidence-based changes 50–1;
    review of 41, 48–50
politicisation of feedback 3, 6–18
Polytechnics and Colleges Funding
    Council (PCFC) 9
positive comments 103, 105–7
postcards 185, 186
posters 165, 167
practice: changes to feedback practice

161; evidence-based changes 50–1;
    impact of the assessment compact
    165; review of 41, 48–50
praxis 123
pre-course feedback moments 97–8
prize draw cards 165, 167
problem based learning (PBL) 195
process: balance with content 118;
    engaging students with the feedback
    process 162; feedback as 41, 42,
    43–6, 48–50, 87, 108
product, feedback as 42, 51, 108
professional bodies 50–1, 208
professional judgement: characteristics of
    65–8; standards frameworks and
    students' understanding of 68, 69,
    72–3
Programme in Course Redesign (PCR)
    191–202
programme-level change interventions
    168, 193–4, 208
programme view of assessment 182, 184,
    185
project type selection 192, 201
promptness of feedback 13, 15, 21–2,
    71, 97, 194
Putnam, H. 200

quality: of feedback 27–8, 61, 135–6;
    judgement in peer assessment of
    complex works 60–1, 62; self- and
    peer review and 46–7
quality agencies 50–1
quality assurance 49
Quality Assurance Agency for Higher
    Education 9
quantity of feedback 135–6

Race, P. 87
Ramaprasad, A. 31, 32, 107
Ramsden, P. 8
readiness for change 147–8
REAP (Re-engineering assessment
    practices in HE) project 145,
    191–202
recognised problem area 196, 201
reference level 32, 107–8
reflection on learning 117
relational process, feedback as 41, 42,
    43, 45–6

research evidence 50–1, 197–8, 201
research-informed teaching 130
resources: communicative 202;
    educational change projects 200–2;
    ESCAPE 181–5, 186
return deadlines 14, 21–2, 194, 195–6,
    204
review of policy and practice 41, 48–50
roadshows 165
rollout projects 198–202, 207; barriers
    to direct action 198–9;
    constructivism 199; decisions 191–8;
    persuasion 199–202
Rust, C. 71, 80, 81, 137
Rutledge, P. 138

Sadler, D.R. 31, 32, 33, 46, 55, 69, 71,
    72, 114, 135
safe learning space 99
scaffolding 78, 129; using exemplars 78,
    133–41, 206
scholarship of assessment, student
    involvement in 77, 80–91
sector-level change 195–6
Segal Quince Wicksteed (SQW) 9
self-assessment 31, 32, 35–8, 39, 206;
    assessment compact 154; capabilities
    206–7; communities of practice
    128–9; community learning and 124,
    125–6; GOALS process 129–30;
    models of 36–8; student involvement
    in scholarship of assessment 81–2, 86
self-critique 28
self-efficacy 137–8
self-evaluation: Agenda for Change 41,
    46–7; capacity development and
    sustainable feedback 113–22
self-generated feedback 100
self-marking 36, 37
self-monitoring 136–8
self-regulation 196
seminars, with inbuilt feedback dialogue
    71
sensitivity to feedback 126
Shay, S. 67
Sheffield Hallam University 22; FAST
    project 162–3; Feedback for Learning
    Campaign 160–71; TALI 163, 164,
    167, 168–9
'showing students where they had gone
    wrong' comments 104–7

situated learning 123–8
skills development: comments 78,
    104–11; departmental planning for
    111
social constructivism 43–4, 67–8, 134,
    138
social interactions 86, 88, 99
social learning 78, 123–32
sound standard model of self-assessment
    36, 37
sources of feedback 41, 46–7
sports science 179–80
staff development 165; Oxford Brookes
    University 152–3, 155; University of
    Hertfordshire 186–7
stakeholders 42, 50–1, 207–8
standard model of self-assessment 36–7
standards 4–5, 47, 92–3, 139; reference
    level 32, 107–8
'standards' frameworks 4–5, 64–74;
    differentiated by teacher 66–7;
    holistic 65–6, 68, 69; principles
    68–73; tacit 66; transparency 65, 73
Strathclyde, University of 191; see also
    REAP (Re-engineering assessment
    practices in HE) project
Student Experience Survey
    (NUS/HSBC) 3, 19–29
student-facing resources 185, 186
student-focused ESCAPE feedback
    hierarchy 185, 187
student involvement 72; in the feedback
    process 162; in the scholarship of
    assessment 77, 80–91
student surveys 51; NUS/HSBC
    Student Experience Survey 3, 19–29;
    politicisation of feedback in Australia
    and the UK 3, 6–18
students/learners 50; awareness of the
    assessment compact 155–6; change
    interventions at the student level 168,
    193; and feedback 34–5; knowledge
    of what is expected of them in
    assessment tasks 134–5; partnership
    with 145, 160–71; responses to
    written feedback comments 78,
    103–12; understanding of the
    assessment compact 156
students union: partnership in
    institutional change 163–70; problem
    of frequent changes of officers 170

subject areas *see* disciplines
summative feedback 24
surface learning 84–5
Surrey University Professional Year
    Programme 194
sustainable assessment 114
sustainable educational change 145,
    190–203
sustainable feedback 78, 108, 113–22,
    206; case study 115–20;
    characteristics 114–15; definition
    113

tacit knowledge 57–9, 66
tacit standards 66
TALI (The Assessment for Learning
    Initiative) change model 167, 168–9
TALK criteria 21–8
Taras, M. 36–7
teacher-focused ESCAPE feedback
    hierarchy 185, 188
teacher-led interventions 88
teacher training 193
teachers/tutors/lecturers 50: achieving
    change at the level of 193; belief
    systems 121; as learners 98–9; need to
    be proactive 209; recommendations
    for written comments 109–10;
    standards and differentiation by 66–7;
    usher role 93, 95
teaching, transmission model of 55–6
teaching and learning environments
    85–7
technical concepts 95
technology distance-learning students
    103–7
technology enhanced assessment 145,
    172–89
telling students 55–6
text-walls 93–4, 99–100
thinking dispositions 124, 126
time: development of students'
    perceptions of standards over 68,
    71–2; limits for delivering feedback
    14, 21–2, 194, 195–6, 204
timeliness of feedback 13, 15, 21–2, 71,
    97, 194
Tishman, S. 126

transformational educational change
    145, 190–203
transmission model of teaching 55–6
transparency 65, 68, 73
Truman, M. 106–7
trust 78, 118, 121
Twigg, C. 191

undergraduate fees 19–20
understanding: clarification of 13, 15;
    lack of understanding of written
    comments 103, 105–7
United Kingdom (UK): First Year
    Experience Survey 14–15; NSS *see*
    National Student Survey;
    NUS/HSBC Student Experience
    Survey 3, 19–29; political history
    9–10; student surveys and the
    politicisation of feedback 3, 6–18
Universities Funding Council (UFC) 9
unjust criticism, feedback as 110
updating of resources 201, 202
usefulness of feedback 21, 26–7, 162–3;
    written comments 103, 104–11
usher, teacher as 93, 95

ventriloquation 128
verbal feedback 23
video-taping oral presentations 119–20
virtual learning environment (VLE)
    69–70
Vygotsky, L.S. 123, 134

Weaver, M.R. 103
Wenger, E. 123–4
Wiliam, D. 31, 32–3
Williams, L. 70, 71
Williams Report 7
Winter, R. 32
Wittgenstein, L. 57
writing styles 47
written feedback 23–4; legibility 21,
    25–6; student responses to comments
    78, 103–12

Yorke, M. 14

zone of proximal development 134